# Yalla!

## A Wandering Jew Survives Palestine, Cuba, Jamaica and America

by
### Alejandro Modena
with Colin Ingram

Robert D. Reed Publishers • Bandon, OR

Robert D. Reed Publishers
P.O. Box 1992
Bandon, OR 97411
Phone: 541-347-9882 • Fax: -9883
E-mail: 4bobreed@msn.com
web site: www.rdrpublishers.com

Typesetter: **Barbara Kruger**
Cover Designer: **Grant Prescott**

ISBN 1-931741-64-6

Library of Congress Control Number 2005931416

Manufactured, typeset and printed in the United States of America

# Dedication

I dedicate this book to my parents Laura Fohrman Modena and Adolfo Modena who gave life to me. I know even though they have passed on they were always guiding me and telling me how to write this book. Every chapter that I wrote I saw that night in flashbacks about them. Perhaps if they had written this story it would have been different.

Sometime I would wake up in the middle of the night sweating, cursing myself and asking myself why was I writing this book, *"Yalla!"* (which means "Let's go!" in Arabic). I finally realized what drove me. I want my children and grandchildren to read this book and to know what life was like in Palestine, Cuba and Jamaica at the times I lived there, because life in each country has changed since then.

I also dedicate this book to my wife Barbara Pollack Modena who helped me to write, and to my friend Glenn Sousa who did research for the book. And last but not least to Colin Ingram, my mentor and my friend, who spent many days and nights editing my writing.

# Contents

# Chapter One, Israel

Israel is the Promised Land, the land of milk and honey, but if anybody had told me in 1933 that he was planning to go to Israel I would have told him that he was crazy. There wasn't any such country. If you looked at a map or a globe at that time you would never find it. The name of the region was Palestine but it wasn't a region of milk and honey; it was a poor area, with many diseases, droughts and social unrest. If people needed to flee from Europe, why go to a poor, miserable place where nomadic tribes were wandering around with guns and might rob, steal, kidnap or kill you? If you looked at a map you would see that it would take you a long time to travel from Europe to Palestine. If I'd had a choice I would rather have gone to the United States, Canada or Australia.

As a human being, besides air, food, water and shelter, you need protection. The pogroms were killing Jews all over Europe and the Nazis were already planning genocide. My parents didn't get protection in Europe so both decided to go to Palestine in the year 1933.

My father went first. He came from Italy. My great-great grandparents on my father's side were wine dealers in Spain who immigrated to Modena, Italy. My family had no permanent last name because in Jewish tradition a person's last name was taken from the first name of the father. But as wine merchants of Modena, they came to be named for their city and retained the same surname through the generations, and that is how I got my name, Alexander Modena.

My father was also a wine merchant and worked in the family business. He had two younger brothers who joined Benito Mussolini's fascist army. My grandmother was proud to see her two boys in the army. They wore their fascist uniforms and marched arrogantly with their leather, front-lacing ankle boots. They wanted to show that they were disciplined and that they appreciated the military life. They tried to force my father to join them, but he wouldn't agree. They thought that it would stifle their own careers unless all brothers were seen as fascist devotees. They threatened that if he wouldn't join them in the army they were going to kill him. If my father hadn't taken the threat seriously and left, he might be skiing in the Alpine slopes then, if he were still alive. Instead, he left for Palestine.

It was early fall in 1933, and it was cold and snowy in northern Italy. My father packed a few belongings in a suitcase and left without saying goodbye to his mother or his two brothers. He left at midnight by train from Milan to Rome. The day was Yom Kippur, the Day of Atonement. It is a Jewish holiday observed with fasting and praying. My father left late at night, just like a thief, frightened for his life and wondering what would happen to him. He was twenty-nine years old, single and unattached.

The train was packed because school was starting and families were returning from vacations. My father was lucky that he was able to get a seat in the coach section of the train. Unknown to him, his uncle, aunt and three of his cousins were on the same train in first class. They were also traveling from Milan, returning from their vacation to their home in Rome. The cousins were about the same age as my father. They lived in Rome in an old Jewish community and were also in the wine industry. They lived next to a synagogue and while they supported it money-wise, they only went to the synagogue at the high holidays.

They were enjoying the train ride. The parents and two of the three children were eating a late supper that they had brought with them. They were eating pork on Yom Kippur. In the Jewish religion you aren't allowed to eat pork. The oldest son was the only one from his family who was observing the Jewish holiday by fasting. My father was also fasting, not because he was a religious man but because the kitchen on the train was closed and he had brought no food with him.

My father was asleep. The earlier arguing with his family about joining the army had left him exhausted and he needed that sleep.

He didn't know what he was going to do when he arrived in Rome. He thought maybe he would visit his uncle in Rome and ask him what to do.

My father's problem, in comparison to the mounting conflicts in the rest of the world, was a small problem, but to him it looked like a big problem. His leaving home seemed to have solved the problem. Running from his brothers and his mother wasn't the best solution, but at that moment he saw no other choice. I don't know if my father exaggerated when he thought that his brothers would kill him if he didn't join the army, but he knew that it was very important to have the whole family in the army. His brothers had had to convert from Jewish to Catholic in order to join the Fascist Party. In order for his brothers to be promoted they had to have the complete cooperation of their family. In contrast, my father thought that his family should know the truth about the fascists; that they were planning the genocide of the Jews.

Earlier generations of my father's family in Spain had suffered from the Inquisition and had been forced to move to Italy. In Spain at that time there had been only one religion–Catholicism. In order to live in Spain, Jews had to convert to Catholicism or face torture and death. Often, torture and death of converted Jews occurred if they were suspected of being insincere Catholics. This story had been passed down to my father and he felt the same thing could happen in present-day Italy. Although the Italians weren't as anti-Semitic as the Germans my father saw the handwriting on the wall. We know now that a modern fascist state carried out the systematic murder of a whole people for no reason other than that they were Jews.

As the night fled by on the train, all of a sudden a loud bang woke my father. He and the other passengers fell from their seats. The windows had broken in my father's cabin. Some passengers had gotten hurt but my father had only a few bruises. All the passengers were cold and eager to find out what had happened. It was dark, not yet morning. He knew that it was still Yom Kippur because the Jewish holidays start at sundown and end at sundown the next day. In a few hours the sun would shine and they would be able to see what had happened. My father and the rest of the passengers sat and waited for morning. No one had come to tell them what had happened or to offer medical help. Some passengers were speaking tiredly with one another. There were some children crying in the cabin, screaming a monotonous, steady complaint; but as soon as their mothers gave them some food they calmed down and fell asleep again. The smells of urine and of unwashed bodies were in the cabin. The only good smell was of tobacco and brandy that had spilled from the dining car. My father found his suitcase safe under his seat so he fell asleep again. Before he fell asleep he thought, "Wouldn't it be nice to sleep in a soft bed and in my own room? I could have joined the Fascist Party and worshipped Mussolini, 'Il Duce.' I could have worn the brown uniform and served my country."

Finally, morning arrived, slowly at first but then faster, just like water pouring from a water faucet. At first it was dripping, then it was running very slowly then it was pouring and you couldn't stop the water just as you couldn't stop the sun from shining.

My father found out that his passenger train had collided with a freight train. The accident involved eight passenger cars hauled by a single locomotive colliding with twenty cars of a freight train hauled by two locomotives. The accident occurred only a few miles from Rome. The passenger train had accidentally been switched from the main line onto a siding where the freight train was stationed. Two of the crew, the engineer and a trainee engineer were killed, as well as four passengers. My father later was astonished to discover that the dead passengers were members of his family: his uncle, his aunt, and two of his three cousins. The whole first class cabin was smashed. My father wondered if it had been an act of God punishing those sinners who had eaten pork on Yom Kippur. They'd all had a terrible death. The heavy wooden roof had collapsed on them. It had smashed them, and everywhere there was blood and scattered body parts. The sole survivor who had occupied my relatives' cabin, the oldest son whose name was Moses, lived because he wasn't in the cabin at the moment of the accident; he was fasting and couldn't stand the attractive smell of the food so he was walking from one car to another.

My father and some one hundred passengers were taken to the local hospital. Soldiers helped to take the passengers to the hospital. When my father saw the brown-uniformed soldiers he thought that his brothers had sent the troops to bring him home or to kill him. He heard the noise of the marching boots and tried to block their sound. He knew how vicious they could be.

Most of the passengers were released shortly after the accident. My father was very lucky that he was alive and safe.

When he left the hospital he wandered around and wondered what to do. On his third day in Rome, staying in a cheap hotel, he bought a newspaper and was shocked to read about the death of his relatives in the train accident. He decided to visit his cousin Moses, who lived in Rome, out of respect for the deaths of his relatives. When my father saw Moses he realized that although he, himself, had problems, Moses had bigger problems. Moses had to bury his family and liquidate the business.

My father stayed with his cousin in Rome, helping to liquidate his assets. He knew that he, himself, was still in danger for his life. Luckily he didn't go to the burial because his mother and brothers were there and surely would have dragged him off; or worse, turned him over to the military.

His cousin Moses became more religious after the death of his family. He told my father that God had punished his family for not observing the Jewish dietary laws. Moses said in order to atone he felt he must leave Italy and go to the Holy Land. Another reason was that he, too, feared the Italian fascists. He knew that my father was a fugitive. My father joined him, and in the fall of 1933 the two young men boarded a ship in Genoa and sailed to Jerusalem. Moses had money and he invested in properties in Jerusalem. My father didn't have any money. Moses offered assistance to my father but he was too proud to accept it. Instead he joined a kibbutz, a collective farm or settlement.

That was his only choice. My father came to Palestine during the Depression years. If you couldn't find work in the United States, in Palestine it was even harder. Many young men and women who came to Palestine from Europe and couldn't find work and didn't have any money decided to live together, both to survive and help build the country. That's how the kibbutzim were born.

At the same time that my father fled to Palestine in 1933, there was a young lady, twenty-five years old, searching for her beloved prince. That young lady was my mother.

She had lived in Poland in a Jewish ghetto in the city of Brodea. My mother's desire to help others had an early start. During World War I, in 1917, at the age of nine, my mother, Laura, decided to become a volunteer at a local hospital. She wrote letters for the wounded soldiers. She brought flowers and fruit to them and tried to be helpful. At the age of fifteen Laura's mother was all alone and expecting her ninth child. When her mother was in labor, Laura sent her brother to the hospital to call for help. Neither the doctor nor the midwife came to help deliver the baby. Forced to rely on herself, my mother was successful in delivering her sister. Everybody heard her success story and people started to hire her. She wasn't afraid to do the job. Laura became a lay-midwife, since she had no formal training in midwifery. Then she decided to become a doctor.

At an early age my mother had decided to go to school and not become an illiterate woman. She graduated with honors from secondary school. Although she knew that the only profession for a woman in Poland at that time was to be a mother and raise children, she applied to and was rejected by medical school in Poland both because she was Jewish and because she was a woman.

Nevertheless, my mother was bright and determined to make her way up and out of the ghetto. She left Poland and went to study medicine in Czechoslovakia, where there were fewer restrictions. Once again she graduated with honors as a doctor. Her parents were genuinely proud of her accomplishments.

When I heard about my mother's life in Poland I became enraged! Here was a country, short on doctors, thousands of people needing medical attention, and yet they insisted on preventing all women and Jews from practicing! What stupidity, I thought! What mindless prejudice! Neighboring Czechoslovakia was not a paradise, but compared to Poland it was an oasis of enlightened thinking.

After she graduated from medical school in late autumn of 1933 and before deciding what to do, her parents gave her a cruise on the Mediterranean Sea. She gathered together a few of her belongings, traveled overland to Italy and boarded the same ship from Genoa that my father and Moses had taken earlier. She arrived in Palestine and fell in love with the country and decided to stay. She left the ship and never came back, in spite of her family in Poland. This was a free country for her. She didn't see signs saying, "Don't Buy from Jews," or "A Poland Free from Jews Is a Free Poland," or "Unemployment is Thanks to the Jews." This was a country where she could smell the fresh air and be proud to be a Jew.

She got a job as a nurse in a sanatorium in Jerusalem. The only way that she could practice medicine as a doctor in Palestine was if she had a college degree from England. She didn't want to go to England so she became a nurse. She was lucky that she got a job during the Depression. As a young woman she was able to support herself and she only worked forty hours, five days a week, which was less than most others. On the weekends she traveled all over Palestine. One day she traveled to my father's kibbutz. An accident occurred and my father got hurt that day. My father, not accustomed to labor, had tried to fix a roof, and instead had fallen from the ladder. He bruised his face, cut his lips and strained his arms and legs. Since they didn't have any doctors or any nurses and they had a lot of sick people, my mother volunteered to stay in the kibbutz. She took care of my father and other kibbutzniks. One day she shaved his mustache and noticed he had a birthmark under his mustache, the same kind of birthmark she had on her right arm. It had the appearance of a port wine stain. She showed her birthmark to him and they believed that they had been marked for life together. My mother asked him, "Were you teased when you were young?"

My father replied, "Yes, I was. In Italy they called it the "devil eye." My parents couldn't keep anybody to take care of me when I was a baby."

My mother laughed. "Were the people that superstitious?"

My father answered, "The Southern Italian people were, and that was where we got our maids from. We lived in Northern Italy and the people from Northern Italy accepted us the way we were. But at school they teased me and told me that the devil had marked me."

My mother looked at my father and said, "I'm sorry."

My father replied, "Don't be sorry. I'm lucky that I met you and we don't have to look further for other people. I know you are the one because we share our birthmark."

My mother laughed. "You're really sure about yourself, aren't you? Remember, I'm Polish and my parents would never allow me to date an Italian."

My father looked at my mother with loving eyes and told her, "We don't have to tell them. We are adults." They kissed and then started to date. Little did they both know that the war had already started and the Jewish people were being taken to concentration camps, where my grandmother and some of her children died. My grandfather and two of his sons escaped to the United States.

I don't know if it was physical attraction or spiritual belief or destiny. Maybe it was a little of each that brought my parents together. I don't care. The most important thing is that they gave me life and it is a precious gift.

Both my parents believed that they had chosen the right place to live–Palestine, now Israel–and they could call it home.

I remember a story that my father told me when he was in Italy and when he went to the vineyard to choose the right grapes for the wine they made. My father noticed that the grape pickers were always singing. They sang beautiful arias from famous operas and he imagined that he was at La Scala, Milano's famous opera house. Even though all the men were far apart from each other, they always seemed to be singing the same song at the same time. The grape pickers told him that the music was in the air. They took great pride in their land. Every once in a while they would bend over and cup their ears to the earth and tell him that they heard an act of a famous opera coming from the earth. My father also wanted to hear this beautiful music that they were talking about. He bent over and placed his ear firmly against the soil but couldn't hear a sound. He was sad, and he asked the grape pickers why he couldn't hear any music. They told him, "You can't hear the music because you are a Jew and this is Italian land. Only natives, only those who belong here, can hear this special music." My father realized that no matter how hard he tried to be an Italian, he would always be a foreigner.

When he arrived in Palestine and started working the land, he heard music, and he knew that this, now, was his home, even though he didn't speak Hebrew and didn't know the words. He started humming the beautiful music and he sounded just like a cantor singing in the temple on the High Holy days.

My mother had the same experience in Poland. When she went with a bunch of Polish girls to the fields to pick berries, she saw that the girls bent over and cupped their ears to the earth and told her that they heard Chopin's music. My mother tried the same thing and thought that she was deaf. The Polish girls told her, "You are a Jew and this is Polish land. Only natives, only those who belong here, can hear this special music." Once my mother reached Palestine and she was working in the fields, all of a sudden she heard some hidden melodies that she didn't know the words for and she began humming them. Then she knew that she had found her home.

# Chapter Two, The Will to Live

I am a boy, a real boy. In the Jewish religion both boys and girls are very important, but boys are the ones that keep the family name alive. Jews recognize boys at birth in the ceremony of naming the child. The name is important for a person's development. It makes its bearer both identifiable and unique. I am Alexander Modena. I am a Levite and Kohayn, a descendant of ancient Jewish priests. Biblical law requires that every son of a Jewish woman be circumcised on the eighth day after his birth. It is the sign of the covenant between God and the Israelites. At thirteen I celebrated my *Bar Mitzvah*. I was considered to be an adult and was asked to read the Torah. I was able to participate in a *minyam*, a quorum where ten men are necessary in the Jewish religion to pray to God.

I was born in 1935. I was a handsome baby and eager for the adventure of life. My parents saw a different picture. They saw a premature baby whose survival was in doubt. I could hardly breathe. I was born in the beginning of my third trimester, two months early. At birth I weighed three and a half pounds and my height was 18 inches. But even though I was premature, I was lucky. I was born with the amniotic sac still around me. In those days it was considered a sign of good luck. I was fully developed but my lungs were weak.

I saw it differently than my parents. I was eager to get out of my mother's tummy. I was afraid that I was missing something and I wanted to see the world. My mother wasn't afraid to hold me. I told her, "Look at this handsome boy, blond hair, rosy checks, blue eyes and slim. What else do you want?"

The doctor told my parents that the only way to save my life was to put me in an incubator. My mother was against the idea because she knew from her medical training, studying medicine in Czechoslovakia, that most babies placed in incubators at that time became blind.

Years later the blindness was linked to the excessively high flows of oxygen delivered to the baby. My mother instinctively kept me out of the incubator. She kept me close to her and kept me warm in the hospital. She put a lamp in my crib. That and her body heat was all I needed. She breast-fed me and I was content.

When I was born and the rabbi saw me, he didn't give my parents any hope for my survival. In spite of this I was determined to show him who had the last word. Although it was later than normal, two months later, I was large enough and well enough to have a *B'rith-Milah*, the Jewish rite of circumcision. *B'rith-Milah* means covenant in Hebrew. I believed in myself and I knew I would grow up to a be a fine man.

My parents checked on me constantly. My mother asked my father, "Is he really ours?"

My father replied, "Of course he is ours." Once again my parents counted my toes and fingers and the end result was twenty. My nose was perfect. I had my mother's nose and mouth. I got my father's eyes and forehead. After two months of living in the hospital, gaining weight, in the eyes of my parents as well, I was perfect. I ate, I burped, I pished and pooped, and slept.

It didn't take too long for the nurses and doctors to fall in love with me. They came to see me every day, not only for a checkup, but also for a social visit. As they came to know me their feelings deepened. They couldn't wait for me to wake up so they could play with me. I opened my eyes, looked around, and listened to the nurses singing me lullabies in Hebrew, German, English and other languages. They let me grab their fingers and they let me suck them. I was fascinated with their faces and sounds. I was allowed to be part of the hospital world. There were three nurseries; one for the healthy babies above nine pounds, the middle nursery for the healthy babies below nine pounds and the third nursery for intensive care where I was. Every baby was in a bassinet. I was proud of myself. I was in a blue bassinet–I was a boy. I continued to gain weight and I had great willpower and a determination to live. At that time very few kids survived being premature at birth in Palestine.

One day before I was born, at the end of winter and beginning of spring, when the days were longer and hotter in the beginning of my mother's trimester, she had gone to see her cousin Donald to get her money that her father had given to Donald's parents in the United States. Every month my grandfather, Abraham, gave Donald's parents money to send to Donald so that he could give it to my mother in Palestine. My mother needed a large amount of money in order to pay for my delivery at the hospital. My parents lived in a kibbutz but they were not members of the kibbutz, so they had to pay for hospital expenses.

Years later when I was older my mother told me the story.

"I remember the day when I knocked at Donald's door. It was in the morning just a few hours before I started to work at the infirmary in the kibbutz. The doctor told me that walking was the best medicine. I knew that I was going to collect my money from Donald, pay the hospital, see the doctor for a checkup and then walk back to work.

Donald half-opened the door. He didn't let me in. I greeted him, 'How are you, Donald? Did you hear from your parents?'

Donald looked at me and said, 'I am fine, Laura.'

'Are you letting me in?' I asked him.

He replied, 'No, I am planning to leave in a few moments.'

'Donald, this is the third time that I have come for my money. You know that your parents got the money from my dad and they sent it to you.'

Donald didn't reply.

I told him again, 'I need the money to pay the hospital. It is due today.'

Suddenly I felt a strong force pushing me backward. I fell immediately. I began to feel labor pains and I saw a pool of blood coming from between my legs. I looked up to call for help and I only saw Donald slam the door. I prayed to God and asked him to give me a healthy baby. In spite of the fall, I got the best. I got you, Alex."

When my father found out what happened he was ready to confront Donald. However, Donald quickly left the country and came to the United States without paying the money that he owed my mother. My parents didn't tell my grandfather about the embezzlement–they were very ashamed that a such a thing could happen in the family. It took them five years to pay their debt to the hospital. That's why I am an only child; they couldn't afford another.

My mother didn't enjoy living in the kibbutz. She felt that there wasn't any challenge in life. Everything was done for you. You got a place to live. If you were single you lived with two other roommates of the same sex. You ate three meals a day at the dining room. You worked six days a week. My mother worked as a nurse and if there were not any sick people, she worked in the laundry.

My mother and father didn't have a private wedding. At the kibbutz there were only mass weddings. My parents and five other couples got married together. At the kibbutz everything was shared. You shared your clothes, food, housing and children. The children didn't live with their parents. They lived with their peers in the dormitory. My parents weren't allowed to have a child in the first year of marriage, only in the second year. The kibbutz couldn't afford to have any more mouths to feed.

The kibbutz had one hundred members and, finally, fourteen couples were allowed to have a child. My parents were among the lucky ones. When my mother found out that she was pregnant it was an overwhelming experience for her. She told me that from the moment she first learned that she was pregnant she wanted to see me. My father made sure that my mother stopped smoking and began eating well.

My birth was a culmination of a miracle. I wasn't crying at birth; it took several minutes before I started to breath. My skin was slightly bluish-gray. Once I started breathing everything was okay for the moment. But the odds of survival were against me. What kept me alive was my will and determination. Despite sickness, hunger and poverty, I survived.

At the kibbutz we did everything as a group. The kibbutz hired a rabbi who did the ceremony of naming the babies. Naming is an important part of this process. A boy is named at his *Brith*. A girl is named in the synagogue on a *Shabbat* following her birth when her father is called to the Torah. Each parent was called to the Torah to present their baby to the kibbutz. Each parent had a written speech which they read and saved to read again at the boy's or girl's *Bar* or *Bat Mitzvah*. My father read his speech: "Alexander, my mother and I are giving you this name to honor my father whose name was Alexander. Just like Alexander the Great he was a great warrior. He died defending his mother and, Italy, in World War I. And you, my son, are also a great warrior. You fought a difficult battle to survive your premature birth. Mom and I love you very much. Remember to fight for your motherland, Palestine, that one day will be Israel."

After the ceremony it was a Jewish custom to plant a new tree when a baby was born. When the child grew up and was ready to be married, branches cut from the tree were used to hold up the *chupah*, a canopy. In our kibbutz, each grade of kids had a name. Our group of kids was named "Grapes." We had a green flag embroidered with purple grapes. When the adults addressed us, instead of calling each kid individually, they yelled, "The Grape Group." My father and the other proud parents planted grapevines in the garden, so eventually we would be able to collect grapes and make our own wine. We consumed wine for dinner and for the holidays, including *Shabbat*, every Friday night. I wondered if fourteen grapevines would produce enough grapes to produce wine for the whole kibbutz. But we didn't have enough money to buy more than fourteen grapevine plants. As I grew, my parents took me to my grapevine and made sure that I knew that we had to water and fertilize it. It was a competition amongst the adults and the kids. The one whose grapevine was the biggest and healthiest bragged about it.

My mother started breast-feeding me at birth in the recovery area and kept breast-feeding until I was one year old. At six months she had started to give me the bottle. I didn't want the bottle, I wanted the breast. I cried and held my breath. I had the last word. My mother continued breast-feeding me to the age of one. Once I started to walk I took away food from the other babies in my dormitory. When we were in a playpen eating cookies, I would take them away from the other children. At the age of one you couldn't tell that I was born premature. My mother worked in the nursery and fed me extra food. It was the law of the stronger. I learned at an early age to satisfy my hunger.

My mother breast-fed another child whose mother's milk had dried. The child had been crying and my mother couldn't stand the

crying. The crying was a hunger cry and it was sad. When the
children were older and the kibbutz didn't have any food, they gave
the children bottles with sugar water. It was because the year was
1937 and there was a famine in Palestine. My case was different
because my father had two jobs, one for the kibbutz and another to
help feed the family. Whatever he made working outside the
kibbutz he was able to keep. My mother fed me extra outside the
nursery.

But in spite of my father's two jobs, none of us had enough
to eat and the cries of the children were unbearable. My mother
blamed herself when she stopped producing milk. She would
have breast-fed all fourteen children in my nursery if she could.
Sugar water was not enough. When we were outside the building
we ate dirt. Sometimes we ate worms or ants. We swallowed our
tears and we comforted each other. Our eyes were always sad;
they were the eyes of hunger. The adults were also hungry and
seemed unable to ration the food that would have lasted longer.
The adults tickled us and tried to make us laugh, but all we
wanted was food.

We were just like termites devouring the food. Whoever fed us
was our pal. That year there was a great drought that destroyed our
harvest and left us hungry and ruined. The kibbutz lost its food
reserves as well as the grain that they would have used until the
next harvest. It had hardly rained that year at all. We were against
an invisible force that tried to destroy us. We hardly had any water
to irrigate our fields.

We were hungry all the time and no matter how much we ate it
never was enough. Our mothers held us and let us sit on their laps
to comfort us. Sometimes they let us suck their nipples even though
they knew their breasts were dry and there wasn't any milk. Feeling
the breast and sucking the nipples temporarily comforted us.
Holding us close was enough for us to fall asleep. Our mothers
pretended that they were feeding us and they told us to suck and
swallow the precious milk. For the moment we were happy.

We prayed, and the following year was better. It rained and our
land was fertile and produced fruits, and we forgot the drought.
After living in the kibbutz for five years, in 1940 we left it just as
World War II started.

For the five years I had been alive, I was surrounded by sickness, hunger and poverty. The odds of my survival as a premature baby during a famine had been slim. Yet there must have been something inside of me that willed me to live and grow, and as a toddler I took advantage of everyone and everything to achieve that. At that age there was no moral imperative, just an instinctive knowledge that the strong survive, and I was going to be among them.

# Chapter Three, The Kibbutz

In 1933, the first years that my parents were married they were very close to each other. They worked hard but as long as they had each other they were happy. But gradually they needed something more to fill their lives, and the following year, 1934, they were starving for some culture. They were both very spoiled. In Poland my mother had gone to a coffee shop every Sunday afternoon and had coffee and cakes with her friends. Sometimes she went to the movies or a concert. In the kibbutz there were no coffee houses, movies or concerts, and she had not been able to make close friends.

In Italy my father had gone to luxurious restaurants on Sundays. He went to the La Scala opera house in Milan and saw the best operas. He lived like a spoiled rich boy. He only had to snap his fingers and the maid brought him anything he wanted, like clothes, books, magazines or drinks. In the kibbutz he had to do everything for himself. He had to wash his clothes and wash dishes in the kitchen. In Europe, both my parents had slept on silk sheets; here in the kibbutz they didn't have any sheets at all, they slept on a bare mattress and a blanket. They used the sheets for babies' diapers

In 1935 the kibbutz had a baby quota; no more no less than fourteen babies were allowed to be born. There were six girls and eight boys. I was the number six baby. I was supposed to be number nine but I jumped my turn because I was born two months prematurely. When I was born, at first all the attention was on me. My mother had so much breast milk that she was able to breast-feed me and another child. Her name was Ada; I thought she was my sister.

I developed normally even though I was premature. At six months I had very clumsy hand movements. I used a palmar grasp just like I was wearing mittens. At nine months I was able to pick up small objects. At ten months I was able to maneuver myself into a sitting position. At a year old I started to crawl and at a year and half I started to walk. From all the kids in the group I only played with Ada.

In 1936 all the proud parents celebrated the first birthday of their children. On my birthday, for one day I was the center of attraction. My mother dressed me in a new outfit. For once I didn't have to share my outfit with any of the other kids. This outfit was mine. When I outgrew the outfit my parents had to give it to another child; they weren't allowed to keep it. They sat me on a high chair and the rest of the children were on the floor. I felt that I was a king for the day. All day long the staff sang me happy birthday. They fed me a birthday cake and all the other kids who were able to eat the cake joined me. My mother had a free day. She didn't have to take care of the other children.

For my first birthday I got a package of clothes from the United States from my grandfather and aunt. The clothes were useless. The climate in Palestine was mostly hot, with dry summers and mild winters. I got heavy sweaters and wool coats. My parents wondered if those people knew which part of the world we were living in. My family lived in Chicago and they thought that I was freezing.

However, the wool sweaters and coats weren't wasted. Thanks to Jewish ingenuity they used the materials to make stuffed animals. They made teddy bears, dogs and cats, and stuffed the cloth animals with chicken feathers.

There were several carriages available for the babies. Each proud father wanted the best carriage for his child. The kibbutz rotated the carriages and we had to wait our turn. When it reached my turn I had already outgrown it. I started walking at a year and a half.

When my parents arrived in Palestine the immigrants were just learning to speak Hebrew as a national language. Before that in much of Europe it was forbidden to speak Hebrew except in the temple for prayer, since Hebrew was considered a holy language. Although I was learning Hebrew in the kibbutz in school, my mother spoke to me in German because that was the only language in which she was able to communicate with my father, since neither of them could speak Hebrew. She hated to speak Polish, since she had hated living in Poland. I was a baby and mixed Hebrew and German together. Most of the people in the kibbutz came from different countries, and their children also mixed different languages: Russian, Polish, Czech, to name a few. So maybe I wasn't so wrong with the way I spoke.

In 1938 I was three years old. I didn't sleep or live with my parents, I lived in a nursery with thirteen other children. Most of the time they were the only comfort I got. I had to share my clothes, food and toys with the other children. Once a day after dinner my parents took me out for an hour or two to be with them. They fed me extra food, played with me with my private toys, and I had some nice clothes to wear that I didn't have to share. Even so, I didn't feel close to them. Whoever paid attention to me, I called them "Mommy" or "Daddy." Some of us were so hungry for attention that when our parents approached another child in the nursery and comforted him, we had tantrums. My mother and father had to frequently reassure me that they were my real parents.

My father had two jobs, one in the kibbutz where he worked in the dairy farm and took care of the cows, and another outside the kibbutz where in his spare time he worked with other farmers. The money that he earned in his second job was spent for extra food for me and my mom. In spite of that we were always hungry. The kibbutz had a debt from buying building materials: machinery, breeding animals, seeds and plants, and they had to repay it. They paid with goods like milk, eggs, bread, fruits and vegetables that the kibbutz produced, creating severe food shortages for its own members. Though we were mere toddlers we had to sacrifice our milk. We gave it to the babies. When we were crying, our caretakers gave us sugar water. Being hungry we ate whatever they fed us. Everyone hated being poor and hungry, but no one had options.

Our kibbutz was in a fertile valley, but the main problem was how to obtain water for the arid fields. Hundreds of years ago there was a great population living in this region, but once they lost their water the population moved away or succumbed. Now the kibbutzniks dug canals with their bare hands and shovels because at the beginning they didn't have any other tools. Both men and women carried loose dirt from the canals. When that arduous task was finished they saw water rush through the canals to their thirsty crops. Bountiful harvests of beans, melons, tomatoes, corn, cucumbers and lettuces rewarded their labors, but they had to sell them in order to pay their debts.

For the first five years of my life I lived in the kibbutz, but I never liked living there. My mother didn't like it, either, and I am sure that her dislike had an effect on me. Sometimes at night, when I sleep, I have nightmares about our hard life in the kibbutz, even to this day.

One small pleasure was at the age of three when I was so proud of the wooden toy tractor that my father made for me. After working sixteen hours a day, six days a week, he had found time to surprise me and presented me with it. At that time at the kibbutz we didn't have many toys; whatever we had were made for us by the members of the kibbutz. The girls had corn dolls which were made from the ears of corn that we had for dinner. The dolls' clothes were made of whatever remnants of material the women could find. The girls held onto them for dear life. When they went to bed, they sucked their thumbs and held their dolls with the other hand. My own security blanket was not a soft toy or a blanket, it was my wooden toy tractor. When I went to bed, I also sucked my thumb and held onto my toy tractor. I didn't let any other kid in my age group touch it. I was like a lioness protecting her cubs. When I ate or was fed, the toy tractor was next to me. I talked to it just like it was a person and I pretended that it was my best friend. If somebody tried to take it from me, I had a tantrum. The wooden toy tractor appealed to a lot of the other kids, but I wouldn't share. One day the older boys pried it away from me and broke it and told me that they were teaching me a lesson, not to be a show-off. I felt as though they had stabbed me.

As an adult I know that I should have shared my toy with the other kids. But it was a special toy that my father had made for me and I just wasn't able to share it with anyone else.

When I was four years old we moved from the nursery building to the toddler building. We were toddler age or pre-kindergarten;

kindergarten and first grade children were also in our building. We started to learn reading, writing and arithmetic. We had recess and we played with the older children in a big play yard all fenced. I wasn't in my mother's classroom anymore; she took care of the babies from the age of birth to three years old. Sometimes I snuck out and went to my mother's nursery. She would hug me, give me a cookie and take me back to my group. She could have been any other woman as long as she hugged me and gave me a cookie and comforted me.

One of my favorite fruits was apricots. We didn't have them often but when we did, we devoured them. The whole dining room was full of the sweet aroma that we cherished. We gobbled them just like a bunch of animals and we spit out the pits and saved them to make whistles. We had very few toys in the kibbutz and this was a chance for us. We washed the pits and let them dry for a few days. Then we started rubbing them on the cement floor. We were only four years old but we competed with the older children in making apricot pit whistles. We rubbed a pit for hours until there were holes in both ends. Then we took a nail and we cleaned out the meat of the pit and we ate it. Finally the holes in the pits were big enough so we could blow air through them. It was hard to make a sound but once we mastered it we were proud of ourselves.

The girls collected pits and made holes in them as well, but instead of whistles they made necklaces and bracelets. The girls were all excited to wear them. What little we had we made use of it.

Life was very simple. Six days a week we did the same thing, Sunday through Friday. We got up at seven o'clock and washed and dressed for breakfast. Breakfast was from eight to nine. At nine o'clock we went to school until twelve o'clock. In between nine and twelve we had a snack. Twelve to one lunch. From one to three we took a nap. At three o'clock we had another snack. From four to five we took a bath and five to six was dinner. At six o'clock our parents took us for one or two hours to their house, and at eight o'clock our parents took us back to the dormitory where we slept until the next day.

Saturday was a special day; it was the Sabbath, and if my parents didn't have any work on that Sabbath I was able to spend the whole day with them. It was very rare that I had both my parents to myself. They took me from the dormitory to their house. It was a one-room apartment, with a shower and toilet. My parents had a large bed, a table, three chairs and a dresser where they hung their clothes and kept their linens and towels. They had just a few dishes for meals. Even though it was measly, I loved to eat the food that my parents prepared for me.

After eating breakfast we took a walk to the supply room. My parents got their supplies, like sewing materials for my mother to sew a blouse or a dress for herself. My father got some wood so he could make me a wooden toy. Sometimes we got plants or seeds that we planted in front of our house. We also got paint and we painted the inside and outside of our house. We had lunch at the kibbutz dining room, where I ate with my parents and Ada and her parents. My mother made several dresses for Ada. Ada told everybody that she was my sister. I wondered how, since I had a mother and a father and so did she; but I believed her. We ate dinner at our nursery and after dinner our parents put us to bed. Saturday was a long day for our parents and for us.

If I had been raised outside the kibbutz, I would have lived in the same room or apartment as my parents and would have been a part of their daily routine. They would have taken me shopping for food, for clothes and wherever they went. I would have had the comfort of living in a family surrounding. In the kibbutz, neither my parents nor I made many decisions; everything was decided for us. We didn't have to think very much, just do our jobs. The kibbutz was not the ideal place for children or adults. In those days many members were there out of necessity–it was a means of survival.

# Chapter Four, Why?

All of the kids in the kibbutz were in the same situation–poor and hungry. We dressed in the same kinds of clothes, ate the same food and were taught the same things in school. Yet some of the kids were kind and helpful to other kids, and some were simply mean.

I remember one night around midnight when the older kids came into our room and harassed us. They made noises like wild animals; monkeys, coyotes, hyenas and owls, and told us that those animals would get us. They held the corners of our sheets and threw us up in the air. Sometimes we fell on the floor and hurt ourselves. When we cried, the older boys called us crybabies. At an early age I learned to lock the door by putting a chair under the door handle. I wondered where the adults were that were supposed to protect us. The older boys would yell at me and tell me to open the door, otherwise they would get even with me. But I didn't open the door, I pretended that I was asleep and I didn't hear them. During the day when I left the room, the older boys pushed me and when I fell down, they mocked me, "Why are you so clumsy?"

It wasn't worth it to complain to the adults because they didn't do anything. Instead of attachment to our parents, each one of us was attached to a toy or a blanket because our parents weren't raising us. We only saw them after dinner for an hour or two, and then they went back to their quarters and we went to bed. The nurses that took care of us were always tired. There were only two of them and fourteen of us. They bathed us, changed our diapers, dressed us and fed us. They did our laundry and kept our rooms clean. It was a hard job and it was no wonder that they were too tired to play with us. They didn't have time to comfort us when we got hurt; instead, we comforted each other and we learned at an early age to take care of ourselves.

My parents and teachers noticed that I was a loner and a daydreamer. They tried to involve me in different projects. But it was my father who got me involved. He worked on the dairy farm, in the barn, feeding the cows. He washed them, milked them and every year he made sure that the female cows got pregnant and had calves. I saw bulls impregnate the cows, but I couldn't comprehend the parallel between the cows and human beings. Finally, at the age of four, I found my first real friend. It was not one of the kids in my group, however, and it was not an adult and it was not a toy or imaginary friend. It was a real friend and he didn't betray me. Our friendship was a priceless gift that I treasured and shared.

For my fourth birthday I didn't want a birthday party. I wanted to spend the day with my parents, but both had to work. However, my father promised to take me to the barn on my birthday to watch the birth of a calf. When I was younger I was afraid of the cows–they seemed so big–but when I was older I realized they were nice. I couldn't wait to see the birth. I got up at six o'clock in the morning, walked from the dormitory to my parents' house and I greeted my father in my pajamas and asked, "Is it time for the cow to give birth?"

My father replied, "Not yet, son. Happy birthday, get dressed."

I was impatient . "Do I have to go back to the dormitory and get dressed, Dad?" I asked.

My father replied, "Yes. We have plenty of time."

I couldn't wait. As boys in a hurry are wont to do, I dressed with the inside clothes outside and the outside clothes inside. I wore shorts and a t-shirt and sandals. When I finished dressing, I ran to the barn.

My father looked at me and said, "Alex, look at the way you are dressed. You are now four years old and you should know better how to dress."

I undressed in front of the cows and dressed properly. Then I saw my father and the mother cow lying on the floor and I yelled, "Is she giving birth?"

"Not yet," my father answered.

I waited quietly, sitting on the hay, cloaked in silence, staring at the cow. Finally, the cow started giving birth. Tears ran down my cheeks when I saw the cow laboring hard. The barn was completely silent. None of the other animals made a sound. My father put his big loving arms around me and told me, "Any moment, now, you will see the miracle of birth." All of a sudden I saw it. The calf slid out real quick, feet first. It was weak and shrouded with the placenta. It could hardly walk, but his mother licked the blood off of him and helped him to stand up. The calf tried to walk soon after birth. Its legs wobbled and it fell a lot.

But before long, the calf was walking and drinking its mother's milk. He was black with white spots. I asked my father if I could take care of the calf, and he agreed. I decided to call him Black.

I fell in love with Black. I don't know what I liked best about him; his black eyes, his soft black fur and, when he was older, his watery tongue that licked me and removed the flies that bit me. His tongue felt like sandpaper, but I liked it.

There were millions of flies in the barn, and Black protected me from them by wagging his tail at them. I felt comfortable lying in the hay with him and looking at the sky.

The calf followed me around just like a puppy, which was unusual. Rarely did a calf become attached to a human being. I learned to milk the cows, which helped my father. I made sure that some milk was left to feed the calf. For breakfast, my father would bring me some bread to feed me. I always gave some to Black. When Black got milk from his mother, I would suck the other udder and get milk next to him. When Black would begin to suck, his tail would wag and hit me. His eyes would look at me, perhaps wondering if I was stealing his milk.

Black was a great pet. The bond that we shared from the first day of his birth turned into the same connection that develops between two close brothers. Sometimes I brought Ada to the barn, and bragged about Black to her. She wasn't interested, but when I taught her to suck on the udder to get milk, she got all excited. I told her to keep it a secret, and she did.

During the first spring of Black's life he learned many things. He learned to chase the other kids that teased me. He learned that he must not annoy the cows.

Black understood human speech–at least my human speech. Whatever I told him, he did. I would tell him, "Eat, drink, come, or go." Surprisingly, Black waited patiently for my commands. He would moo when he didn't like somebody. Sometimes I took naps with Black; I would lay on the hay next to him and I felt great. Black liked to take a bath at the pond with me. He would follow me at an eager trot and wait for me to scrub him vigorously. He enjoyed splashing and swimming in the pond. Sometimes he would give me a ride, and I looked like an Indian prince when I was on his back. I was surprised that he didn't throw me off of his back. I guess that was because we were so close to each other.

I remember playing soccer with Black. I got a soccer ball for my fourth birthday and I managed to avoid sharing it with the other kids. I didn't trust the older children to play with my soccer ball, but I trusted Black. I taught him to kick the ball to me. I would kick the ball to him and he would return it to me. I pretended that I was a big soccer player and Black was the enemy. He enjoyed playing with me; I could see it in his eyes.

At school I was very quiet. I barely talked because I hadn't mastered the Hebrew language. My parents spoke to me in German and the kibbutzniks all spoke to me in Hebrew. I mimicked the words but they sounded garbled. In contrast, Black never laughed at me like the kids did. He enjoyed listening to me. I'd tell him stories and we would laugh. If I got hurt and bled, Black would lick my wound and his saliva was like an antiseptic. Alcohol and iodine didn't work as well. Sometimes, I used to put blood and dry manure on my wounds and, believe it or not, they healed.

I hardly played with any of the kids from the kibbutz, even though I was with them day and night. I ignored them. Once I got Black, he was my real friend. I told him all my secrets, and sometimes I thought that Black was laughing with me or crying with me.

The older kids teased me and made fun of me, but Black didn't. Whatever I told him, he kept secret. Whenever I did some schoolwork, I showed it to Black. He rewarded me by licking me. He was so proud when I showed him that I could write my name. Nobody else rewarded me; after all, everybody in my class knew how to write their names, so it wasn't such a big deal. But for me, it was!

Sometimes I would steal some bread with butter and sugar on it and bring it to Black, even though I was hungry myself. I hid it in my pocket and Black found it. It didn't occur to me to wonder if it was unusual for a child to spend so much time with an animal–Black was my companion. Sometimes if I came late to the barn it seemed like Black was angry with me. I wondered how he knew the time, since he didn't have a clock or a watch.

One day Black and I were playing soccer. I kicked the ball to Black and he hit the ball high, and before I could stop the ball it hit a glass window. Black was frightened by the loud noise, so he ran to the barn and I had to face the crime.

My teacher caught me and asked me, "Alex, did you break the window?"

I was eager to catch Black and I replied to her, "Not exactly. Can I go now?"

"No, Alex, you can't go now. Did you break the glass window?" I didn't reply. Then she grabbed me and yelled at me, "I am losing my patience. Did you or didn't you break the window?"

I didn't look at her as I said, "Black did it."

"Don't expect Black to pay for the window."

So instead of taking naps in the afternoon and playing, I had to work for three hours a day at the chicken house.

The hens lived in wire cages with sloping floors, and the eggs rolled to the front of each cage. I collected the eggs and packed them into egg cartons. I also washed the food containers and checked the containers for water and food. This wasn't fun, it was work, and I hated it. This made me dislike living in the kibbutz even more.

I remember the time there was a yellow fever epidemic. I had a very high fever and, even though sick, I ran to Black and he cooled me off by licking me and taking a bath with me in the pond that the kibbutz's livestock used.

Yellow fever is characterized by alternating high and low fevers. It is an acute, destructive, infectious disease caused by a virus transmitted by a mosquito, and mosquitoes breed in swampy water.

We had several swamps in the kibbutz that we had to drain. As soon as the rain started, the hard ground didn't absorb the water and the water stood there. It was the ideal place for mosquitoes to breed. The mosquitoes carried yellow fever, bit us and we got sick.

We were very lucky that some Australian soldiers were camped close by. On their free days they volunteered to work in the kibbutz. Some of the soldiers got romantically involved with the single young women at the kibbutz. The soldiers had had the same problems in Australia as we did in the kibbutz. They had many swamps and the only way they could permanently drain the swamps was by planting eucalyptus trees. We in Palestine didn't have any eucalyptus trees and we had never heard about them. The Australian soldiers, who had been mostly farmers and shepherds before the war, helped us. They had their families send eucalyptus saplings to us at the kibbutz. They told us that the trees would grow very quickly. Beside giving us shade, they would give us lumber and the oil from their leaves and seeds could be used as an antiseptic, a deodorant, or a stimulant. The faster-growing trees would protect the orange and lemon trees from the wind. They helped drain the swamps because they required much water to grow, and after they were planted the land became dry and the mosquitoes no longer bred there.

Our lack of lumber was not unique to the kibbutz; it was all over Palestine. The Turks, in World War I, had cut all the trees down. They had used them to burn for heat and cooking and so we didn't have any wood to build houses. But in a short while the eucalyptus trees grew big enough to provide us with lumber.

The Australian army camp was next to our kibbutz. We supplied them with electricity and water. We kids would watch them and imitate their combat maneuvers. From a passive group of children we became very aggressive. We went from verbal fights to physical abuse. We would pick up sticks and hit each other for no reason than that we were trying to imitate the Australian soldiers. We watched them digging trenches and we started to do the same. We were hungry and we begged for food. The Australians always treated us with kindness and gave us sweets. The food rations that a soldier had for breakfast, lunch and dinner could have fed all fourteen of us kibbutz kids.

The Australians also tried to learn to speak Hebrew. They used to imitate us when they heard us singing nursery rhymes like "The

Little Goat" and many others. This was the first time that they encountered the Hebrew language and their pronunciation sounded very funny to us. They supplied us with toys like jumping ropes, bicycle wheels, and soccer balls and basketballs. They built a basketball court for themselves, and they let the kibbutzniks use it.

My mother, for the first time since she was in the kibbutz, enjoyed being there. She joined the women's basketball team and, surprisingly, she was very good and could shoot baskets even though she was only five feet tall. The team competed around the area with other kibbutzim and they were number one. They didn't have any money for a trophy, so the generous Australians ordered trophies and presented them to each member of our team.

The Australians even gave us a piano. They ordered it for us all the way from Sydney and this was the present they gave the kibbutz in 1940, when they left us after staying for five years. Several members of the kibbutz who had taken lessons before they had come to Palestine started to play the piano and gave lessons to the children. I really enjoyed playing the piano with my father, but I didn't have any talent. I tried to imitate what he did with his fingers but I was very clumsy.

Sometimes I pretended that I was a bullfighter and teased Black, but he never hurt me even though as he grew larger he could have. Black only saw the first spring, summer, autumn and winter of his life. When the calf was one year old, the kibbutzniks slaughtered him and sold the meat because money was needed. The cow almost stopped her milk because she missed her calf. I was completely heartbroken. My father was afraid that Black's mother would stop producing milk, so he took the calf hide and pretended that it was Black, that Black was alive. The mother cow fell for that trick and produced milk.

Even though the barn was full of cows and calves it looked empty to me because Black was missing. It looked depressing. It may never be fair to judge the adults for what they did but then I did judge them. They shouldn't have killed Black.

I had decorated Black's spot in the barn. I had hung multicolored paper chains and pictures. After his death I destroyed the decorations and while I was tearing the paper chains and pictures down, I told myself how much I hated the grownups in the kibbutz. God made those animals, I thought, and we didn't have the right to kill them. I knew that Black had feelings, and he was my pet and companion. I thought that I should have run away with him and joined a circus; that way he would have lived.

The kibbutz provided my food, clothing and shelter. They tried to comfort me, but a huge void was created in my world. I remembered the times when I had tied Black to a toy wagon and Black had pulled me, and when I had play-wrestled with him. After Black was slaughtered I decided never to eat meat. We rarely ate meat at the kibbutz anyway, but on those occasions when we did, the kids teased me and told me that we were eating Black. I would run away from the dining room to the barn, crying. Black was the only real friend that I had had.

My father couldn't take my grieving any more, and he believed it would help if we pretended to bury Black. I could choose a burial plot and decorate it and put a wooden sign with his name on it. I asked my father if he would do that for me, but I didn't want anybody except my parents and Black's mother, the cow, to attend the ceremony. My father dug the grave and then my mother and I covered the dirt and pretended that we buried Black. I was the only one who said a few words.

"Black, I know that you are not in the human heaven, but God will make an exception for you and allow you to be in heaven. I love you." I was surprised that I didn't cry. I knew that Black deserved a burial. This was the first time that I faced death. I was not even five years old.

To provide a diversion, my mother decided to take my father and me to Poland. I was all excited because I was going to see my grandmother, uncles, aunts and cousins. But when my mother went to the embassy to get a visa to go to Poland, it was denied. We were lucky; the year was 1939 and Germany had attacked Poland and my entire family was killed.

My family in Poland were unknown to me and far away. Black was my real grief. I grieved for him for a long time. Sometimes I would start to cry without knowing why. My father stopped taking me to the barn. My new inspiration was to be a policeman. I started to collect toy guns. Some other kids who were the nicer ones gave me some guns and I was happier.

In 1940, when I was five years old, my parents decided to move from the kibbutz. Even with the diversion of the basketball team, my mother disliked living on the kibbutz, and I was still sad about Black. My grief over him had never gone away. The kibbutz had killed my pet. Some kids had dogs and the kibbutz didn't kill them; some kids had cats and the kibbutz didn't kill them. They only killed Black, my pet calf. I had heard that in some countries they eat cats and dogs. I felt that the kibbutz could have killed them and sold their meat instead of killing my calf.

# Chapter Five, Ali and Me

The year was 1940 and I was five years old. It was summer and the days were long and hot. My family and I were moving from the kibbutz to the city. I had lived all my life in a kibbutz in a safe environment of barely one hundred people, all Jews, who spoke the same language and wore the same clothes. I was afraid to live in the big city where thousands of people lived. Traffic jams, stores, automobiles, buses, were all new to me. My parents, trying to comfort me, told me that it was going to be okay.

My father borrowed a horse and a buggy from the kibbutz to move our belongings to the city. My father let me drive the buggy. I was very proud of myself, only five years old and already driving.

Our belongings consisted of very few things: a bed, a mattress, a cot where I slept, a broken table and three different chairs. The chairs were two folding chairs and one fixed one. We also had four pillows, three blankets, a toy chest filled with broken toys, our clothes, towels, and sheets and dishes. None of the dishes matched; it was a *mishmash*, a mixed-up mess. The cups were solid colors and the plates all had different designs. We didn't care how the dishes looked; they fulfilled their purpose. Pots and pans and utensils were included. We also had some food: a loaf of bread, some goat cheese, a jar of olives, a jar of strawberry jam, a fried chicken and some baked potatoes. That was all the food that my parents were able to gather from the kibbutz. Before I left the kibbutz I had a healthy breakfast, a bowl of hot cereal and hot chocolate. We were moving to a town not far from Nazareth, a mixed town where Jews and Arabs lived together.

After traveling an hour in the buggy, as we approached our new house, suddenly a dark-skinned kid dressed in a white robe ran across the street. I almost ran him over, but he was quick and escaped our buggy. I stopped our buggy short and it almost turned over. Once my father realized that the other child was all right he asked me, "Alex, are you okay?"

I answered, "Yes, Dad, I am fine. Is that an Arab boy? What is he wearing?" I asked. I had never seen an Arab child in the kibbutz.

My father replied, "He is wearing a robe."

I parked our borrowed buggy in front of a light green building. In front of the building was a wire fence with a metal gate. There were some olive and palm trees and a well-trimmed lawn. The Arab boy was still there, and my father started yelling at him in Arabic, "Inti Maznun?" (Are you crazy?), but the kid didn't care. I could see that he knew we were his new neighbors.

My father told me that we were going to live in this three-story building. After living in the kibbutz in a one-story building all my young life I was frightened at seeing a three-story building. I asked my father which floor we were going to live on and he told me the third floor. This scared me even more; I could see myself falling from that great height. I had always been afraid of heights. When we went swimming in the kibbutz at the water tower, I was afraid to climb the ladder and I didn't go. I don't know why I was afraid but I always was.

Jews and Arabs lived in the same buildings in this town. Each floor of this building had one apartment that consisted of three bedrooms, a kitchen, bathroom, hallway and a balcony. A Jewish family lived on the first floor, a father, mother and three adult kids. An Arab family lived on the second floor, a father, mother and three children. The children were two girls and a boy. On the third floor was another Jewish family of a husband and wife. My parents and I lived in the third bedroom on the third floor. We shared the kitchen and bathroom with the other Jewish family.

I started to climb the staircase and counted the stairs out loud in Hebrew. "Ajad, Chetaim, Chalosh, Arba, Jamesch, Seis, Seva, Chemone, Techa, Eser" (One to Ten). The Arab boy followed me and repeated me, counting the stairs in Arabic: "Waahad, Theen, Talaate, Arbea, Xemse, Sitte, Seba, Tamaanye, Tiesa, Asara." I was annoyed. He followed me to the empty apartment. He was a pest. He pushed me. I kicked him. I was a big hero in front of my father.

My father told him to go home, but the Arab boy followed us like a puppy. I studied him for a moment. There wasn't any love or kindness in my heart, but I pretended to give him a warm smile. He didn't smile back. My parents started to move the furniture and belongings, and the Arab boy helped us carry my toy box. Once he saw my toys his eyes opened wide. I had guns, pistols, metal handcuffs and lead soldiers. I had a soccer ball also but the Arab boy wasn't interested in my soccer ball, only the toy guns. I had a dart gun. He grabbed it and started shooting darts at me. My father scolded him in Arabic and told him never to aim a gun at a person. The boy laughed and ran home. I was happy to be alone with my parents in our single room. I was really afraid of the Arabs, because I had never seen olive-skinned people wearing strange clothing.

Everybody in the kibbutz was European. My father told me that anybody who was born in Palestine, now Israel, is a *sabre*. A *sabre* is a native of Israel. The word comes from a cactus fruit which is soft and sweet inside and hard outside.

This was the first time in my lifetime that I had touched an Arab. The family who were living in the two rooms next to us were very friendly. When we arrived they greeted us with a prepared lunch and then left us alone. It was a lunch basket with a *challah* (a Jewish bread made specially for Sabbath), honey, apples, a bottle of wine, some candies for me and a note in Hebrew, "Beteavon" (Welcome), from Judy and Martin Cohen."

It was very hot. It wasn't *khamseen*, the hot wind emanating from the Western Desert, but we were sweating and restless. Finally we settled down. I was drinking cold water from the faucet and eating my lunch. This was a special meal. I had never had challah and honey, and my parents hadn't had wine for a long time. My parents hung some pictures on the wall, pictures of some relatives from Europe–Poland and Italy–that my parents had told me about. My favorite picture was "Black and Me" (my pet calf and me). I asked my parents if I could go outside and check out the neighborhood. They attached a tag to my clothes with my name and address on it, and told me to be careful.

I left the house and I saw some Arab children eating watermelon. They were wearing different colors of *galabeyyas* and *keffiyehs*, the light, full-length robes worn by men, and the head pieces to protect them from the sun, sand and wind. The kids were barefoot, while I wore tennis shoes, shorts and a t-shirt.

The watermelon looked good and I was salivating. The same boy who had followed me to my apartment said to me in Arabic "Biddak?" and gestured to ask if I wanted some. I nodded, yes. I spoke my name, Alex, and the Arab boy told me his name was "Ali." He gave me a piece of watermelon. I didn't speak Arabic and he didn't speak Hebrew, but we were able to communicate. We were eating watermelon, spitting the seeds, and some of the water of the watermelon was dripping on the floor, and staining the sidewalk. When we finished eating the watermelon we dropped the rinds on the ground and we started playing tag. We tickled each other and made funny faces. Ali's father yelled at us and told us to pick up the rinds and throw them in the garbage can. We didn't pay attention since we were engrossed in our game. Ali's father noticed our lack of response so he sent his older daughter to clean the sidewalk. While we were playing tag, the daughter, dressed in a loose cloak, started picking up the rinds and hosed the sidewalk.

I was amazed that the boys didn't have to clean the place but the girls had to do it for us. While we were playing tag I noticed that Ali's sister looked at us with envy as if she wanted to play with us. She knew she wasn't allowed to run and play on the street. Ali grabbed the hose from his sister and wet her. We were all laughing. She left wet and was laughing also. At least she'd had the chance to play with us for a moment. Ali didn't let go of the hose; he wet the rest of us, too. It was hot and the cold water felt good. It didn't take long to dry our clothes.

I noticed some Jewish schoolgirls and schoolboys throwing pebbles and playing hopscotch. I approached them and even though I spoke their language, Hebrew, I felt they didn't want me to play with them.

In fact, I was hypnotized by Ali. I felt that this was the place that I belonged, and Ali and I would be great friends. I felt like we were magnets to each other, and whatever he did excited me.

Just then my father called me and asked me to go with him to return the horse and buggy. I asked my father if Ali could join us, since he was our neighbor. My father asked Ali's father if Ali could come with us, and then Ali joined us. I let him drive the buggy. I was surprised that Ali wasn't afraid to go to the kibbutz. When we arrived he acted as if he owned it. The kids that I had grown up with were curious to see an Arab boy. They touched him and felt excited and brave that they could touch an Arab boy. Ali didn't care. He was used to being watched and touched by strangers.

After we had moved in to our shared apartment I slept on a cot instead of a crib as I had done in the kibbutz. The moment I woke up the next morning I looked for Ali, just like I used to look for Black in the kibbutz.

Both Ali and I were five years old. I was blond with gray-green eyes and light skin. Ali was dark with black hair and bright, black eyes that were filled with curiosity. Ali's hair was cut short, free and uncombed. My hair was cut as short as Ali's but was combed. We both were slim and active, but while I was a country bumpkin, Ali was street smart.

That next morning I grabbed a piece of bread and goat cheese, ran down the stairs of the building and I met Ali. He shared his breakfast with me. We traded our food and his tasted better than mine. It was pita and falafel. I petted Ali on his head just like I used to pet Black. Ali had replaced Black in my mind and my heart.

Ali had two sisters. The older one was named Lylla and the younger one was Nadine. Their hair was long and the ends of it were tied in rubber bands.

At home, Ali was served first for breakfast. When he finished, the girls served themselves. The girls had to make Ali's bed and clean his room. They weren't allowed to play outside. Ali went out into the street without asking his parents' permission. After breakfast we went to my house, took some toy guns and played cops and robbers. Sometimes the girls joined us, when we played inside, but we never let them have guns. They pointed their fingers like pistols. We played for hours in Ali's apartment.

When Ali brought home some of my toy guns his father scolded him. His father was a religious man, a Muslim who prayed five times a day. He told Ali that he was a peaceful person and Ali should follow his lifestyle. The more Ali's father preached and forbade him to play with guns, the more Ali was obsessed with them. When we went to visit the toy store Ali grabbed the rifles or pistols. He knew every gun or pistol by name. Even though he couldn't read and write, he recognized them from the pictures in a gun magazine. I on the other hand wanted marbles, kites, tops, puppets and wooden puzzles.

Summer ended and the Jewish holidays started. After the Jewish New Year and Day of Atonement, in the month of Tishrei in the Jewish calendar (September), we started school. Ali celebrated the Jewish holidays with me. He went to the synagogue with me and we sat next to each other. Even though at first we couldn't speak the same language we became good friends. Ali spoke Arabic and I spoke Hebrew, but children speak their own language and we understood each other.

At school while I was drawing flowers, trees, houses, dogs and cats, Ali drew guns, pistols, and other weapons. He enjoyed stories about the war, World War II; I wasn't interested. But we both collected army memorabilia, which was easy to get. Most of Ali's army memorabilia I kept in my house because his father didn't allow him to keep those things.

We were inseparable. We went to school together and we did our homework together. I remember every Friday we saw a British Army convoy pass by. We followed them and begged for Chiclets. Each box of Chiclets contained two pieces of gum. What Ali and I collected we shared. The gum had to last us for a week. Once we ran out of gum, if one of us still had a piece of gum, when he finished chewing the gum he would wash it and give it to the other. If one of us swallowed the last piece of gum we considered it a crime. I gave Ali a smack if he did it and he did the same to me.

We were growing very, very fast. I particularly remember one day when I was six or seven and Ali and I were playing hopscotch. His older sister, Lylla, wanted to join us. She was eleven years old. Her mother had sent her to buy milk, and the milk was in a metal container. Lylla joined us in the game. At one point she fell and spilled the milk. She was afraid to go home not because she spilled the milk, but because she was jumping and had allowed her skirt to ride a few inches up her thighs.

When Lylla had spilled the milk on the sidewalk, she made a puddle. The milk started to run downhill. All of a sudden I saw flies, mosquitoes and spiders rushing to drink the milk. They had a party. I wondered where were they had been hiding. I also saw some ants on the sidewalk. It was a hot day and we were sweating and we imagined all those poor insects also sweating and thirsty. I asked Ali if he would contribute some money to buy milk to replace what Lylla had spilled. He told me, "Why should I?"

I ran home and broke my piggy bank and quickly was able to collect some money from other boys and girls. I replaced the lost milk and I thought Lylla was spared punishment. Ali didn't contribute any money and instead he told his parents what Lylla had done. When Lylla arrived home her mother yelled at her, "Shameful, shameful." Then she slapped her and didn't let her leave the house for a month. Lylla was only eleven years old.

For weeks after that, every morning I saw the milk mark on the sidewalk and it reminded me of Lylla's punishment.

Ali was the gutsiest of all the kids in the neighborhood. When it was really hot, he opened the fire hydrant, and all the other kids came by to cool themselves. It was against the law but Ali didn't care. He was always full of fire and energy, and that's what excited me about him.

I remember one day when Ali and I went to a party. We played games, ate cake and when the party was over and we were ready to leave, the adults gave each child a balloon. Ali and I got yellow balloons. Ali wanted a green balloon. He saw a boy with a green balloon. Instead of asking the boy to exchange his yellow balloon for the green, Ali shouted at the boy, "Give me the green balloon." The boy didn't want to give Ali the green balloon, so Ali popped it.

The boy started to cry and Ali laughed. He told him, "Next time when I tell you to give me, you give me!"

My best friend and constant companion Ali, had a cruel side that I did not understand and that I chose to ignore for many years to come.

# Chapter Six, Hardship

Both my parents thought that because the war had started, they wouldn't have any problems getting a job, but they were wrong. It was very hard to get a job. My parents were young and alone in the city for the first time since they came to Palestine. Far from the support of their own parents and their peers, they tried to survive. My father was a college graduate with a degree in business and my mother was a doctor. She couldn't practice medicine with her Czech diploma; she needed a British diploma in Palestine, and besides, nobody had jobs for doctors or university graduates. Everybody was looking for common laborers who could dig ditches, pick fruits and drive trucks. My father was strong but was used to doing only office work. He didn't last too long digging ditches. He had blisters on his hands and pain in his back and couldn't compete against an experienced Arab common laborer.

My father thought that he would be able to support the family and my mother would stay home taking care of me. They both were dreamers. Life in the city was expensive, what with rent, electricity, food and clothes. In the kibbutz they hadn't had to worry about those expenses; they had all shared the expenses and profit.

Now my father got up early in the morning before sunrise, looking for work. The streets were empty and you could hear his steps walking on the sidewalk before the *muezzin began* calling his flock to gather at the mosque and start the morning prayers. There were several men waiting to be picked up to work in the fields. My father pleaded with the owners to hire him and promised them that he would work longer and at a cheaper rate, but they didn't hire him because he looked too neat and tidy, and the owners didn't believe that European immigrants would work as hard as Arab laborers, even though the owners were European immigrants, themselves.

Sometimes Father was lucky and the city hired him to sweep the streets. When he got a job we ate well, with potatoes, eggs, bread and jam, but the city only hired him once a week. It was very painful for me to see my father without a job.

My mother got a job in the hospital as a visiting nurse. She needed a bicycle in order to do her job. We didn't have one and we hardly had any money to buy one. My mother went to a pawn shop and pawned our sheets and blankets and got a bicycle. It was autumn, it wasn't cold yet so we didn't need our blankets to keep us warm. If we were cold we wore our sweaters. We also used our towels to cover ourselves.

We were happy that Mom got a job. She earned enough to pay the rent, electricity, water, garbage and clothes that we bought secondhand.

Then Ali and I started school. We walked to school together, and Ali always put his arm around my shoulders and gave me the comfort that he would protect me from older boys who used to pick on me. Ali's older sister also walked with us to school. Ali went to the Arab section of the school and I went to the Jewish section of the school. During recess and lunch we met and we played. We played tag, hopscotch or jump rope. I noticed that when we played tag Ali was very rough with the other children but gentle with me. He would hit them hard and he would shout, "You are *it*." I didn't question that at the time–I just accepted it.

My mother and father left early in the morning to work. My parents took me to Ali's apartment where I slept until it was time to go to school. Five people normally shared their bathroom and now there were six of us, but we all went in our turns; first the boys, then the girls and then the parents.

If my father didn't work he walked to school with us. I was very happy that my father kept me company. Sometimes he would get a job at school as a janitor. I wished he could get a steady job. He didn't get paid much but he was able to get us a little extra food like bread, cheese, olives and milk.

When my father didn't work and I didn't go to school he took me to the park and we played soccer. I didn't take Ali with me because I wanted my father to myself. When I was with my father I was the happiest kid in the world. Even though we didn't have much money we had each other. I was very lucky that I had a soccer ball; very few kids in my neighborhood had a ball. My father used to kick the ball to me and I kicked it back to him. We used to run the field and pass the ball to each other. Sometimes I tried to take the ball away from my father but because he was bigger and taller it was very hard to take the ball from him. I enjoyed playing goalkeeper since I was able to use my hands and I tried to stop the ball. We alternated and when my father eased up enough to let me score a goal I was in heaven. He would yell loud and clear, "Goal! Goal!"

My father taught me to dribble the ball down the field with my feet. It was hard. I learned to control the ball without using my hands. I used my feet, head, legs, and chest to advance the ball.

There was a very special relationship between us. I didn't get material things but I got his undivided attention.

At the park we saw a billboard saying, *"Join the army, we need you."* I asked my father, "Are you going to join the army?"

He replied, "I don't know."

"Dad, are we winning the war?"

"I don't think so."

"Dad, what will happen to us if the Germans come here?"

"Alex don't worry, the Germans will never be here."

We continued playing soccer, and when we were through I noticed some dead trees at the park. The trees had lost their leaves and the branches were brown and woody. The leaves were dry on the ground. I remembered just a few months ago when the trees had stood tall with healthy green leaves. I knew the trees had been happy they were alive.

I asked my father, "How did the trees die?"

He told me, "They got a disease and died."

I said, "Can I get a disease and die?"

My father replied, "No, I won't let you get a disease and I won't let you die. Your mother is a nurse and she will take good care of you."

Satisfied that I would not die, I once again looked at the dead trees and I told my father, "We should have prevented this. We should have taken better care of the trees."

As Dad and I were talking, Ali arrived at the park. He broke some branches and made two sticks and pretended they were swords. He asked me if I wanted to play pirates with him. I told him, "No." I took the soccer ball and went home with my father.

That year was 1941, and Ali and I were six years old. We both were in the first grade. I noticed that Ali's school was harder than mine. Ali studied Hebrew and Arabic, but I only studied Hebrew. We were reading the same reading book. The name of the book was *Javeri*, "my friend" in Hebrew. I also noticed that Ali was learning to add and subtract while I was still learning to recognize the numbers. I don't know if Ali was smarter than me but his school was more advanced than mine.

We started school at eight o'clock in the morning, but first we had our daily prayer. For us Jews it was *"A-don o-lam, a-sher ma-lach, b-teh-rem kol y-tzir nivra; L-eit na-a-sa v-chef-tzo kol, a-zai meh-lech sh-mo nik-ra,"* which means "You are the Eternal God, who reigned before any being was created; when all was done according to your will."

Ali's morning prayer was in Arabic, *Ala Kabir*, which means "God is great." We both faced East because Mecca, a holy city for the Muslim, is to the East, and for the Jew the Wailing Wall is also to the East. After we finished praying we listened to the radio world news, for even at six years old we wanted to know about the war. Then we started to write our alphabet. Ali did both Hebrew and Arabic, I did only Hebrew. At ten o'clock we had recess and the Arab and Jewish schools mixed. Ali always greeted me and we played together. If I had any treat I shared it with Ali. After recess, in our class we read, played with our toys or studied science or health. Ali did reading in Arabic and Hebrew. From twelve to one we ate lunch and played outside. I only played with Ali; otherwise, I was a loner. Back in class, from one to three my class studied the Bible and we listened to records and we drew pictures. Ali, on the other hand, studied the Koran. He told me that he had to memorize ninety-nine ways to say the name of God.

In the Jewish school we ended by singing, *"O-seh sha-lom bi-m'ro-mav, hu-ya-a-seh sha-lom a-lei-nu v'al kol Yis-raeil, vi-m'ru: Awmain,"* which means "May the One who causes peace to reign in the high heavens cause peace to reign among us, all Israel, and all the world."

I got used to living in the big city, where thousands of people lived. I was fascinated by the traffic jams. I loved to go to the stores, and when I had some money I treated Ali and myself to a candy.

I hardly saw my mother. She worked very hard but got paid very little. All I knew was that she visited the homes of all the children in the neighborhood, both Jews and Arabs. She made sure that the children were vaccinated and went to school, and that expectant mothers got prenatal care.

I have neglected to mention the importance of the bicycle. I remember that there were four members in my family: my father, mother, me and the bicycle. We ate and slept in the same room with the bicycle. It was necessary for her job, and it allowed us to survive. Although my father had told me that the Germans would not conquer Palestine, I still expressed my worry to my mother. She told me that if by some chance the Germans conquered Palestine, that since we had a bicycle we could all ride together on it to a safe place. It didn't occur to me then how the three of us and all our things could fit on one bicycle.

Every morning I made sure that the bike was with us. At night before going to sleep I looked at the bike and it reassured me that we were safe.

# Chapter Seven, The Bicycle

That day was a good day for me. I was in the second grade and the year was 1942. It was also a good day for my father. It was the second day that he worked as a janitor at our school. If we were lucky he would get a permanent job there. The pay wasn't great but my father was able to get leftover food to take home.

For lunch that day at school we had a choice: pita falafel or spaghetti with tomato sauce, and chocolate pudding or halvah (a confection made from ground sesame seeds and honey) and milk. As always I ate lunch with Ali. Ali had spaghetti and chocolate pudding and I had pita falafel and halvah. We usually shared our lunches, but Ali didn't care for the pita falafel. He told me, "My mother could do better."

After lunch we had physical education. We had track events, including running races. Although I was considered one of the best runners in my school, I had always thought that Ali was a faster runner than me, but that day I beat him. Ali couldn't claim that he lost the race because he didn't have tennis shoes because we both ran barefoot. Once I knew that I could run faster than Ali I felt great. So far I'd had a great day; the food, my winning the race, and because my father was working.

My family consisted of my father, mother, me and the bicycle. I considered the bicycle a part of my family because the bicycle was so important; without it we couldn't make a living. The bicycle never complained to us and it was very easy to get along with.

When I came home after school that day with my father, I saw my mother sitting on our broken chair. I wanted to tell my mother that my father had brought leftovers of my favorite food from school and I had beaten Ali in track. But she was sitting like a beaten animal, crying and looking a mess. She was on edge and ready to scream at my father and me. The room was a mess. The bed wasn't made, the dishes from breakfast weren't washed and a stack of clothes were on the floor. My mother had millions of things to do but she was sitting and crying.

I knew if I opened my mouth I would irritate her, but I was a child and I couldn't keep my mouth closed so I started talking to her. I talked and I talked and my mother and father asked me to be quiet, but I wasn't. I was too happy and excited, and I wanted the whole world to know that I was one of the best runners at my school. I nagged my parents to give me some halvah.

They told me to go outside and play. I told them very rudely, "Why should I?" My mother slapped me and told me to be quiet now. The hard slap caused my nose to bleed and I started to cry. My mother was also crying. She was yelling at me, "Go and play outside, Alex!"

I didn't know why my parents didn't want me around. I felt so hurt. A moment ago I was on cloud nine, happy, joking and laughing; now they slapped me and yelled at me. I had believed everything was perfect. Both my parents were working and I was doing well in school. We didn't have to worry about the rent and food. I asked myself, "What happened?" Then my father informed me that our bike had been stolen. At that moment I didn't care. All I wanted was a piece of halvah.

Later on I realized that without a bike my mother would not have a job. The bike was our bread and butter. I knew how much we had loved our bike. Every morning my father had checked the tires and made sure the bike was spic-and-span clean, even though it was old and shabby looking. Sometimes I had helped my father wash the bike and polish it. It was our lifeline. I remember when my mother had a flat tire and she'd had to walk in the heat, sweating and walking the bike home cursing it. My mother was lucky that when she got the flat tire the air escaped slowly and she didn't fall down. When she brought it to the apartment my father removed the tire from the wheel and put it in the bathtub, which was full of water. We put some air in the inner tube held it in the water so the hole would bubble and then we could tell where the leak was, and then we patched it. We were poor and we couldn't afford to buy new inner tubes for the bicycle tires. At that time rubber inner tubes cost almost as much as a new bike. We had an air pump and my dad let me pump air into the tire. I felt that I contributed to keeping up the bike.

I had dreamed that my father taught me to ride the bike, and that I traveled around the world. I went to Poland and saved my mother's family from the death camp. I rode my bike so fast that the Germans couldn't catch me. I called our bike "a friend," and friend it was. Just as I had confided in and shared with my calf-friend, Black, years earlier, I had done the same with our bike. I used to show the bike my schoolwork papers, and if I got a bad grade I promised the bike to do better. Sometimes when I got goodies like candy, or cookies, or chocolate, I pretended to share them with the bike. I told all my secrets to the bike since it was my friend. I changed the ribbons on the handle bars and I put stickers on the bicycle tubes.

The bike was an old one, a man's bike, but my mother didn't care. She had a basket in front of the bike where she carried her documents and medicines. Sometimes the chain broke, but my father would fix it. The bike was painted blue but the color was fading. The whole family loved the bike.

My mother told me that once she had found that the bike was missing she reported the theft to the police. She had then asked her boss if she could work inside the hospital instead of visiting homes. She also asked the hospital to lend her a bike. All the answers were, "No." My father asked my mother to beg her boss to keep her on but my mother told him, "She doesn't need me. She has more nurses than she can handle."

"What are we going to do without your salary?" he asked.

"Dolf, I don't know." My mother was sobbing.

Father told us, "Let's have dinner and then we will feel better."

After supper I went to Ali and I told him the bad news. I didn't want to cry. I tried to hold my tears but once I told him I started to cry. At first Ali didn't know what to do for me. He offered me his last pack of gum and told me, "Chew it and then you will feel better." Then Ali took me to the mosque, the Islamic house of worship.

The mosque consisted of two parts. The tower was the most prominent feature of the building. A man called a *muezzin* called Muslims to prayer from a balcony on the tower. The second part of the building was the domed prayer court. On the floor of this mosque was a beautiful handmade rug. Ali told me that the rug was made in Iraq by children aged three to five years old. The walls of the mosque were ornamented with engraved names of Allah in Arabic calligraphy. I was fascinated with the beauty of the mosque.

Before Ali started to pray in Arabic, we washed our hands and feet. Ali told me that Abu-Hurayra, companion of the Prophet Muhammad, had said, "The Messenger of God told us that God has ninety-nine names, one hundred minus one. The one who names them all enters paradise." We thought that if we recited the 99 names of God we would find the bike. Ali knew only ten. We started to recite them: "the Compassionate; the Merciful; the King; the Holy; the Source of Peace; the Preserver of Security; the Protector; the Guide; the Mighty; and the Overpowering." When we finished reciting the ten holy names I was sad because I believed that only ten names would not help us find the bike. Ali told me not to worry; he would ask his sister to help him with God's other names. I asked Ali to recite God's names again and again; I wanted to be sure He heard us. I approached one worshiper who understood Hebrew and I asked him if Ali was pronouncing God's names properly. The man assured me that Ali knew God's names. I felt good since we were doing something.

We ran home and asked Ali's sister, Lylla, to name God's other names. She told us that she wanted a penny a name. At that time a penny was a lot of money; you could buy an ice cream cone for a penny. Ali and I had a few pennies between us and we couldn't pay her a penny for each name. Ali hit her and told her not to be so selfish. After arguing for a long time we settled that she would tell us the additional names she knew and we would buy her an ice cream cone.

Ali told her the names he knew and she added: "the Creator; the Maker; the Forgiver; the Wise; the Loving; the Governor; the Glorious; the Powerful; the First; and the Last." Her voice was monotonous; she recited the names of God without any feeling.

I still wasn't happy but I knew we had started our mission. I knew that it was a great task to do, but I was determined to find the bike. The only way I knew was to ask God for help. I knew my whole family was depending on that bike.

I took Ali to the synagogue, the Jewish house of worship. It had a Holy Ark in which the rolls of Scripture were kept; a lamp that burned all the time to symbolize the constant presence of God; and candlesticks for use on the Sabbath and festival days.

The congregation was divided by a screen, with the men sitting on one side of it and the women on the other side. The only prayer that I knew by heart was *"Sh'ma Yis-ra-eil; Adonai Eh-lo-hei-nu, Adonai Eh-chad!"* (Hear, O Israel: the Eternal One is our God, the Eternal God alone!) I added a few of my words: "God, please let us find the bike in one piece." Ali recited the prayer with me. We both felt good. We were doing something, we weren't sitting idle.

I asked Ali, "What if they took the bike apart and sold the parts?"

Ali reassured me, "I don't think so. It would take too much work. And if the bike was taken apart and the parts sold, it would mean bad luck."

I added, "Probably the man needed the bike so he could get a job."

Ali looked at me and said, "I think he stole it and sold it."

I told him, "It is so sad that now we've lost our linens and our bike." In order to buy the bike we had pawned our linens.

Every day before we went to school we visited the mosque and we prayed. We learned eleven more names of God, "the Great in Majesty; the Most High; the Most Great; the Light; the Fashioner; the Sustainer; the Reckoner; the Majestic; the Generous; the Watcher; and the Answerer." Ali told me, "Because God is the Watcher and Answerer, very soon we will find the bike."

I waited for two weeks and still we didn't find it. I started to doubt God. Meanwhile, my mother didn't work. She felt that somebody had violated her. She felt that it was the end for us. On top of all of this my father lost his job as a janitor in our school and he couldn't find another job even though he was willing to do anything.

That year was 1942, the year that many members of the kibbutz deserted it. Both men and women joined the British Army as a way to support their families. The kibbutz couldn't support them. Everything they grew was unsalable. They grew watermelons and grapes but the Arabs undersold them. The Arabs had been farmers for hundred of years and the Jews at the kibbutz had only started a few years ago. There wasn't any market for the fruit that they grew so they let it rot.

Back in the city, it had been several months since the bike had been stolen and Ali and I were still searching for it. We stole some balloons and told ourselves that as soon as we found the bike and my mother started working again we would pay for them. We needed the balloons to send them to God with a message. We printed in Arabic some of God's other names: "the All Embracing; the Prevailing; the Advancer; the Delayer; the Outward; and the Inward." We put the messages into the balloons, inflated them, tied them to hold the air inside, let them loose to fly away and hoped God got the messages.

Ali and I knelt down and prayed. I promised Ali that I would pray with him five times a day, at dawn, midday, midafternoon, sunset, and nightfall.

I had changed. From a noisy, active kid I turned into a shy, frightened kid. Since my mother had lost her job my father hardly worked. Everything he earned was barely enough to pay rent and utilities. We hardly had any food to eat. My parents dragged me to a soup kitchen, a Catholic soup kitchen that served everyone.

I had never been in a soup kitchen. I felt that I became a beggar and so did my parents. They told me, "This isn't going to last too long; we are going to find jobs and live like kings." I was afraid that some of the other kids in my school would see me and make fun of me. I didn't want Ali to know how poor we were.

The soup kitchen was only open two days a week, Monday and Friday. It was in a room in the back of the church. We ate and prayed. They gave us packages to take home, which had kasha, canned milk, grits, bread and jam. I hated the kasha, it was brown

rice and noodles, but it tasted like dirt. But when you are hungry
and your stomach is empty you can't help yourself. I enjoyed the
grits because my mother mixed them with jam that was nice and
sweet. At that time we never had fruit, meat or vegetables. I got
those at school but in retrospect I wonder how my parents survived
with our meager dole.

Most of the people…Jews, Arabs and Catholics…who visited
the soup kitchen were just like us; trapped in the Great Depression,
unable to get work to feed their families. The children and the
adults were very quiet and all were ashamed to be there. The nuns
were polite and caring for those of us who were so desperate.

Now I started to doubt the Jewish and Muslim Gods, so I went
to ask for help from the Catholic God. In our neighborhood there
were some Catholic children that went to parochial school. We
played with them, especially at Christmas time when they got new
toys. I asked them if they would pray for me to help me find the
stolen bike, and they led Ali and me to their church and then left us.
I was nervous and embarrassed to enter the church because I had
never been inside a Catholic church before. After Ali and I rang the
doorbell we hid. When the nuns opened the door we giggled. They
called us, "Don't be afraid, welcome." We stayed hidden and when
they closed the door we rang the door bell again. I was afraid to see
those nuns again, afraid they would punish us for hiding. But they
didn't and we went inside.

There were fifteen steps leading up to the door. I was scared
before I entered the door but once I was inside I was struck by the
richness of the decoration, and by the pictures of the Old and New
testaments. Some of the pictures were very scary to my seven-year-
old mind. When I saw a man hanging on a cross with blood I was
terrified, but once I got used to the church I enjoyed the paintings.
"This is the place that God will help me find the bike," I thought.

Some of the Catholic kids who were there told us that we had
to light some candles and pray to God, and they showed us how to
do it. I wanted to light all the candles and hoped that God would
answer my prayers soon. Once I found out that I had to pay for the
candles I lit only one candle and prayed to Jesus Christ.

I don't remember the prayer, I only know that I crossed myself
and Ali refused to do it. I told Ali, "I don't care, as long as I find

the bike." When Ali left the church I went back and I kneeled in front of the altar and begged for help. I talked to God: "God help me find the bike. I am not asking for much, after all the bike was ours." I cried. I wanted a world of peace and harmony, and I wanted our bike.

❦

I wasn't happy because we were living like beggars. My parents were constantly fighting. My father wanted us to go back to the kibbutz but my mother had hated it there. I tried to hide underneath the bed to get away from the shouting, door banging and screaming.

Although I had had nothing to do with the theft of the bike, still I blamed myself as if somehow it was all my fault. This was made even worse by my mother telling me that without the bicycle we couldn't escape if the Germans came for us. The bicycle had been our salvation.

Several times I visited the Catholic church and I tried to pray to God. Since I didn't remember the prayers I thought God wouldn't listen to me. I begged some Catholic kids to go to church with me and help me to pray to God. They told me that they would rather play soccer than go to church with me. I thought if I bribed them they would pray with me and we would find the bike.

In our neighborhood we had a grocery store. The grocery store had several glass containers filled with candies. There were hard candies, chocolate candies, jelly candies, etc. Ali and I drooled when we saw the older kids who worked there cleaning the glass containers and eating the broken candies. We didn't have any money and we wanted some candies. We would touch the glass containers and pretend that we were helping ourselves to the candies. We didn't actually ask for candies, but our eyes were begging. When some of the customers gave us candies we stopped breathing and held our mouths open. We wished that we were older so we could work as bagboys. Sometimes we helped the older people by carrying their groceries to their homes. If we were lucky they would tip us. Whatever we made we used for buying candies.

I saved my money and I bought some candies and I approached and bribed some of the Catholic kids. We went to church and started to pray. I repeated every word they said: "Our Father which art in heaven, hallowed be thy name…" When I finished that first sentence they all yelled, "Glory hallelujah!" We continued praying, "Thy kingdom come, Thy will be done, on earth as it is in heaven." I asked them, "Is that all?"

"Stupid." They told me, "There is more. Do you have any more candies?"

I replied, "Yes, I do. I have a long stick of a peppermint candy."

"Give it to us, otherwise we aren't going to tell you the rest." I gave them the candy. I was sad because I had given them my last piece of the candy, and I wanted to end the prayer and find the bike.

They started again, "Give us this day our daily bread. And forgive us our trespasses, as we forgive those that trespass against us. And lead us not into temptation. But deliver us from evil. Amen." I rubbed my forehead with a knuckle and I ran home. I went home, I laid on my bed and I cried.

Sometimes when I walked on the street and I saw people riding bicycles I wondered if one might be our bike. I wondered if I called its name it would be returned to us. But the bike didn't have a name. It only had a license number, and I didn't remember the numbers. Was it 1721 or 1271? I didn't want to ask my mother; I didn't want to show my family how ignorant I was.

<hr/>

Finally, my mother was able to get another job. In spite of her medical skills, she was only able to get a job at a bakery. Every morning she would pick up bread and deliver it to the neighbors. She gave them credit and charged them for the delivery service. She didn't earn much but we survived. My parents and I knew that the only way we could get ahead was if we got a bike and my mother could work for the hospital again. I got frustrated and blamed myself that we lost the bike. I thought that I should have quit school and watched the bike instead.

Even after the bike had been missing for weeks, Ali and I were still on a quest to find the remaining names of Allah. Ali asked his teacher to write more of God's other names, and the teacher did: "The Sublime; the Amply Beneficent; the Acceptor of Repentance; the Dominant; the Bestower; the Provider; the Decider; the Knower; the Withholder; the Plentiful Giver; and the Abaser." Ali told me that we had to burn the list in order to reach God, but we didn't have any matches. I told Ali we could go to the church and get some. We went to the church and took some matches, but when we struck the matches they didn't work. We knew we had committed a sin by taking the matches. We took the paper with the list of God's names and bought a candle at the church and let the paper burn. Then we hoped it would be effective, since it was an Arabic prayer, done by a Jewish boy and an Arab boy, in a Catholic church.

Then I had another idea. I thought that maybe if I stopped talking for a whole day God would help me find the bike. I didn't talk for a full day, which was very hard for me. But He didn't help me find it. Then I thought if I fasted for a day He would hear me and help. I fasted, and that was very hard also, but He still didn't help me.

I was obsessed about the bike; I couldn't forget it. One day it was in our room, the next day it was gone. Bike, bike, bike–that was the only thing in my mind.

On the money side things weren't getting better. My father only worked once or twice a week. He pawned his suits that he had brought from Italy. I was sad because I had been so proud of him, seeing him wearing a suit in temple for the Jewish holiday. Now he was considering joining the British army, not because he was patriotic but because that was the only way that he could support us.

I begged Ali for another list of God's names. Ali was sick and tired of me and yelled at me, "Alex, you don't know when to stop."

I replied, "Ali, if somebody stole your father's taxi, would you give up?" Ali looked at me and said, "I am sorry," and got me another list of God's names. This one said, "The Exalter; the Honorer; the Humiliator; the Hearer; the Seer; the Judge; the Just; the Informed; the Clement; and the Great." We took the list written on a piece of paper and instead of burning it, we buried it in the Muslim cemetery. Since burning hadn't worked we hoped that the dead people would help us find the bike.

Then there came still another list from the Arabic with God's names: "The Forgiving; the Rewarder; the Resurrector; the Witness; the Real; the Trustee; the Strong; the Firm; the Patron; the

Giver of Life; the Giver of Death." We took this list and we buried it in the Jewish cemetery.

After all of our efforts nothing had worked. I was angry, and I asked my rabbi what to do. The Rabbi replied, "God helps the ones who help themselves."

There were thirty or so more of God's names which we never got, but now I was going to heed the rabbi's advice. I decided to look for the bike in the neighborhood. I asked Ali, "What would you do if you had taken the bike?"

Ali replied, "I would take it to the pawnshop where they would pay me good money and wouldn't ask me where I got it."

So Ali and I went to the pawnshop and, sure enough, we found it! I recognized it by the blue ribbons on the handle bars and the stickers that I had put on the bicycle tubes. I was excited that God had finally helped me to find the bike. I touched the bike and called him My Friend. I asked him if he missed me and did the thief treat him well? Ali and I ran and told my mother and she went to the police, claiming her bike. The police didn't do anything. My mother and I then went to the pawnshop and spoke to the owner. "Sir, this is my bike. It was stolen from me a few weeks ago."

The owner replied, "The only way you will get the bike is if you pay for it"

My mother raised her voice said, "Sir, do you sell stolen merchandise and will you please tell me who brought you this bike?"

The owner said to my mother and me, "Lady, if you raise your voice I will have to call the police and they will kick you out." I started crying and now I wondered if there really was a God. My mother pleaded with the owner, asking him to identify the thief and give her back the bike. The answer was, "No."

I started to hate God.

At home I looked around the room and I saw my father and mother and I didn't see the bike. My father told me, "It is our tragedy. It is what it is. It isn't necessarily what you'd like it to be."

The next morning my father enlisted in the British army, knowing that was the only way he could support his family. My mother and I were sad and we blamed it on our luck. We had gone downhill since our bike had been stolen.

Meanwhile, Ali was in heaven. He loved the army and army games. He wanted to be a part of the army base and he felt he would be closer to the army now that my father had joined.

Because of the loss of our bike I lost my father, we lost our livelihood and I lost my faith in God.

I never learned to ride a bike in Palestine, I only learned thirty years later. I was teaching a special education class in California and my students, who were as afraid to attack new skills as I was, bought me a bike and they taught me how to ride it. Every day when I looked at the bike it reminded me of the bike we had in Palestine.

# Chapter Eight, The Army

Everyone says that Israel is the land of milk and honey, that people are honest and religious, and it is the birthplace of the three major religions in modern life: Judaism, Christianity, and Islam. But at an early age I discovered that this country, then known as Palestine, had more than its fair share of thieves, murderers and corrupt political officials. I thought that we could trust everybody in the city the same as in the kibbutz. At the kibbutz we never locked our doors, but in the city we did. When my mother's bike was stolen, I lost a piece of my innocence. I saw that the world could be very cruel. Why couldn't the hospital allow my mother to work inside? After all, she was trained as a medical doctor and could be very useful, but they had no job for her without a bicycle.

I learned at an early age not to trust anybody. Once I found our bike in a local pawnshop, then I knew that a local person had stolen it. I wondered why the police didn't do more to help my mother recover the bike. This experience made me more self-reliant and began to build my mistrust of our neighbors. I didn't trust any of our neighbors, except Ali and his family, because he was my best friend.

My mother was devastated after somebody stole her bike. Things were not getting better even when both of my parents were working; they hardly made ends meet. Some months we couldn't pay the rent and we knew that the landlord would soon evict us. We pawned our table and chairs in order to pay the rent. I collected bottles in the neighborhood and redeemed them for the equivalent of pennies and nickels. Ali was my partner. Sometimes we helped Ali's father to deliver groceries and the people would tip us.

My father joined the army, not because he was a patriot but because that was the only way he could support his family. He was placed in a Jewish Palestinian unit in the British Army. He got paid three months in advance so we were able to pay our debts. My mother and I believed that as long he was in the army we would get part of his salary and would be able to live above the poverty level. We would be able to pay the rent, electricity, water and garbage and have food on the table. We would be able to buy secondhand clothes and once a month we would even be able to go to the movies.

My father was in the infantry. He took basic training for nine weeks and then waited to be sent to Egypt. As long as he was stationed in the base in our town I was able to see him every day. He came home in the evenings and had dinner with us and would tell us about his new experiences.

"The job of becoming a soldier in my mind is similar to the job of training mules for pack work. Every day for two weeks a new piece of equipment was issued to us which had to be placed in our pack according to the soldier's handbook." The full backpack weighed 55 lbs. and my father told me besides that he had to carry a rifle and ammunition. "I realize," he said, "that snails and turtles don't exactly lead a life of ease when they carry such a large load."

Once Ali saw my father in uniform he thought my father was great. My dad took Ali and me to his army base and gave us a treat; we rode on a jeep and a tank and ate lunch with the soldiers. Before we left the base some of the soldiers gave us an army cap, buttons and some empty bullet shells.

Sometimes Ali and I would shine my father's boots or shoes and we did this with pride. I did this because I loved my father and Ali did it because he pretended he was in the army. Ali told me that when he grew up he was going to join the army. He would travel all over the world in his army uniform. He told me that he knew that wearing the army uniform would make the girls drool over him. I didn't care about joining the army, but since my father joined the army I had learned a lot about it. I learned how to salute officers and I knew all the ranks. Before my father joined the army I didn't care what rank I played as long as we played army, but now I told everybody that unless I was an officer I wouldn't play. Since I had most of the toy weapons, the other kids let me be an officer.

I had an air about myself. I thought that I was better than anybody in my entire school except Ali and the other children whose parents had joined the British Army. I watched the older kids wearing their parents' uniform shirts. I begged my father to let me wear his army shirt even though it was many times too big for me. It was a long sleeve khaki shirt with a collar and two pockets. My father told me, "Alex, I would let you wear my army shirt, but not for the purpose you want."

"Dad, don't you want me to help in the war?"

"Alex," my dad said, "wearing an army shirt doesn't make you a soldier. You are getting too big for your britches."

In spite of my father's admonition I put on his shirt, folded the sleeves and tucked the shirt inside my shorts. I must have looked like an inflated balloon, but I said to him, "Don't I look great? Can you get one shirt for me and one for Ali.?"

My father untucked the shirt and replied, "I'm not getting one for you or for Ali."

I got angry and I told him, "When you leave, I am going to be the man of the house, and the only way I can protect Mom is if I have an army shirt."

My father said, "Alex, there are better ways to take care of Mom. Meanwhile, I'm still here. I'm not going away so quickly."

I started crying. "Dad, I know you are leaving us. Why can't Ali and I have an army shirt?"

He must have grown weary of my pleas, for he finally relented. He kissed me and he said, "Okay, Alex, I will get you and Ali shirts."

I was sad and so was my father, but he got them for us. Now I had an army shirt. All of a sudden the older kids accepted me and I felt like a big shot.

At the army base I saw my father digging trenches, so as the "officer" I ordered my "soldiers" to dig trenches. I saw my father filling sacks with sand so we did the same, with empty sacks and shovels we were able to steal from the base. We put several sand sacks in front of our house. I watched my father marching and I marched with my soldier friends. We were prepared to fight anybody who would try to attack us.

My father told me that he lost all his sense of individuality and privacy when he was drilling. He felt like nothing more than a pair of feet with a serial number attached thereto. There was close order drill, then extended order drill, calisthenics, a bawling out by the sergeant, rifle nomenclature, combat exercises and kitchen and latrine duty. He was a private and at the lowest rung on the military ladder.

I wished that my father had failed the physical checkup and stayed home. I wished that they hadn't called his name for the first group of men to be sent to the front. I wished he hadn't answered, "Here!" when they called his name. All the men in my father's group were privates, with the classification of riflemen, and because they were grouped alphabetically, all their surnames in his group began with M.

In age, the majority were over 30, and most of them were married with children. Because of their late entrance into the war, they were infantry replacements–not as punishment, but because the army needed infantry replacements above all others.

My father spent his last day with us before leaving for Egypt. He took me out of school and told me, "Today is a special day. What would you like the three of us to do?" I didn't reply because I was sad and I knew that this might be the last day I saw him alive. In my heart I was also mad at my mother because I knew that if she had allowed us to return to the kibbutz he wouldn't have had to join the army. I thought how selfish she was. This was the first time in my life I felt strong hatred–I hated my mother!

I said, "This is your day. What would *you* like to do?"

It was a beautiful day. He took us to the beach and we went swimming, but I wasn't able to enjoy it. I tried to hide my tears in the ocean water but my father came near me and asked, "Alex, are you crying?" I told him the salt water got in my eyes and I couldn't help the tears. Even though my father was only five foot four inches, in my eyes he looked six feet tall with a large, solid frame. He spoke almost in a whisper, forcing me to bend over because I wanted to catch every word; I wanted to remember him the way he was.

For dinner he actually took us to a restaurant. I had never eaten at such a place before. Food was served to us, and my eyes were bigger than my stomach. My plate was full of food, worthy of a king, but I couldn't eat–even the luxury of a rich custard pudding. My mother told my father, "It's all right, we will eat it later," and we took the food home.

At one point my father said to me, "Alex, I cannot leave you like this. I know that you don't want me to go to Egypt, but I must." He grabbed my left hand and told me, "I have a secret for you." I was very curious about the secret and what it might be.

I asked him, "Dad, what is the secret?"

He replied, "It's called the kissing hand." He opened my hand into a fan and kissed the middle of my palm. Then he closed my hand in a fist and told me not to open it. He smiled and said, "Whenever you feel lonely and need a little loving from me, just press your hand to your cheek and think, 'Daddy loves me, Daddy loves me.' And that very same kiss will jump from your hand to your face and fill you with warm thoughts." I smiled and it wasn't quite as hard for me to part from my father after that. I held my hand tight. I didn't want the kisses to escape. I forgot to ask him what would happen when I washed my hands; would I lose his kisses? I decided that he would have told me if that was so, and was very happy with my closed palm.

When my father left us for Egypt, my mother, Ali and I went to the army base to say goodbye. My father kissed me on my forehead, and he kissed me again and again and he told me, "I love you, Alex, I love you, Alex, I love you," and he was crying. I don't know why I was silent; I didn't say a word to him. I didn't kiss him back. I froze. My mother asked me to kiss my father and say goodbye to him. I couldn't say a word; I felt that this was the end. This was the first time in my life that my father had left me. Ali and my mother said goodbye to my father but I couldn't. I felt that any moment we all were going to cry, but none of us did. I held my pain tightly inside of me, unable to kiss my father or even speak.

We dragged our feet and tried to have a last look at him. My mother told me, "Alex, remember your father. He is a handsome, robust man. I don't know how I will live without him."

We walked so slowly. A five-minute walk took us almost half an hour. We didn't want to lose his image. I started to be impatient with my mother and I told her, "Let's go home, I'm tired." On the way home it was like a heavy weight in my stomach, trapped, with nowhere to go, no escape from a grief that was both intolerable and unknowable to an eight-year-old.

When I looked at the room without my father it was terrible. It was an empty room, even though it had two beds, a table and chairs. My father wasn't there. I was still a little boy and I needed the pampering and security that a father gives to his child. All of a sudden, being without him, I was lost. I was already missing his morning wake-up, calling me: "Alex, Alexander the Great, wake up, my dear son." Even though I was awake I pretended to be asleep waiting to hear the loving voice of my father calling me, "Alex, Alex, wake up." He would put my clean clothes that I was going to wear that day on my bed and then shared the food that we were going to eat for breakfast. We hardly had any food, but the little that we had he made sure that my mother and I got. I always gobbled it and I felt that I never had enough.

As my father was undergoing training and preparing to leave I had been sad and afraid for him. I knew the army was dangerous, but the idea that someone else in the world might hope for my father's death had never crossed my mind. When he actually left, I began to understand that others were in fact not only hoping for his death but deliberately lying in wait to shoot him on the battlefield. I was profoundly shocked.

When my father was sent to Egypt, life wasn't easy for me. I envied Ali having a father so close to him. I hated when Ali fought with his father. I told Ali if my father was with me I would never fight with him.

Ali laughed and he said, "Alex, who are you kidding? I've seen you fighting with your parents."

He was right, of course, but I thought to myself it would be wonderful to be living in a world where no hateful words were ever spoken, and no hands raised in anger. I looked at Ali and I said, "I miss my father and I hope he isn't fighting."

Ali said, "What is the good of being a soldier if you don't fight and die for your people?"

I started to cry and I said, "I don't want my father to die."

Ali said, "I don't mind if I die. I am not afraid." Then Ali took a cigarette, lit it and started to burn himself. "You see, it doesn't hurt." I took the burning cigarette and I burned myself and I felt the pain. I don't know which I felt more, the pain of missing my father or the burning of my hand. I looked at Ali and I knew that Ali would be an excellent soldier, but I knew in my heart that I wouldn't.

⋯⋯⋯

During his army service, on those occasions when he was able to write, my father kept a diary. After his unit had left Palestine he wrote: "To get to Cairo we were virtually poured into trucks so tightly that we had to breathe by the numbers–one, inhale; two, exhale! I was amazed by the army's ability to move thousands of men from place to place. Then came a feeling of emptiness, utter emptiness, which came with the knowledge that I was leaving behind everything dear to my heart, especially my wife and son, embarking on an adventure from which I might never return.

"One morning I found myself once again loading onto an army truck. However, it was only a ten-minute ride. We were dumped off at a very shabby railroad station and herded into very disreputable looking freight cars! Forty of us were sitting on cracker crates.

"We were traveling west through Egypt, passing little agricultural settlements. The native kids were running along the tracks begging for candies or cigarettes. They were dressed in the barest of clothing; a gunny sack if they were lucky. Shoes were something they didn't know existed. They were dirty–no, filthy–with no more desires than something to eat occasionally and a place to sleep when night overtook them. A sudden shudder went through me, and I thought that if I was killed the same could happen to my beloved son, Alex.

"The train was moving slowly and there was time, more than ample time, to ponder what kind of a soldier I would be."

# Chapter Nine, The Wrestler

My father was away in the army, stationed in Egypt, and for the first time in my life he had left us. I worried about him because I knew that sooner or later he would face the enemy, and I wondered if he would survive if he had to fight.

Ali didn't care. He was safe. If the Germans came to Palestine they wouldn't harm him. The only difference in his life would be that instead of learning English he would have to learn German, and in addition to praying to Allah he would salute Hitler. I wondered if Ali was loyal to his people or his religion; I thought that he was loyal to the one who fed him.

Ali was fascinated with the army. He was always daydreaming about the war. He didn't care which army he belonged to as long as he was a general and he won the battles. When we played army and we played against each other, I took the Allied side and Ali took the German side. He and I gathered quite a collection of army memorabilia. I got a toy machine gun. Ali and I took the machine gun apart and put it together blindfolded. Ali told me, "We should be prepared to fight the enemy." Most of our daily conversation was about weapons. Ali let me store his toy guns in my house since his father didn't want him to have any guns.

Playing war was one of our few distractions. Anything exciting was rare in the community. If a dog was hit by a car or a cat had kittens, it was an exciting event and the whole school was involved with it.

At this time what I started to dislike about Ali was his wrestling. At first he wrestled for fun, just horsing around. Nobody got hurt and every time that Ali won he was happy. But then some older boys, probably in the seventh or eighth grade, saw Ali wrestling and they had a plan. They asked him if he would like to wrestle for them for money. His sponsors would bet on Ali when he wrestled other kids. Ali couldn't believe that they considered him to be so good that they would pay him.

At first Ali won every match when he wrestled kids the same age as himself, but when he started wrestling older kids, he lost, and when he lost his sponsors beat him up because they lost money. Each time he lost he would get hurt and I couldn't stand seeing him getting hurt. I told him to stop it, but he didn't; it was just like an addiction.

I thought about ways to stop him, and I decided that the only way that I might stop Ali from wrestling was if I challenged him and won. Ali was surprised that I would dare to fight him; I was his best friend and he had confided in me and used me sometimes as a guinea pig, trying to practice his blocks and holds.

When they heard about it, all the kids at school were excited because Ali and Alex, who were known to be best friends, were going to wrestle each other. The whole school was excited over our match. I had never wrestled Ali except in play, but from practicing with him and watching him wrestle other kids, I knew every movement he had. And also, before my father had left he had showed me how to defend myself by teaching me a few wrestling holds.

The day after I challenged Ali, his sister, Lylla, knocked at my door and asked me to let her in. "Alex, if my parents knew that I came to visit you by myself they would kill me." A decent Arab girl never visits a person of the opposite sex without a chaperone.

I asked her, "Why are you here?"

"Alex, please don't wrestle with my brother. He is practicing with my sister and me. He is using us as guinea pigs, and I don't want you to get hurt."

"Lylla, don't worry, everything will be fine." I said, and I paid no further attention to her. I hadn't told my mother that I was going to wrestle Ali for money because I knew that she would stop us.

The day before the wrestling match I had a talk with Ali. "If I win the match, will you quit wrestling for money?"

Ali laughed and said, "You will never beat me, and it is none of your business how I earn my money."

I told Ali, "When I see you hurt, it hurts me. Why do you want to get hurt?"

Ali replied, "This is just like taking candy from a baby. Why shouldn't I wrestle? I'm good at it."

I asked again, "Ali, If I win, will you stop wrestling?" He never answered me.

I knew that Ali was strong. He was taller and slimmer than me. He was very confident and started to sass me. He had several fans that cheered him: "Ali, you will not falter and will not fail us. Ali, you are the greatest." He raised his arms as though he had already won the match. He was so cocky that he paraded around the school shouting, "I'm the greatest!"

It's funny how a little excitement made Ali and I celebrities. Overnight we were the talk of the school. I didn't enjoy wrestling, but I wanted to teach Ali a lesson that he should stop wrestling for money. I didn't want him to get beaten by his sponsors when he lost.

Then came the day of the match. Three boys ages seven to ten massaged Ali and made sure that he was relaxed. They made faces at me and they called me a loser. They were whispering some secrets to Ali. I was frightened, and I asked myself, "Am I doing the right thing?" I completely lost confidence in myself. I didn't have anybody to support me and advise me. Ali had the crowd behind him–he was their hero.

Two older girls tried to spook me. They grabbed some papers and tore them to pieces just like confetti and threw them at me yelling, "This is what Ali is going to do to you." They had never seen me fight before and had no idea what I could do. Ali, however, had performed many times in front of them.

Although I was scared, I didn't panic. Besides, I knew my strength and I was determined to win the match. If Ali won he would be impossible to live with. His older sister surprised me. She bet against me instead of keeping neutral, as I thought she would.

Wrestling was a way of making money at our school. Because Ali was the favorite, I had a hard time getting sponsors to sponsor me. The only way that I got some was that I promised them if I lost I would pay them back. I didn't know how I would find the money, but I was desperate. Ali only fought for the money; I, on the other hand, was just trying to keep him from getting hurt.

We started wrestling in the back yard of the school. Ali and I were standing and facing each other, cautiously. The kids were restless; they wanted to see some action. We started walking in a circle. Ali started shouting some crazy sounds that didn't make any sense. I knew he was trying to frighten me. Then he suddenly tried to grab my ankle with one hand and use his body to drive me backward, but I blocked him, and his move wasn't successful. The kids were happy to see some action but the fight was slow. Everybody was giving us advice and it was difficult for them to watch a match lasting so long. Most of Ali's other fights had been short because he had guile and conned his opponents, and that made the match uneven. That's what everyone had thought when, before we started, Ali had started dancing and jumping his victory dance. How could an inexperienced fighter like me dare to fight with Ali?

Now we were running around in circles in the ring, trying to tire each other. We were both sweating and panting, but I was outrunning Ali. For a moment I thought I could surprise him, but instead he grabbed me and threw me to the ground. As he got down lower to take advantage of my position, I saw my chance and caught Ali's wrist and started to bend it. I wanted to finish the fight. I bent it more, until it almost broke. Ali fell to the, crying, and I won.

Ali's sister, Lylla, spit at me because I had humiliated her brother. I didn't take the money I had won. I didn't want wrestling money, and I went home. It was only Monday and I didn't talk to Ali all week. I kept away from him.

Friday after school, the boys always chased the soldiers' jeeps, begging for gum. In the past, whatever Ali and I had picked up we had always split. The gum had to last us for the whole week. This time I wasn't lucky; I only picked up two packages of Chiclets. I saw that Ali had picked up many more.

He looked at me and asked, "Alex, how many did you get?"

I answered, "Only two."

Ali told me, "I got twelve, here are five for you. That makes seven each."

I took the five packages of Chiclets and smiled at Ali. Ali put his arm around me and we walked home, and tears were in my eyes.

When you are seven years old you only live for the moment. Ali and I were again best friends.

# Chapter Ten, The Pawnshop

In most neighborhoods, after your home, the most important buildings are the grocery store, the bank, the post office, the drugstore and maybe the bar. But not in our neighborhood. In our neighborhood the pawnshop was the center of our world. Both Jews and Arabs were in the same boat and used the pawnshop often. If you wanted to hear the news or the local gossip you went to the pawnshop. The owner was the only one who had a radio and a few chairs where you could sit and listen to the news. At that time, radios were very expensive, and in our neighborhood nobody else was able to afford one.

If you had asked me if we were poor, I would have replied that I didn't know. I didn't even know what the word meant. Twice each month the pawnshop was very busy, at the beginning and in the middle of the month. The beginning of the month was when everyone pawned their treasures to pay their rent and utility bills. By the middle of the month they had received their salaries and were able to redeem their valuables. The cycle repeated itself every month.

We had a cubicle where my mother pawned our precious belongings, such as linens, dishes, clothes, furniture and, sometimes, her jewelry that the owner kept in his safe. The only one who made money was the pawnshop owner. His policy was if you didn't redeem your belongings after six months, the items were for sale. My mother had a gold bracelet and her wedding ring that my father had given her on her wedding night. When my parents were in a financial bind and there was nothing else to pawn, my mother pawned the gold bracelet. Several times we almost lost it. Once, the pawnshop owner called my mother to inform her that

several people were interested in buying the bracelet and if she
didn't come with the money he would sell it. My mother
desperately looked for money so she could redeem her bracelet.
When she went to the pawnshop she asked the owner to let her wear
the gold bracelet one last time, because she believed she was going
to lose it. He allowed her to do that. When she put the bracelet on
her wrist, the light reflected very sharply off of it. In that light, she
seemed to see the faces of her family: father, mother, sisters and
brothers that she had left in Poland. She touched the bracelet and
remembered when she had been wealthy. Then, she had been well-
dressed, well-fed and a gold bracelet had meant nothing to her.
Once she had lost a gold bracelet and she wasn't concerned. When
the maid found it and returned it, she didn't care. Now, this bracelet
was the only thing of value that she had left.

With interest, the pawnshop owner charged almost double the
amount that we had borrowed. Where was she going to get the
money? My mother didn't know if her family was still alive in
Poland, and her family in the United States seldom wrote to her. In
desperation, my father went to the kibbutz where they had lived for
seven years, and by persuasion and good luck, they lent him the
money without charging any interest.

The pawnshop owner was a Jew from Syria, named Ibraim. He
had immigrated to Palestine in 1930 at the age of thirty
and he had gotten married ten years later to an orthodox Jewish girl.
The marriage had been arranged, because otherwise no woman
would have married him because he was a hunchback, short and fat.
But since he was a successful businessman and wealthy, it was a
different story. His face was full of warts so he had covered them
with a full beard. He had little hands and little feet and, with a large
head, looked like an ugly dwarf. But since he was a successful
businessman and wealthy, it was a different story.

Perhaps to compensate for his small size he spoke very loudly.
If you didn't see him, you could hear him. He was a womanizer and
he tried to touch every woman's butt. Every woman felt that he
undressed her with his eyes. He would stare at any woman and look
at her from bottom to top, very slowly. When he had finished
looking at the woman, he would lick his lips and then compliment
her rudely.

My mother hated to go there by herself. She always took me with her. He wouldn't dare touch my mother in front of me. Some women let him touch them. They thought that he might treat them better by lending them more for the pawned items and charging them lower interest.

After we left the pawnshop, my mother would ask my father, "How do I look? The pawnshop owner was ogling me. He makes me feel dirty."

My father replied, "You are beautiful, Laura, and you are worth looking at."

Ibraim's family owned pawnshops in Syria and he had expanded the chain of shops into Palestine. He had two boys, both younger than me. They were normal, not hunchbacked like their father. They were happy kids. Their father gave them anything they wanted. But I had something that Ibraim's sons wanted and couldn't get. I had a colorful t-shirt; royal blue, and the rest of the shirt had stripes of many colors, starting with dark blue, green, orange, royal blue, blue-green, and then the pattern repeated itself. I called it Joseph's Shirt, and it was my favorite shirt. I had won the shirt at a Purim carnival. It was the only new shirt that I had; the rest of my clothes were secondhand.

One of Ibraim's sons begged his father to buy the shirt from me, but I didn't want to sell it. I felt that for the first time in my life I had something that Ibraim wanted. Every time I wore the shirt, even though I was hungry and thirsty, I felt great because this was my treasure.

We needed money, and my mother had already pawned everything that she could pawn. She asked me if it was okay to sell the t-shirt. I told her, "No."

"We're hungry, and the shirt will buy us a loaf of bread, six eggs and a pint of milk," she said, and went on to say that if we got the pint of milk we could dilute it with water so it would last longer. I did not cry in front of my mother, but I cried inside. I told myself that at least I would be contributing food on the table. But for some reason we never pawned that shirt, and after a while I finally outgrew it and I gave it to Ibraim's son. I wanted to show Ibraim that I was a better person than he was.

When I was older and I had money, I searched far and wide and finally found the exact same shirt that I had had years ago, only in a larger size.

As a child, most of my clothes had been donated by American churches. Sometimes the nuns had come to our school and brought clothes to us. Ali and I did not care about clothes as long as they fit us, but other children were embarrassed to wear charity clothes.

Nadine, Ali's sister, wouldn't wear any of the charity clothes, but took some to use the material to make some of her dresses. She would tear the charity clothes and then sew them together and make skirts and blouses for herself. Her clothes were very picturesque. I gave her some of my torn shirts and I later recognized them as part of her blouses or skirts. We were very poor, but we children didn't realize that we were poor because we were all in the same boat.

Ali and I loved to hang around the pawnshop. We asked the owner, Ibraim, if we could sweep the place and then, as a reward, play with the toys that were pawned. The Catholic families pawned their children's toys, like bicycles, tricycles, electric trains and dolls that the kids had gotten for Christmas. Ali and I would play with the electric trains for hours, but we had to supply the batteries and they were expensive. I remembered a trick I had seen the older kids do; we would find old batteries that were dead and we put them in an oven and baked them and they became as good as new.

The pawnshop was in a big room. When you entered you saw cabinets containing merchandise that was for sale, and behind them the owner had a table where he sat. He had a cash register that only he knew how to open. Behind the big room he had three bedrooms, a kitchen and a bathroom. He also had a big fenced-in back yard which was where Ali and I played with his sons. We were never allowed to enter the bedrooms. Supposedly, that was where the family lived but later on I found out that was also where he kept stolen merchandise.

When I found out that he had our bike and he wouldn't return it to us I was devastated. My mother went to see Ibraim and pleaded with him for the return of the bike, but he refused. I decided to take action. I told Ibraim, "I'm taking the bike home."

Ibraim replied, "Alex, go home before I get mad. *Yalla raah minon*," he said, which means "go away."

I got angry and I started yelling, "Ibraim, you know that the bike belongs to my mother."

Ibraim looked equally angry and told me, "Alex, this bike is mine. I bought it. I don't work for charity. If the bike was yours, it would have your license on it. This bike doesn't have a license."

I looked at the bike and I said, "This bike is mine. You can see my names on the handlebars of the bike."

In spite of this proof, Ibraim laughed and said, "Alex, I wonder why I let you hang around here and let you play with my children and their toys."

I replied, "You let me hang around here because I'm a good worker. I sweep the floor and put away things and you don't pay me."

Ibraim came back at me, "Alex, I let you listen to the radio and I don't charge you for it."

I left the pawnshop and I swore never to put my foot in that place again. But Ali continued going to the pawnshop. Ibraim hired him and, perhaps purely out of spite, paid him for sweeping and helping at the store. I really resented Ali for doing that.

The pawnshop remained the most important shop in our neighborhood, even though everyone knew what he had done to us. They were all dependent on Ibraim's good will for survival.

At about the same time as the events at the pawnshop were occurring, my father had continued writing in his journal. "The railroad station seemed utterly useless as we got off the train, only 20 miles from the front lines! No more train rides from here. This was the last stop before we reached our final destination. From here we'd be assigned to regular fighting units, especially those that had suffered losses from enemy action. Our equipment was checked once again. We were issued new rifles and even taken out to a range for a little practice. It was hot but not too windy, and the sand didn't blow at our faces.

"We had two days of this so-called final conditioning and then one morning we were called out to hear the names of the first group of men to be sent to the front. My heart dropped to my feet and buried itself in the sand as I answered, 'Here!'

"Trucks were waiting for us. There was another roll call and as each man answered to his name he climbed onto the truck. There were no smiles among the men as they quietly helped each other onto the trucks. I glanced around at the faces of the men in my truck, looking deep into the eyes of each one, hoping to see something I knew wasn't there–a look of confidence, or at least a bit of humor!"

# Chapter Eleven, The Plane

The year was 1943 and when I looked at myself in the mirror I didn't like what I saw. I was eight years old and I was in the third grade. People who knew me said that I got my smile from my parents, so I got my frown from them also. In fact I was a miserable wretch. Tears were in my eyes for no reason. I was worried about my father and I didn't realize how this affected me. Both at school and at home I daydreamed. At school I would sit down at the desk and I would twirl my pencil and sometimes chew it. While chewing my pencil I felt secure and the pencil was tasty. If I wore a long sleeved shirt I would suck the sleeve of my shirt and sometimes I would pick my nose. I couldn't do any work, I was numb. If the teacher scolded me I would start crying and I would leave the class. The same thing was happening to me at home. At dinner time I would twirl my fork. I could hardly eat anything. I felt I had knots in my stomach. When my mother would ask me what happened at school, I didn't reply and then I told her to leave me alone. There were tears in her eyes. She hugged me and told me everything was going to be okay. She held me tight and kissed me. I felt her wet tears on my check and I knew she was also afraid. We went to sleep and we slept in the same bed. We were both afraid of the same demons.

I was worried about my father. I knew my mother was also worrying about him and that rubbed on me. At school I hated to listen to the radio news. Everything was sad; we were losing the war, and sooner or later I knew that my father was going to be on the battlefield. At school all I heard was that so-and-so fathers had died and I thought that this could happen to me. I hated to see the army mailman knocking at the neighbors' doors, certain that he was informing them about the bad news. When I saw him I prayed that he didn't knock at our door. I was growing up too fast. I tried to think about pleasant things, but I couldn't when my father, Dolf, was away fighting a war.

One morning I washed myself, got dressed, ate breakfast and went to school, just like every school day. Ali and his two sisters joined me. Today was show-and-tell, which was the best part of school for me. Ali and I shared our treasures, which we showed individually in each of our classes. I showed my goodies in the morning at first period and Ali showed his after lunch. The reason I enjoyed show-and-tell was that I never knew what the other children had brought from their homes because they brought them in brown bags. There weren't a lot of rules about show-and-tell. It was an amateur show and you always got a good grade. It was a bit disorderly and unpredictable. The girls usually brought their dolls or stuffed animals. The boys brought army toys, balls, or pets like lizards, puppies or kittens. I usually brought my army toys.

One of my classmates brought a German helmet. I wondered where he had gotten the helmet. It probably had belonged to a German soldier who was killed in a battle in the desert in Egypt. Ali's father told me that after each battle the Bedouins would take the remnants from the battlefield and they would sell them to whomever paid the highest price. Ali and I were jealous. We wanted the helmet and we tried to convince the boy to give it to us. We invited him to play army with us after school. He hardly had any friends and, since he was the owner of the German helmet, we made him the captain of one of the teams and convinced him that he should leave the helmet in my toy chest. For a week we brought him treats, like the gum that we collected from the British soldiers. Ali was even willing to do the boy's homework because he was not a good student. But none of our ploys worked; the boy outsmarted us. After all our attempts at bribery, he took his helmet home anyway.

One particular morning I had eaten well–hotcakes and hot chocolate–even though I was still worried. While walking to school with Ali, all of a sudden we heard a strange noise: "zum, zum." We wondered what it was; we had never heard that noise before. We looked up at the sound of the noise and we saw a brown plane flying very low, above us. Ali screamed, "The Germans are coming."

Lylla and Nadine became hysterical. "They are coming and they will kill us."

Both at school and at home that was what we heard; that the Germans were going to kill us.

"Ali, you are crazy. I don't think that the plane was a German plane," I shouted at him.

"Alex, I know that it was a German plane. It had a swastika on the tail and a black and white cross." Ali was all excited; he was jumping and yelling. I looked again at the plane and saw that it was still flying low. It was the first evidence that a war was raging nearby. I had never seen real planes before but I recognized them from pictures in a magazine.

Ali was right, it was a BF 109F Messerschmidt, a single-engine plane, colored brown. When I saw the swastika and heard the buzz and roar of the plane, I froze, and I wondered why the pilot didn't drop bombs and try to kill us..

I was getting sick to my stomach; it was my nerves. I couldn't believe that the Germans were here. I knew that they were only 30 miles away from Cairo. I had heard it on the radio news at school that week. I was surprised that the British, who were supposed to protect us, had let the Germans penetrate our airspace. We'd had faith in the British but now I began to wonder how secure we were.

Lylla was sobbing and started to kneel and pray. Nadine followed her and told us, "I'm too young to die. I don't want to die."

Lylla said, "The pilot ran out of bombs but he will come back and kill us."

Ali told his sisters, "Shut up. You don't know what you are talking about."

Lylla grabbed her brother and the three of them started to pray. When they finished, we went to school holding hands. We knew that the school was the safest place to be, indoors and under cover.

When we reached our school we saw pamphlets flying over our heads that the German plane had dropped and we tried to catch them. The flyers were on multicolor papers. Some kids caught the flyers and told us that they made excellent paper planes. At school we didn't have any colored construction paper and were hungry for pretty things. When I saw the large assortment of colored paper I was speechless with surprise and pleasure.

Everybody was yelling about the German plane and wondered why the plane hadn't dropped bombs; we were an easy target. Our teachers and principals hadn't prepared us for the war in case we were attacked. They had told us we were invincible and the German could never attack us. I started to doubt them.

The words on the pamphlets that we got were divided into three sections. Each section was written in a different language: English, Arabic and Hebrew. There was also a picture of Hitler embracing some children. When Ali saw Hitler's picture, he spat on it. This was the first time that I saw a picture of Hitler. He looked so nice and friendly I wouldn't have minded shaking his hand. I started to read the Hebrew part of the pamphlet;

"Friends, Jews, Arabs and Christians: We the German people are your friends. Please surrender and don't fight. The time has come for you to be free from England. Heil Hitler."

I asked Ali to read me the message in Arabic, but Ali refused to do it. I thought that maybe the Arabs had gotten a different message than the Jews, but Lylla told me the messages were the same.

Besides the pamphlet, the German plane had also dropped candies and watches, just like the Israelites got Manna from heaven when they wandered forty years in the wilderness of the Sinai dessert. All of a sudden my sadness disappeared and I started grabbing the candies and the watches. I was laughing. Our spirits lifted up. I felt that I was not a weeper or a beggar anymore. I thought the Germans were great and wondered why we were fighting them. I was won over to their side for a few candies and a watch. At that time very few kids had watches. A watch was usually given as a *Bar Mitzvah* gift. I thought I was a big shot, wearing a watch, even though I was dressed in rags. Ali told me, "I'm not going to show the candies and watches in show-and-tell. The older kids will take them away from us."

Soon after the pamphlets, candies and watches had fallen on the ground, some British soldiers drove by in their jeeps with loud speakers, yelling, "Don't eat the candies, they are poisoned, and the watches are bombs." Some of the soldiers showed us their scars and told us about the watches that they had picked up in the battlefield.

Ali and I were hungry for sweets and when we had first seen the candies we had filled our pockets with them. I was afraid that they would drop dead in front of our eyes. I thought that the Germans didn't have to bomb us; they were killing us with poison candy. Ali told me, "At least we will die with a full, sweet stomach. I'm so hungry sometimes that I don't mind dying." I wondered if all of the children in the world were hungry, just like Ali and me. I told Ali that one day I was going to be a millionaire and I would feed all the children in the world with candies, and I wouldn't mind if they had rotten teeth. Ali laughed. "If they have rotten teeth, they will fall out and they won't be able to eat any food and they will starve to death."

When the soldiers approached us, they told us to give them the candies and watches and if they weren't poisoned and didn't have tiny bombs they would return them to us. The candies were bonbons; the real thing, chocolate with fruit filling. They smelled like real chocolate and the fruits smelled like apricots and cherries. They were creamy and juicy. Their smell drove us crazy. I knew those bonbons, I had had them before. I could never eat just one or two, I always filled my stomach. I knew that they would explode with flavor in my mouth.

The wrapping paper was shiny silver with designs. Even the wrapping paper was a treat for our eyes; on those few occasions in the past when we had had wrapped candies, we used to collect them and use them for special prizes.

Some of the other children couldn't wait and started eating the candies. I looked at Ali and I closed my eyes. I was trembling. The thought that he would eat the poison candy frightened me. In my mind I saw Ali pleading for just one piece, his empty stomach immune to the harsh words of warning that were being shouted at him. He asked the soldier, "How do you know for sure that the candy is poisoned?" The British soldier responded, "Are you willing to take a chance?"

Ali hesitated giving up the candies and watches to the British; he hid some in his pocket. I worried about him as I emptied my pockets and gave the British the candies and watches just like a good kid. I told the British, "Do not deceive us. It is very hard to part with these candies because we haven't had any for many months." Nadine and Lylla gave their candies to the British soldiers. We were just like timid dogs.

The whole thing was a terrible tease; we had held, we had smelled, but we hadn't eaten the candies. Now, sixty years later, I still cannot eat candies both because I am diabetic and because the taste makes me think of poison like the Nazis put in the gas chambers.

Then many of the parents arrived at the school and I saw them hugging their kids. The grownups were crying; they couldn't help themselves. I wondered if my mother would be there. I knew if my father had been there he would be looking for me. I searched for my mother and I was getting mad at her. I felt that I was alone and nobody cared about me. I wondered who was going to take care of me if the Germans were here. After being elated by the papers, candies and watches, they were all gone, and now I felt not only disappointed but all alone and miserable. I saw Ali's parents but I didn't see my mother. I was embarrassed to ask Ali's parents and Ali if they had seen my mother. All of a sudden somebody grabbed the back of my t-shirt. I turned and saw my mother. She was crying, and she hugged me. I instantly became happier. Then the bell rang, my mother and I separated, and we kids went to class. Once the parents saw that their kids were okay they left. The truth was that the kids calmed their parents.

⁕

This was what was happening to my father at this time, from his notes from the battlefield. He was tired, and the ominous rumble of artillery on both sides should have kept him up all night but it didn't because he could sleep almost anywhere. Now and then, the faint chatter of machine gun fire echoed through the mountains, probably a reconnaissance patrol hitting a little opposition.

The next morning he awoke ready for battle. He was checking his equipment, rerolling his pack, and drawing the essential ammunition from stocks. His rifle was polished, his bayonet was oiled and he was given two pairs of heavy socks that he stuffed in his pockets. In Egypt, it is very hot during the day but at night it is freezing cold. So extra clothing was necessary. He was ready.

As they marched towards the battlefield, they encountered bunches of Italian soldiers dropping their guns and surrendering to his troop. They were begging for water and his captain told my father to give a cup of water for each rifle that he collected. He couldn't believe the sight. The Italian soldiers were coming from everywhere, begging for water and food. My father's commander recognized the usefulness of his ability to speak Italian and assigned him to interrogate the prisoners.

He told himself, "This is not so bad. Interrogating is a safe job. And we are starting to win the war."

# Chapter Twelve, A Difficult Time

I wonder why the years 1942 and 1943 happened the way they did, when I was seven and eight years old. Early in my life, my parents and I struggled to survive. My father's enlistment in the Jewish Division of the British Army was not to fight the Germans but to better take care of us. Work was almost impossible to find, and when our bike was stolen, my mother couldn't get work either. As long as my father was stationed near home my mother was healthy, but as soon as my father left us for Egypt she fell apart.

For no reason, my mother would start crying. She was very agitated. She would start a job, like straightening the room, but she didn't have the strength to finish it. The few clothes we had were on the floor. She didn't seem able to wash them and return them to the drawers. Our one bedroom was a mess, had an awful smell of dirt and you could see both the roaches and the spiders having a feast. We were living in the Middle East where, unless you were very clean, flies and cockroaches were everywhere.

After my father left us our daily routine changed dramatically. We got my father's paycheck regularly and my mother was able to quit working and should have been able to be a mother. While financially it was easier for my mother, emotionally it was very hard for her. I went to school and then the rest of the day I was on the street. My mother hated me being out there; she didn't want me to be raised like a street kid. But it was actually safe to play on the street. Beside my mother I was alone except for Ali. He was lots of fun, always craving excitement. He was full of energy and that kept me busy and for those times I didn't think about my father. We both collected bottles and cashed them in. With the money we got we would buy candies. At first the candies tasted sweet but, somehow, they reminded me of missing my father and the taste was bitter.

My mother became severely depressed. She missed him. She would stay in bed all day, sleeping or crying. She wore her red robe all day, and I didn't like that. She used to sleep during the day and was awake at night. She would demand that I talk to her, but I was usually so tired I fell asleep on the floor. I can still remember her talking to me, "Alex, am I good mother? Alex talk to me, I don't know what to do."

I wanted her to keep quiet and I rudely yelled at her, "Shut up!" All I wanted was to sleep.

I was always hungry. I didn't take baths or showers and my clothes were very dirty. Even Ali's parents couldn't stand that I was so dirty and they sent me home and told me that when I was clean I could play with their children. But my mother was too depressed to keep me clean and I didn't seem able to do it myself.

My mother didn't drink but otherwise she acted like an alcoholic. I hadn't realized that she was so dependent on my father. She also worried about her family who were in a concentration camp in Poland. Later on we discovered that they all had died in Auschwitz.

It is very painful for me to describe that year, 1942. To this day I still can't speak about it out loud, but I can write about it.

I came to school in filthy clothes and wasn't bathed. I was the last one to enter the classroom. I dragged my legs and my heart wasn't in it. There was a boy who shared a seat next to me but now nobody wanted to sit next to me because I was so smelly. I didn't care. I was in my own little dreamland. I would dream that I was with my father, playing soccer in the park. Those soccer days were the happiest days of my life. The teacher and the kids all started calling me *zevel*, which in Hebrew means "garbage."

At the start of the school year I had been one of the top students. I was reading two or three grades ahead of my class and I was a good speller. But now on I didn't do any work. I had completely lost interest and didn't absorb my subjects. I was scribbling on my papers and counting down the minutes when they fed us and when school was over.

I missed my father terribly when he was in Egypt. I wanted to join my father's army division;. I was determined to be with him. I thought I could get a ride on a train and be with him, but I knew I couldn't because I had to stay with my mother.

The teacher would speak to me but I blocked him out. I would sit quietly and I wouldn't move a muscle. Day after day I would come to school filthy and smelly. My classmates would hold their noses. I, too, felt that I was *zevel*. Sometimes I ran out of the classroom and I ran to the park. I pretended to play soccer with my father. If Ali saw me leaving school he followed me and we played tag. Ali was a real true friend. The only reason that I went to school at all was because I got a free lunch and also because I couldn't stand seeing my mother so helpless and sad. I told my mother that the kids and teacher called me garbage. My mother replied, "That's nice, they could call you worse things." She was in a daze.

At school both the Jewish and Arab kids would push me and one time I fell down and had a bloody nose. When I went to see the nurse, she took care of my wound but ignored my filthy appearance. I wondered why nobody came to my rescue. I wanted to be clean and wear clean clothes like the other kids but somehow I couldn't help myself. I wore my clothes maybe for a week or two. Sometimes I peed in my pants and I smelled like urine and I still didn't change my clothes. I slept, played and went to school with the same clothes. My fingernails were long and dirty and so was my hair. I didn't care. I wept silently. I wanted to be accepted by my classmates, but I knew I wasn't.

Plus I had a sick mother and I had to take care of her. All of a sudden I was the adult and my mother was the child. In my eyes she looked ugly, sick and dirty. I knew that she was hungry for an adult companion but I was only a child. I thought about reporting her for neglect, but if I did I believed the authorities would lock her away and then I would have no one. What could I do? At least her body was with me even if her mind wasn't.

When I was little, my mother used to put me on her lap, a place that I had outgrown. I had enjoyed her thoughtless caresses and still wanted her to baby me, but now she pushed me away from her. Did she know that I was also falling apart? Ironically, before my father left, my mother used to check and report to authorities about neglected kids. Now here I was a neglected child. As I grew thinner, what others noticed about me were my huge, sad eyes.

Every month I had to help my mother dress so she could go to the army base to collect our army check, because the rest of the time she stayed in bed. When she cashed the check she had to pay a commission, otherwise nobody would cash our check. Once we paid all our debts, little money was left.

Once a week we got a letter from my dad. He started by telling us how much he loved us and he missed us. He described Cairo, the Nile and the Pyramids. In spite of our pitiful emotional condition, my mother and I wrote back to my father. I started to collect the large, colorful stamps that came on my father's letters from Egypt. I was all excited that my father had the chance to visit the Pyramids. All I knew about Egypt was what I had learned in school about the Jewish holiday, Passover. I had learned that my predecessors were slaves in Egypt, and helped build the Pyramids and then were freed.

We hardly heard from our families in the United States and Italy. My friends told me that I was a liar and that I made those imaginary people up to be my family. I didn't care since I had never known them. All I cared about was my father because I missed him. Every night I looked at his picture and I talked to him.

One day I came home from school and my mother was still in bed. She pleaded with me, "Alex, go to the grocery store and get us some food; here is some money."

I told my mother, "You go. I don't know what to get." I was angry.

My mother raised her voice and shouted, "Alex, I am sick. Please be a good kid and bring us some food."

I yelled back, "I don't want to go and I don't want to be a good kid. I am a little boy and you are supposed to take care of me."

Rather than arguing with me, my retort seemed to shock her out of her lethargy. She got her act together. She got up, got dressed and took me to the grocery store. When we were there she asked me, "What do you want for supper?"

I told her, "You aren't going to get me what I want, I'm sure of that."

"Try me," she said.

"I want a gallon of strawberry, vanilla and chocolate ice cream."

At that time a gallon of ice cream was very expensive. We usually got tiny portions; with a gallon you could feed twenty kids.

To my surprise, my mother bought the gallon of ice cream. We rushed home, got two spoons and we started to eat the ice cream. We ate the entire gallon of ice cream! For some reason that ice cream changed everything! When we finished, my mother gave me a bath and washed my clothes in the same bathtub.

We started to live again. We started to laugh. Life had been very sad, and then we had been terribly extravagant. The money we spent on the ice cream could have bought bread, jam and milk, and it could have fed us for three days. When we ate the ice cream we were just like animals. We ate with such fervor that we even enjoyed chewing on the ice cream container.

Next morning I went to school nice and clean, but on that day the nurses found out that the whole school was infected with lice. They started shaving our hair right then and there. Ali and I didn't mind; it seemed different and fun to be bald. Both Arab and Jewish boys didn't mind having their heads shaved. The Jewish girls didn't like it but they didn't protest too much. But the Arab girls were hysterical. Nadine and Lylla screamed and kicked and tried to run away. When the nurses finished shaving Nadine's and Lylla's hair, Nadine said, "Now you're shaving my hair. What are you going to do to me next?."

When Ali and I heard Nadine say this we got mad at her. We told her, "They are trying to take care of you." Nadine didn't answer us.

Once both the boys' and girls' hair was shaved the girls wore scarves. The boys grabbed the scarves from the girls and everybody saw them bald. The girls started to cry and we laughed at them. That night Ali's father spanked us and we promised never to do that again.

With our regular army check, my mother slowly redeemed all our belongings from the pawnshop and then promised me never to go to Ibraim's pawnshop again because of the bike. I was getting along better with my mother and I wasn't fighting with her anymore. Once in a while she would pick me up at school and get me a treat from the bakery. We would sit together and enjoy a cake and a soft drink.

Now my hair was growing back and I was doing better at school. I actually started to laugh again. My mother got a job at the army base, where she sorted uniforms and fitted the recruits' clothes. The only reason she got the job was because my dad was in the army.

I remembered one of the letters that my father wrote my mother, asking her for her picture. She wrote him back, telling him, "The best picture is the one you take with your mind, and it stays with you."

In one of his letters my father told us, "I discovered that women make life and men take it away."

My mother replied, "Why did you let your son play soldier? Why didn't you encourage him to play a rabbi or a farmer?"

When I wrote my father I drew pictures. When I drew pictures about the war my mother tore them up and told me to draw happy pictures like houses, trees and flowers. I did this but my heart wasn't in it.

A month letter we got my father's last letter.

"Dear Lola and Alex: Today my sergeant told me to write you my will. In twenty hours we are leaving Cairo and we will face the enemy. Lola, I remember you the way I left you: short, slim and smiling. I knew that once I left you, you would cry, but while I was still there you held your tears and you didn't want me to see you unhappy. Alex, although you are very young, you are very wise. Take good care of your mother. Remember this, Alex. If you grab a handful of sand in your hand and hold it tight you will spill some sand, but if you hold it in an open hand you will keep the sand. The sand is your mother; be gentle with her. If something happens to me, Lola and Alex, return to the kibbutz. They will take good care of you. Love and kisses, Dolf."

When my mother and I got the letter and we read it we started to cry. I asked my mother, "Can we have ice cream?" Through her tears she replied, "Alex, take some money and get us a gallon with the three kinds of ice cream." This time I went to the store without protesting, got the ice cream, and again we ate it together.

# Chapter Thirteen, Alone

Perhaps it was easier for the ones who left but harder for those who stayed behind. The ones who left were preoccupied and excited about doing and seeing new things, but the ones who stayed behind were in the same environment, and were always aware that the others were missing.

First my father left us for the army. Then Ali left me for Bethlehem. Ali was my best friend, we were inseparable and I never kept a secret from him. I shared my food, clothes, money and my spirit with Ali.

My father was in Egypt in the British army. A month earlier he had written us that he had left Cairo and he was actually in the battle zone. He wasn't supposed to tell us where he was going but somehow his letter got by the censors.

"They are sending me to El Alamein. El Alamein is an Egyptian city 65 miles east of Alexandria. Even though a few months ago the British took it, the Germans and the Italians are trying to take it back. It is very hot during the day. You can fry an egg on the street and at night it is freezing cold.

"Even though I have several free days I am not using them foolishly. I am saving them so I might be able to come home and spend some time with you."

***

I was the child and she was the adult, but even after my mother had come out of her depression, sometimes we switched roles. At the age of eight I had enough sense to take care of both of us; but I took care of us as a child would view that care, not an adult. Food was the most important thing in my life, and I didn't pick a balanced diet for us but a sweet one. Life was bitter, so picking candies, chocolate and cookies at the store was my priority. I had a nourishing meal at school so I treated myself to sweets when I shopped for my mom. I remember making myself a sandwich, taking two slides of bread, smearing jam on them and putting "life saver" candies in between the bread. That was our supper. Either because of her sadness or because of what I served, my mother sometimes lost her appetite, and when she didn't eat I ate her food.

At first I used to love to read. That was how I escaped reality. I never owned a book. I told myself that we didn't have shelves for the books, but the truth was that we couldn't afford them. Instead, I would write my own books and read them to Ali. Ali loved those miniature books that I wrote and illustrated. Most of the books were stories about surviving. I described myself lost in the desert or on an island, hungry or thirsty, and finally finding a jeep or a boat that took me to civilization. Ali also wrote his own miniature books, but always about the war and soldiers. He wrote that he was a general, and thanks to his skill he always won the battle. I wished it was true and Ali was on my father's side, so my father would come back.

I found out from a letter that my father, besides dodging bullets and marching through blinding sandstorms, hardly ate. He had lost fifteen pounds. He hadn't been fat when he joined the army so he couldn't afford to lose that weight. I hoped my father would be given leave to come to see us, but it wasn't to be. Instead, when my mother went to the army base to collect her check, there was none for her. They told us that they didn't know what happened to my father, that he was missing in action and they considered him officially lost. Incredibly, rather than offering my mother any compensation the army no longer considered him a soldier and they refused to pay us his salary. My mother asked them if he was dead and they told her they didn't know.

It was just like a bad dream. We waited and waited and waited, in limbo. The waiting and not knowing what had happened to my father was the hardest time in my life. My mother's job hardly supported us. I told her, "Let's go to the kibbutz, like Dad told me. They will take good care of us." But we had another idea. Apartment houses were in short supply and anybody who had a room or an apartment was very lucky. There was a great demand for them, and we thought we could sublet part of ours.

In our town, every five or ten blocks there were bulletin boards where the movie theaters advertised the current shows. The local people also advertised on the local bulletin boards for rentals, goods for sale, job information, persons seeking work, etc. My mother put an ad on one of the bulletin boards, written in three languages: Hebrew, Arabic and English, because those were the official languages of the country. I helped my mother to write in Hebrew, "A room for rent, located at (street and number so and so), please stop to see it between 5 p.m. and 7 p.m." Lylla, Ali's sister, wrote the ad in Arabic and my mother in English. I misspelled several words in the ad, but I didn't care.

After a week of advertising we rented our room to a Moroccan Jew. Her name was Rita and she was a belly dancer. We had a perfect arrangement with her. She worked at night at the local bars and came home at eight o'clock in the morning and she slept to three o'clock in the afternoon. During the day my mother was at work and I was at school. At three o'clock when my mother and I came home, Rita helped us to clean the house, washed the clothes and made dinner. The kids in the neighborhood loved her, especially Lylla and Nadine. She taught them to belly dance and she let them try on her outfits.

On Monday morning when I went to meet Ali to go to school, he informed me that he wasn't going to school that day. He and his family were going to Bethlehem. His uncle, his father's younger brother, had died. Since they were Muslims the family was obligated to bury their uncle as soon as possible, within a day of his death. I asked my mother if I could join in with Ali's trip to Bethlehem. She was all excited and told me, "Yes, you will be able to see the holiest part of Palestine; behave yourself." She gave me some extra clothes to take along, and some money.

The trip took four hours. I found out that Bethlehem in Hebrew means "house of bread;" in contrast, in Arabic, it means "house of meat." It is the birthplace of Jesus Christ. Besides being a city, Bethlehem is a religious shrine, and lies south of Jerusalem in the Judean Hills. Narrow streets weave up and down the hillsides. Jews, Muslim Arabs and Christian Arabs lived in harmony.

Ali's uncle left a wife and five children, all under the age of five. The funeral service took place in a mosque. Women and men sat separately in the mosque. Some of the women wore a veil or scarf. Both men and women sat on the floor, leaving their shoes at the door. The service was short and consisted of ritual chanting and recitation from the Koran.

Before being taken to a cemetery for burial, a deceased Muslim's body is washed with soap or some other detergent or disinfectant, and cleansed of all visible impurities. When the body is thoroughly clean, it is wrapped in one or more white cotton sheets covering all the parts of the body. The body is placed in a coffin facing toward Mecca.

At the mosque, the body was covered with flowers and handwritten cards. The family all wore black. At first the body in the coffin was in the mosque. Then it was moved to the burial grounds and a short ceremony was held. Visitors returned to the mosque for more prayers, and people came to console the family. The family hired professional weeping women from Egypt, and it seemed to me they did an excellent job.

They served us a meal at the mosque. Whenever her children stopped crying, the widow would hit them to remind them to keep crying. She scratched her face, causing blood to come out, and pulled her hair.

Ali didn't cry. He told me that he had never known his uncle. He had never before left his hometown and neighborhood and was all excited to see the country. For three days people came to feed us. We visited the cemetery and we recited the Koran in front of the grave.

On the fourth day, Ali's parents, sisters and I left Bethlehem without Ali. His aunt had a kiosk located in the downtown area known as Manger Square. In the kiosk they sold soft drinks, candies, cookies, sandwiches, potato chips and souvenirs. Ali remained in Bethlehem to help his aunt take care of her business. In the morning he went to school from seven to eleven. At twelve o'clock he opened the kiosk and worked till eight o'clock at night. While working he found time to do his homework.

Ali and I thought that we would never see each other again. He was just like a brother to me. When we parted we both were crying. I had lost my father due to war, and Ali, due to a death in his family.

I didn't realize how dependent I was on Ali, and Ali on me. We supported each other, both physically and emotionally. I had a very hard time relating to other kids. Before meeting Ali, Black, my pet calf, had been my closest friend. After Black was slaughtered, I had replaced him with Ali. In my mind I believed that I would never see Ali again. Ali let me know that he felt the same way. He tried to brag and told me, "I'm a big shot, managing a business." But I knew that he was really unsure of himself and wanted my support. I, on the other hand, was scared to go to school without Ali. We had been a unit, and we had supported each other. With my father gone, and now Ali gone as well, I felt helpless and very much alone.

# Chapter Fourteen, Refugee

The year was 1943 and I was eight years old. My mother wasn't able to support us since she had lost my father's army income, so she and I left our home in the city and we moved back to the kibbutz. Each one of us carried one suit case. The night before we left I packed my belongings. Even though it is so long ago, I remember every item: five shorts, two slacks, ten t-shirts, five sets of undercwear, sandals, two sweaters, ten pairs of socks and a few toys. It was so sad to see how little I owned. My mother wasn't any better off; she only owned a few dresses, two sweaters, some underwear, three pairs of shoes and a purse. She had a few coins, a gold bracelet and her wedding ring. In her purse she put some pictures of Dad and her parents. She only owned a few basic toiletry items like toothbrush and toothpaste, soap, a brush, a comb and a lipstick. It was obvious we were poor.

It was mid-morning. We could not afford to take a taxi, so we walked the two or three miles to the kibbutz. I didn't complain since I knew my mother would probably tune me out no matter what I said. The day was sunny so we didn't mind walking in the fresh air. We knew that neither rain, snow, sleet, or hail would greet us; it was the end of summer and the only thing we might encounter would be a sandstorm, but nothing happened. We had a bottle of water that we shared and we made sure that the water would last us until we arrived at the kibbutz. We didn't see any trucks or tractors or horse-and-buggies on the highway; we were the only ones who were walking on the road. To me it was frightening, being alone and not seeing another soul. The land was bare–not a tree or a blade of grass.

Although I knew that this was the road to the kibbutz and safety, I still felt as though we were lost. that we were failures. The clothes that I was wearing were no better than what my poor kibbutz brothers and sisters had worn. My shoes had holes and I had put cardboard inside them. At least I knew that in the kibbutz they could probably repair them and it wouldn't cost us a penny.

When we arrived at the kibbutz it was lunchtime and I was hungry. Just as I remembered, the kibbutz had a wire fence with a main gate, and one member of the kibbutz was guarding the gate. There were also two loose German Shepherd dogs who were barking and smelling us. We seemed kosher to the dogs, and once we told the guard who we were and why we had come, he smiled at us and let us in.

It was hot and the sun was blinding us. I was sweating and the sweat began to soak through my short-sleeved shirt. A water hose was near the guard. He told us, "Help yourself to water." I got the hose and I drank from the end and then turned the stream over my head and face. It felt cool and pleasant.

Near the entrance was the main square where there were several buildings. One was the nursery which had several rooms where there were children from babies to six years old. Once the children started school they moved to another building. Each grade had its own building, with sleeping quarters for five children to a room. There were also bathrooms and shower facilities, and a classroom and a recreation room. The kibbutz had two dining rooms, one for the adults and another one for the children.

Since they didn't know where to put us yet, we went to the adult dining room to have lunch. The room was full with tables and benches. We didn't know where to sit since we didn't want to take someone's place. Finally we asked somebody if we could sit next to him. He told us, "It's okay, I don't care." We had lunch with the adults. I was the center of attraction. They all asked me what my name was and how old I was. I couldn't believe that in three and a half years they had forgotten me. They asked me who my parents were and where I was born. Once I told them that my father was Dolf and my mother was Lola and I was born in this kibbutz, they accepted me.

The men weren't friendly, they were indifferent. They were self-absorbed. They didn't care about us, but the women were eager to find out about us. The women in the kibbutz kept many secrets among themselves and they wanted to hear the latest gossip about my mother and me. They soon found out that my mother hadn't divorced my father and the only reason she had come back to the kibbutz was that she was broke.

In the kibbutz the women fought among themselves constantly and their mouths could be as foul as garbage. Yet there was a line that the women did not cross when dealing with one another. In this kibbutz there were more men than women, and many of the men flirted with the married women. However, if a woman was unfaithful to her husband, he might kill her. Because their own fidelity meant their lives, they rarely gossiped to the men because they didn't want their men to get the wrong impression.

The members of the kibbutz were bored. The women felt that they were confined. The only excitement was when a husband or wife cheated on the partner. Sometimes the couples would switch partners. You could find a woman who had three or four children from different fathers and the kibbutzniks called that family "A Fruit Cocktail." For example there was a woman originally from Germany who was married to a Russian man and had had a child with him. A few years later she had divorced him and married a Moroccan man and had another child. Than she divorced him and married an Australian and had a child with him. The children, even though they were half brothers and sisters, all looked different.

In the main square of the kibbutz there was a water tower where the residents collected their supply of rainwater; in Palestine it only rained three months a year. The water tower was thirty or forty feet high. I used to be terrified to climb the ladder to the top of the tower. Before I had left for the city, the older boys had challenged me to climb the tower. But now I was almost nine years old and I told myself that I would be able to climb the tower. I did, and I felt great when I accomplished the climb up that tower.

Not too far from the tower were several one-bedroom houses where the residents lived. I remembered my parents' first home. It was a brick building with one bedroom, another room used as a shower and a bathroom, and a small kitchen. The bedroom had a queen-size bed, two bedside tables, two standup lamps, an armoire, a table with four chairs and some dishes .

We were lucky to get our old house back. I was assigned to my old class but none of the children welcomed me. I had been gone too long and now I was a stranger. That evening I went back to my mother and I spent the night with her. I couldn't believe how run down our house was. The glass window was broken. I guess that was the first thing that the kids broke when we left for the city. You could find spider webs every place, and mildew. My mother was crying and told me that she was afraid to spend the night by herself. She told me that sooner or later one of the single men would approach her and would ask her to live with him. I asked her about Dad and she told me that she would have to face the possibility that he was dead, as much as she hated to do that. This made it sound as though she believed that he was dead. I asked her if Dad was alive, and, in a sudden reversal, replied, "Of course he is alive! He is alive and well. The British are crooks and don't want to pay me, so they invented the story of his disappearance. They think that he found his family in Italy and went back there."

I started to cry and my mother hugged me and told me to repeat after her, "Dad is alive, Dad is alive, Dad is alive, Dad is alive." I couldn't do it because I didn't believe her. My mother slapped me and ordered me to repeat after her, "Dad is alive, Dad is alive and don't you ever doubt me." I still couldn't do it.

The next morning, before my mother took me to school and told me to do well in school, we had breakfast at the adult dining room. There were ten long tables and benches. Each table had room for ten people. There were ten plates; five of them had-boiled eggs and the other five plates were empty, because they didn't have enough food to go around. My mother, because she was not a member of the kibbutz, felt that she was not entitled to the eggs. I was dying for a boiled egg. My mother told me to sit next to the empty plate.

An older man sat next to us. On his plate he had mashed potatoes, toast with butter and half an egg. He looked pleasant. He turned toward me and asked me, "Sonny, do you want the egg?" I looked at my mother with begging eyes, waiting for her approval. She told the old man, "Thank you, but my son doesn't eat eggs." My mother didn't want to cause any problems with the other members and she didn't want to take something that she wasn't entitled to. I kept nagging her and she slapped me and we left the dining room still hungry.

My mother had a job in the clothing department where the clothes for the children and adults were made and repaired. She was learning how to sew. She told me that our staying in the kibbutz was only temporary. As soon as she was able to support us with her newfound skills, we would leave the kibbutz and return to our apartment in the city. After putting in her eight hours work, she got some paint and started to paint our house. My mother was very handy and she was able to replace the broken glass in the window, and I helped her fix other things.

At that time there was a big demand for uniforms for the British Army. More men and women had enlisted than they had uniforms for them to wear. My mother had a plan to approach the British Army base and contract her services to provide them with uniforms. If she got the contract, we would be able to leave the kibbutz and return to the city. If she got the contract her expenses would be limited because the army would supply her with material and she would be able to find women to work for her at low cost.

Most of the women she planned on using were Arabs like Ali's mother, who had children and couldn't leave their homes, and they would be grateful that my mother was able to employ them.

In the kibbutz the children got up at seven o'clock in the morning, washed, got dressed and ate breakfast until eight o'clock. Then we started school at eight-thirty and ended at twelve-thirty, had lunch and rested until two o'clock. We worked from two to five o'clock. We had many jobs like cleaning our dorms, washing our clothes, helping prepare our food, working in the kitchen garden and taking care of the kibbutz animals. I volunteered to work in the kitchen. I promised myself never to be hungry again. I helped making sandwiches, cookies, salad and soup. At first I would hide food under the mattress in my bed, but once I found ants in my bed I got rid of the food. I didn't want to be scolded.

None of the kids were friendly to me; they didn't trust me since I had left them and then had come back. They all asked me when I was going back to the city. I didn't reply and I didn't care about making any friends. They all pushed me and tried to provoke fights with me. I didn't pay attention to them. Even Ada, my former closest friend, was mean to me. She yelled at me, "Go home, go home, we don't want you any more." Didn't she realize that I was entitled to be there just as much as she?

"This is my country and I belong here," I told them all. I asked if at first they had missed me. They all told me that life was better without me. They told me that they thought I was dead and all of a sudden I came back like a ghost. I started to understand them then because I knew what they had gone through when we left. They didn't really hate me, they were just very accustomed to their own little world, and any change was difficult for them to deal with.

The other children had never left the kibbutz and never knew what was outside the gates, while I, in their eyes, was a world traveler. I had left the kibbutz and I had lived in a big city. When I was born in the kibbutz, my father had planted a grapevine in my honor. Fourteen grapevines had been planted in honor of each child in our group. Our group got a name and it was "Grapes." We had a flag, a picture of grapes and the names of each child in our group. I showed the kids that my name was embroidered on the flag and I showed them my grapevine. They said that since I hadn't taken care of my grapevine I wasn't entitled to claim it.

Three to four months passed at the kibbutz. Mother and I got accustomed to our routine. She had learned how to make clothes from raw materials, and I got used to school and the kids.

The kibbutz had a pet monkey in the cedar and oak park. It was a Barbary Macacque from Morocco, male, three years old. It had thick, dense fur, yellow ocher all over and tailless. The children used to tease the monkey and since I hardly had any friends I decided to help take care of it The monkey lived in a tree house and it was chained to the tree. I started bringing fruit to the pet. At first I threw the fruit to the monkey. Later I was able to put fruit on plates and push them up to him. The monkey would get excited when he saw me. He knew that I had food and water for him. Finally the day came when he let me pet him, play with him and groom him. He usually jumped into my arms and started to talk to me. All the time that I was holding him he would chatter; when I let him go he looked sad and I imagined he was crying.

We went to school six days a week, from Sunday to Friday. On Saturday we rested. I usually spent Saturday with my mother.

Sometimes we went to visit our friends in the city. When we visited the old neighborhood I noticed that our building was falling apart. The stairs were dirty and the paint was peeling from the walls in flaky layers. The mailbox was broken, the iron gate was broken and the grass was dying because the sprinkler was broken. The light bulbs in the stairs were broken and nobody had replaced them. My mother and I acted like big shots; we always managed to bring some food we had taken from the kibbutz. This time we brought two chickens and some fruit. We gave our friend Rita one chicken and Ali's parents the second one.

Rita, the belly dancer, had shared our apartment in the city. She had always hugged me and kissed me. We had taken showers together, and I had seen her naked many times. One day Ali and I had been lying down on the roof, watching Rita, naked and sunbathing. But when Ali started describing her body, I got very excited. He described each part of her body just like it was a dessert. Then he told me about the birds and the bees. He told me that my father put his penis in my mother's vagina and that was how I was born. That seemed bad to me, and I told him that he was a liar; my father would never do that to my mother. I told Ali that I had asked my mother how I came into the world. She had told me that she and Dad were kissing and then he gave her something and she got pregnant and I was born. Ali laughed and told me how ignorant I was. I asked Ali, "Who told you this stuff?"

He said, "The older kids at school told me."

I was angry and wished that I could hit him. Ali was chewing gum. He took one Chiclet and gave it to me. That calmed me down. To this day I wonder, how did Ali get so mature? We lived in the same building and went to the same school, but he was miles ahead of me.

Now, after we had returned to the apartment, Rita greeted us naked. I blushed and I asked Rita why she was naked. She replied, "I am a sun worshiper and your mother and you should join me."

My mother replied, "No, thank you. Get dressed!"

Rita asked me, "Alex, don't you take showers with girls in your classroom?"

I replied, "Yes, we do until the age of eighteen."

"My, my, " Rita said, "aren't you embarrassed?"

I replied, "Those are my sisters and we grew together."

Rita got dressed, and made lunch. All of a sudden I heard Ali's voice. I couldn't believe Ali was back from living in Bethlehem. I was so excited seeing him again. He hugged me and ran his hand through my hair. I asked Mother if I could have lunch with Ali instead of with her and Rita, and she let me go to Ali's apartment. They had chicken and *couscous*. Couscous is an African dish consisting of steamed semolina. I noticed that Ali's mother served the couscous and the chicken to the men, but the women didn't get any meat to eat. Lylla, Ali's sister, told me that her mother searched carefully for the best pieces of meat for her brother and father and she never gave her and her sister any meat. I grew up differently; whatever we had we all shared. Lylla told me that eggs were for her brother, cheese was for her brother, tomatoes were for her brother and when Nadine took some for herself her mother spanked her.

Ali told me that he hated living in Bethlehem. He was living with his aunt who had been in mourning for her husband for forty days. During that time they couldn't play the radio or listen to records. She had worn black and the children were not allowed to play. They had to sit with their mother, crying.

Ali was working at the family's kiosk. Earlier, when I had joined Ali to bury his uncle in Bethlehem, I had helped him take care of the kiosk. Then I had realized that in the plaza people from all over the world came to visit the Church of the Nativity.

The kiosk was in an excellent location. I noticed that the people spoke many languages but a smile spoke them all. So that was why Ali and I kept smiling, and business increased.

Ali told me that his aunt would hit him when he helped himself to candies or chocolate. He couldn't stand it any more so he ran away. He stole some money from his aunt so he could go on the bus from Bethlehem to our town. He told me that he had been working very hard and he hadn't gotten paid.

Ali had brought some sexy French magazines with him, and he showed me the pictures of naked women. We were laughing and really having a good time. I wanted to spend the night with him since I knew that the next morning he had to go back to Bethlehem and I was leaving for the kibbutz. We hugged each other and we knew that this was the adult world and the child must obey the adult's rules.

Before Ali left he told me that he hoped to earn some money so he could buy gold bracelets for his mother and sisters. That was the way Arab women saved their nest eggs.

My mother and I spent the night at Rita's apartment, which used to be ours. We slept in the same bed. Every so often, when I woke before my mother, I laid beside her in the early morning light, studying her face. Eventually her eyes opened, and I could see that she had been crying. "Alex, you're looking at me.," she said.

"I know. I am missing him terrible." I said.

She replied, "At least you had the chance to see Ali again, but I go crazy searching for your father."

Ali and I would rather have lived in our hometown instead of Ali living in Bethlehem and me living in the kibbutz. But in order to live, Ali had to help support his family by working in Bethlehem, and I had to live in the kibbutz because my mother had no other way to feed me. At that early age, being separated from my best friend seemed like an eternity.

---

Now back to my father's diary of that same period.

"I was a prison guard in Northern Egypt, in a town called El Alamein. We were guarding the poorly dressed Italian prisoners who were waiting for food rations. I remember the massive date palms draped over the highway; the straw and mud huts along the side of the road belonging to lowly Arabs; rickety old carts of every description rattling along with little old jackasses pulling with all their might while the musty, bearded native in the driver's seat gave us a perfunctory look. Occasionally a close-veiled woman would be walking behind a cart, obviously the man's wife. As we drove on, little kids, some no older than my son, Alex, would beg us for candy and cigarettes. We tossed a few and the kids went crazy trying to get them.

"My job was very easy, watching the prisoners. As a matter of fact, our whole unit was relaxed. We complained that there was not any action. We spent most of our spare time sunbathing and laughing at each other's stories.

"We had never heard the name of Rommel, and we certainly were not prepared for his rapid attack. I could hear the artillery very distinctly now. Whether it was our big stuff or some that the enemy was throwing at us I could not tell. But suddenly we were surrounded by German tanks, and we who were guards suddenly became prisoners. It happened in the middle of the night. It was dark, there was the increasing rumble of tanks and the grinding of gears and then suddenly, we were captured. In the morning, our prisoners, who had been freed by the Germans, were now our guards. It didn't take long before we were interrogated. Since I spoke Italian fluently the Italian guards considered me a deserter from the Italian Army and began to torture me. They undressed me and hung me from a pole by my feet like a chicken. They urinated on me and beat me with whips. They wanted me to confess to being a deserter. The only thing on my mind was you, Alex. I knew that I had to survive so I could raise my son. I didn't want you to be an orphan or a beggar."

# Chapter Fifteen, Joseph

After spending Saturday in the big city visiting Rita at our old apartment, we returned to our new home in the kibbutz. Ali had already left for Bethlehem. Ali's father had taken him, against his will. Ali had screamed and cried but his father told him to stop it and to obey him. I wanted to rescue Ali, to punch his father and run away with Ali…maybe to find my father in Egypt and for us both to live with him.

Business for the kibbutz was getting better and now they were able to sell their produce. My mother and I were able to catch a ride to the kibbutz in a lorry, an army truck, with a two-passenger cab and a big back for cargo. We squeezed in with the driver. He was one of the oldest members of the kibbutz who had delivered some fruit and vegetables to the local market and was going back to the kibbutz. He hardly spoke with us, but I didn't care; it beat walking three miles. I wondered why he had picked us up and given us a ride since he seemed so unfriendly. He acted like a big shot since he was one of the few in the kibbutz who was able to drive a truck. Five years earlier, when my father had delivered kibbutz products he had driven a horse and a wagon.

I never realized until later years how much I hated my mother because of what she had been making me do. Every week my mother forced me to write a letter to my father, telling him about my average day in the kibbutz. If she didn't like the contents of the letter she made me write it again and again. It was supposed to be a perfect letter. Being a typical boy I rebelled and I told her that I didn't want to write my father, and what was the use of writing since he was dead. My mother slapped me and told me never to give up. Being a stubborn kid, I asked her if we were going to enlarge my father's picture and hang it on the wall just like the Muslims did when somebody died. My mother told me again never to say that my father was dead. I asked her if I was still going to have to say *kaddish* even if he was alive. *Kaddish* is a Jewish prayer recited in the daily ritual after the death of a close relative. When she told me that I didn't have to say *kaddish*, I was relieved.

I kept my eyes on my mother and I asked her, "If Dad is alive, when is he coming home?"

My mother replied, "I don't know, please don't make me miserable."

I couldn't help myself, and once again I said, "He is dead, even though you say he isn't. If he was alive, he would be with us."

This time, instead of replying in anger, Mother replied, "He isn't, because he is smart as a sneaky fox, and he is hiding."

We continued arguing about my father, and I finally wrote my first letter since we had lost contact with him.

> "Dear Dad: Dad, you may know where you are, God may know where you are, but if mom and I don't know where you are, then let's put it this way:
> You and God better be pretty good friends. Love and kisses, Alex."

When I sealed the letter, I kissed the written paper and envelope and hoped that when my father got the letter he would feel my kisses. I made a deal with my mother that I would write my father a letter every week if she didn't check the contents of the letter. I told her that I missed him as much as she did.

My next letter read:

> "Dear dad: I really hate being in the kibbutz. None of the kids like me. In three and a half years they all forgot me. They had already formed their own clique. I thought maybe Ada, the girl that Mother breast-fed, would be nice to me, but she wasn't. The original group of fourteen kids has grown to twenty kids. We got six kids from Europe. They escaped death in the camps and came to our kibbutz by train. There were five girls and one boy.

The girls were from Poland and the boy from France. The boy is Joseph and he is small for his age. He hardly speaks Hebrew and my job is to teach him Hebrew. He speaks French, Polish and Russian. Love, Alex."

My mother didn't bother me anymore about writing my father; as long as she saw a few pages written she was happy and I started to feel good about myself. In school I was repeating the third grade so I was ahead of the kids in math, reading and spelling. Now the kids, instead of calling me *zevel* (garbage), called me *more*, meaning teacher in Hebrew.

Three times a week the kibbutz got the mail from the city. I used to go to the mail house looking for mail. Usually our mail slot was empty. I was dreaming that my father had written us a letter. I thought that maybe he had written us many letters and the letters had gotten lost or the mail plane had blown up and the letters were burned. Martha, who was working at the mail house, already knew our story well and tried to comfort me.

The French boy, Joseph, was my roommate and we shared the same desk in the classroom. Joseph was different from the other children because he didn't have any parents. He didn't know if his parents were alive or dead. The other kids from Europe knew that their parents were dead.

Joseph wore glasses; he was nearsighted and he looked like a little professor. He had long brown hair and brown eyes. When I was writing my dad he wanted to help me write to my father. He told me that he wanted to write to his parents, but he didn't know where they were or even if they were still alive. Once, when Joseph accidentally spilled ink on the table he started to cry. I comforted him and helped him clean the desk. I don't think Joseph cried because he spilled ink on the desk but because he missed his parents so much. I felt like crying too because I missed my father.

Joseph told me that he was born in the city of Lyon. He had started school in a convent in 1940 at the age of five. The convent was also a boarding school. When the Nazis took over Lyon in June, 1940, his parents became partisans and left him in the convent. The nuns and priests took special care of him. He was bright and lovable. His dream was to be an altar boy because that was the world he saw around him. In 1943, after being in the convent for three years, somebody reported that the church was hiding Jewish kids. Joseph, being circumcised, was a target, so before the Nazis were able to get the Jewish kids, the priest was able to find other places for them.

Joseph had been taken from country to country, and at the end of 1943 he landed in the same kibbutz where I was, in Palestine. He didn't have any friends so the teachers paired us. We slept in the same room and we sat at the same desk at school.

My job was to teach him Hebrew and Judaism. He enjoyed drawing, so the two of us made books. I wrote the books and he illustrated them.

> "Dear Dad: You wonder why I am writing you about Joseph. He is the only person that I can relate with. He and I wonder where our fathers are. Joseph told me that he didn't remember his parents. Joseph knew the name of the church where he was hidden, and his number. He also knew that in order for his parents to find him there were three books that had to be matched. In the first book there was a number and his real name; in the second book there was the same number with his parents' names; and in the third book there was the same number with the name of the church where Joseph had been hidden. The books were hidden in three different places, and the combined information could be used to find his present location. Dad, is there a book that I can find that will tell me where you are? Love, Alex"

Already one hundred and fifty days had passed since the last time we had heard from my father. My mother and I made a paper chain and we hung it on the wall. Every day we added another link to the chain. The purpose of making the paper chain was to remind us of the absence of my father. We believed that the chain had a special power and would bring my father back.

Joseph had many nightmares and he would scream and yell his mother's and father's names. My other roommates told him to shut up, but I didn't, since we were in the same boat. By comforting him I comforted myself. I told him how great he was and that he was a survivor, not like other spoiled kids. I told him that he was safe in the kibbutz and they don't allow fat-ass German Nazis in this kibbutz. When I said, "fat-ass German Nazis," Joseph laughed and felt safe being with me.

Holidays were the saddest time of the year for me. Sometimes I would dream that I received a New Year's card from my father for Rosh Hashanah, the Jewish New Year. It would have pictures of pyramids and be written in hieroglyphics, telling where he was hiding and spying on the enemy, and thanks to him we were winning the war. I enjoyed remembering the last good time I'd had with my father, eating ice cream and buying flowers for my mother. But then my father left us–I didn't want to remember that.

> "Dear Dad: It is very frustrating writing you when you don't reply. Love, Alex."

That whole week I was thinking what to write my father next, and finally I wrote this.

> "Dear Dad: We already made one hundred and seventy links to the chain. I cannot wait to burn the chain. We have a sparrow nest in the top window of our house. I hope that very soon we will get some baby sparrows. Love and love and one hundred and seventy kisses, Alex."

Again and again I went to the mail house looking for mail from my father. I asked Martha who was working there if I could help sort the mail. The answer was no, because I was too young. I felt in my heart that my father was writing us many letters. I thought maybe he didn't have any money to buy stamps but once he got paid he would mail us the letters. But still I was angry that he hadn't mailed them.

> "Dear Dad: I hate you. Love, Alex."

*Rosh Hashanah* had gone and *Yom Kippur*, the Day of Atonement, had also gone. This year I was fasting on *Yom Kippur*. I didn't eat or drink from sundown to sundown of the following day. I asked God to help me find my father. I remembered when I had gone with my father to the synagogue and we had prayed for peace. Now at school we exchanged New Year's cards, but I didn't feel like writing to the other kids.

> "Dear Dad: I am sorry that I was so mean to you, but when I am the only one writing and you don't reply I get mad at you. Already two hundred days have passed since we heard from you. Three times a week I go to the post office looking for mail and the answer is always the same: "No mail." Holidays are the saddest time of the year for Mom and me since we don't celebrate it with you. Love, Alex."

*Sukkot*, the Feast of Tabernacles, also passed. This feast we celebrated in autumn. We built and lived in makeshift tabernacles (portable, tent-like structures, symbolizing those used by Israelites wandering in the wilderness). I thought maybe my father was living in one like ours and could take a picture and mail me one, but no such luck. When we had built a tabernacle and were sleeping and watching the stars, I wondered if my father saw the same stars and was thinking about us.

One day I was all excited because foreigners came to visit our kibbutz, and Joseph and I were the tour guides. Even though we didn't speak English we were able to show them around. We told them that this is the "promised land," a "land of milk and honey." We showed them where we grew grapes, pears, apples and oranges. We showed them the chickens, cows, goats and sheep. We also showed them our dormitories, kitchen and dining room, and we treated them to tea and bread with jam.

One of the visitors was a French family, a father, a mother and a little girl. What we noticed about them right away was that they wore gold chains with crosses. The little girl was playing with her cross. It never occurred to us that they might be related to Joseph. We were Jewish and they were Christian. Joseph was all excited because he finally had the chance to speak French. The French family stayed a couple of days in the kibbutz with us. The family was warned that Joseph wouldn't recognize them and not to be overwhelming at the beginning. They should give him time to get acquainted and to accept them. On the second day the mother couldn't control herself and she grabbed Joseph and started to kiss him and told him she was his mother.

"Only a mother knows her child. Joseph, I am your mother." She was completely hysterical and was crying.

Joseph was shocked and angry and he ran away and hid himself in the haystack. The members of the kibbutz asked the French family to leave the kibbutz for a while and promised that they would prepare Joseph to face them. After they had left Joseph was still angry. He told me they were lying, and if they were really his family they would never have abandoned him.

The following week the French family came and brought Joseph presents. I envied him when I saw the bike. I told him, "Don't be stupid. Pretend that they are your parents and take whatever they offer."

Joseph told me, "I want my real parents, not phonies that plan to snatch me!"

Joseph was afraid to go back to France. The war was still on. He didn't want to see killing or live in hunger. He felt safe in the kibbutz. The parents, after much soul-searching, agreed to leave Joseph in the kibbutz for now. They returned to France, and after the war was over in Europe they returned to the kibbutz to claim their child. There was a hearing. The kibbutz didn't want to give him up–they felt he belonged there, but his parents demanded his return.

Joseph was all upset because even though he now realized these people were his real family, he felt the kibbutz and its people were the only safe and secure place he ever knew. His life was here.

I was afraid that Joseph would leave the kibbutz and I would lose a friend. We weren't as close as Ali and I but we were in the same boat; we were searching for our fathers. We didn't have to talk, we knew what the other one was thinking.

His parents prevailed in the hearing and won, but with one condition; they formally agreed to raise him Jewish. Joseph told his parents that he wanted to live in the kibbutz as a Jew, and not as a Christian.

Passover, during which we celebrated the deliverance of the Israelites from slavery in Egypt, was the holiday when I was sure that I would find my father. I went to the mail house, dragging my feet and hoping for a letter from my father. I asked the lady if she had gotten a letter for me from my father. Once again she told me no. I asked her to look again; maybe there was a letter for me. The answer was the same: no. I was ready to start to cry, and I told her; "Two hundred and fifty days have passed and we still haven't heard from my father."

She said harshly, "It isn't my fault that your father isn't writing to you." I gulped and felt my tears dripping from my chin and I left.

> "Dear Dad: Mom and I aren't giving up on you. We know that you are alive and well. Mom wants to join the army so she can find you and bring you back to us. At first I was angry but now I am encouraging her. If Joseph was able to find his parents I am sure we are going to find you. Love, Alex."

Two hundred and fifty two days passed and it was Passover, and we still hadn't heard from my father. All the kibbutz children got new clothes and we looked spic-and-span. The night before, when we were celebrating the holiday with a Seder, a traditional Jewish Passover meal, we ate the foods associated with the Exodus from Egypt. The children not only participate in the ceremony, the Passover ceremony is primarily *for* the children, not the adults.

The children all made *matzos*, which are unleavened bread.

Joseph asked me, "How many matzos did you make?"

I replied, "I don't know."

Joseph bragged, "I made ten and they are the biggest ones."

We asked the Four Questions: The first one: Why on this night do we eat unleavened bread? Because the Jews didn't have time to bake their bread. The second one: Why do we eat bitter herbs? Because bitter herbs symbolize that the Jews had a hard time. The third one: Why do we dip herbs in salt water? Because it reminded us of the Jews' tears. And the fourth one: Why on this night do we recline? Because we are free and can relax.

At the end of the Seder the adults hide pieces of matzo. These are called *afikomen*. The children are then challenged to find and steal the *afikomen*. The Seder cannot conclude until everyone present eats a bit of afikomen, so a "ransom" must be paid to the children who find them to give them back, usually in the form of candy treats.

Some of the winning children grabbed the candies and gobbled them before the others could get any. They acted like animals. I wondered if they enjoyed them. I thought if I got some I would eat them very slowly so I could enjoy myself. I was even then addicted to chocolate, but the only thing that was in my mind during the Seder was that if Moses could free the Israelites from slavery in Egypt, why couldn't God find my father?

<hr/>

It took two years for Joseph's parents to finally get him back. In 1947 he celebrated his *Bar Mitzvah* in Jerusalem at the Wailing Wall, and all of us kibbutz kids were there. Later on, he left Palestine and was living in France as a Jew, even though his parents were Catholic.

# Chapter Sixteen, To Cairo

Because Jews had been persecuted all over the world, you might be led to believe that in Palestine they were tolerant of each others. But the kibbutz where we were staying was very polarized. Even though we were all Jewish we felt persecuted by each other. The Germans Jews felt that they were superior to the Austrian Jews; the Austrian Jews felt superior to the Russian Jews; the Russian Jews felt superior to the Polish Jews; and everyone felt superior to the few Italian Jews.

The German Jews had founded the kibbutz in 1929. Because they needed common laborers, they hired the Russian Jews. Later on the Russian Jews hired the Polish Jews for common labor. The Germans were the leaders and they ran the kibbutz. Any decision regarding the kibbutz was made by the German Jews. I felt the same experience living with the kids. Since I was an ethnic mongrel, they hardly recognized me, being of Italian and Polish blood. I thought that being blond with gray eyes I would be able to mix with the elite group, but they always reminded me that I was an outsider. If I acted silly, they said, "That's what we expect from a mongrel. He's not one of us and he will never become anything. At least he has the camouflage; like a chameleon who hides his color, he will be able to survive in our society."

The German Jews' kids always acted and felt that they were superior. If they acted silly, they were not scolded, but praised for being creative and gifted. The German Jewish teachers always hung their kids' art on the bulletin board. They never hung mine. I didn't care because my parents hung my work at home, but I was always aware of being left out.

I was lucky in the sense that I had left the kibbutz at the age of five and had faced the real world where I was rewarded for being myself and not because of my nationality. In my class at school there were Germans, Polish, Russians and Turks, and each one was rewarded for what he or she did.

When I came back to the kibbutz I was eight years old and had mastered the fundamentals of reading, writing and arithmetic, so I didn't need the recognition that the teacher in the kibbutz gave to the German kids. I realized that some of those kids were pretty stupid and if they were going to be our leaders in the kibbutz, I thought that we were doomed to failure.

Now that I am older I realize that I never felt as if I was a member of the kibbutz. I remember when we celebrated the *Shabbat*. On Friday night when we blessed the wine or the bread , they never called me to lead the prayers. They only called the German kids. Those kids knew that eventually they would lead the kibbutz, and I knew if I stayed in the kibbutz I would have to take orders from them.

Three times a week we got mail from the city, usually in the afternoon. Once the mailman brought us the mail he would stay for dinner. On rare occasions when we got a telegram he would show up early. We recognized him from a distance because he wore navy blue slacks, a white shirt and a navy blue Post Office cap. This time we saw him peddling his bike and looking for my mother. Everybody who was available followed him. Even though they looked down on us, they were all curious to find out what was happening to the Modena family.

My mother was working as a seamstress in one of the outbuildings and she wasn't aware that the mailman was looking for her. She was concentrating on making a bridal dress and she knew that she had a very short time left to finish it. Several members of the kibbutz ran and told her that the mailman had brought her a telegram, maybe the one she was waiting and hoping for. She broke out in tears. She knew that when someone got a telegram it was either good news or bad news and she hoped this was good news.

The telegram was from my father, in the military hospital in Cairo. It was very short. It read, "Alex and Lola, I am alive, Love, Dolf."

My dad was not dead! He was alive!

I was so excited I was jumping up and down. We called the hospital in Cairo and they told us that my father was very sick and we should come to see him. We decided to leave the kibbutz and go to Cairo.

All the other kids knew my father had been missing, and I thought they would be pleased when I showed them the telegram. The kids said, "big deal." They told me how stupid I was writing so many letters without ever getting a reply. I said that my father was a hero and probably got a medal. They all laughed at me and told me that will be the day when an Italian will win a medal. I wanted to beat them up. I held my hands in tight fists and waited for them to approach me, but they didn't. Besides, there were too many of them and, also, I didn't want my father to see me all bruised up, so I swallowed all their insults. I wished that Ali was with me; then we could have fought them all.

❧

During this time in the kibbutz, my mother had learned a new occupation and was already self-sufficient; she was a dressmaker and was now able to support us. She told me that she was ready to leave the kibbutz. When I told my classmates that once again I was leaving the kibbutz they all teased me and yelled, "Go home, go home, we don't want you anymore! We don't want to be friends with an Arab lover." They kept calling me, *Arabi, Arabi*, which is the Hebrew word for Arab. I didn't reply because I was happy that finally I had found my father. None of the adults had bothered to stop their kids from taunting me; as usual the adults favored the German, Russian and Polish kids over a "mongrel."

That same day my mother arranged for us to go to Cairo. We packed lightly. We knew that the next morning we would leave the kibbutz and join a convoy to Cairo. In spite of their having taunted me, all of a sudden I became a celebrity to the other kids. They came to my classroom and asked me, "When are you leaving?"

I replied, "Tomorrow."

"Can we have some of your goodies, like marbles or bottle caps?"

I told them, "I will be back. Don't touch my things."

But Ada said, "Alex, don't be stupid. The moment you leave this place the kids will clean your desk and belongings."

"I will tell the teacher to watch my belongings."

Ada continued, "Alex, please share your treasure with us because this time when you leave the kibbutz you will never come back."

Joseph, my roommate, was mad, and he told me, "You are leaving and you are going to see the world." He was crying and rubbing his eyes. "Every time I get close to somebody the person leaves me. I am never going to see you again."

"But Joseph, aren't you happy for me? I found my father."

"No, I'm not," he said.

"Joseph, every night before we went to sleep, we prayed, wishing to find our parents. Joseph, you did find your parents."

Joseph said, "Those aren't my parents. They are probably looking for a slave. As soon as they get me they will put me to work for them."

"Joseph, remember you told me that when you see your mother you will remember her."

"I was wrong. I don't remember my parents. They left me when I was too young."

I looked at him and I said, "Only a mother will hug and kiss her son like she did with you. They had to leave you because of the war; your parents did their best."

Joseph told me, "All right, all right, I suppose they are my parents. But I don't want to be with them."

I couldn't say anymore, and I was filled with the feeling of having found my own father. I looked inside my desk and I saw the pouch with marbles, the bottle caps, the lead soldiers and the stickers. I knew I had lots of stuff, and even though the other kids had treated me badly, I had found my father, and that was worth more than all those goodies. I acted just like a big shot. I started giving my goodies to the scavengers.

It was easier to leave than to stay. This was the second time in my life that I was leaving the kibbutz. Most of the other kids had never left the kibbutz. They had never seen a train; they probably didn't know what a train was. They had never seen the sea. They had never ridden on an elevator, had never seen stores and had never bought food from a kiosk. Their only contact with the outside world was when other people came to see them. Sometimes a few of the parents took some of the kids outside the kibbutz, but when those kids came back and told us about what they had seen, none of the other kids cared.

Coincidentally, when we left for Cairo it was the Jewish holiday, Passover. We celebrated our ancient people leaving Egypt and going to the Holy Land. My mother and I, on the other hand, were now leaving Palestine and going to Egypt. It was a Tuesday morning and Spring was in the air. Every place you turned you saw flowers. I was excited and I hadn't been able to sleep all night.

The bus picked us up. There were already several passengers that were going to Egypt. Most of the passengers were Arabs. Our bus joined an army caravan. There were tanks, lorries, jeeps and some other buses going to Cairo. It took us four days to get there. The trip was long and tiring. The days were hot and the nights were cold. Now I understood why the Arab women wore many light layers of clothes because during the day they felt cool and warm at night. I had long pants and a sweater. Thank heaven that my mother had brought some blankets.

Among the passengers there was an older Jewish boy who had magazines that I borrowed. The bus was very colorful. We had among the passengers, goats, chickens and pigeons. The bus smelled of animals' urine and manure. The convoy moved during the day and stopped during the night.

Most of the Arabs slept by the bus where they set some tents. My mother and I slept in some third class hotels. As long as we had a bed and could share a bathroom and a shower we were happy.

The Arabs let the goats and chickens wander in temporary wire corrals they set up. I really enjoyed petting the animals. I knew how to milk goats, and for a small price they let me milk and enjoy the fruit of my labor.

There were several Christian monks who traveled with us. They spoke Hebrew so I was able to converse with them. They told me that they lived in a monastery in the desert. I was fascinated by their lives, living in solitude in their small communities. I looked at the similarity of their lives and the lives of most members of the kibbutz; they both didn't make any decisions, and both groups worked together to achieve their main goal. I wondered if the monastery would have helped us financially, just like the kibbutz did every time we needed them. When my mother had pawned her wedding ring and was afraid that she would lose it, the kibbutz lent her money to retrieve it. When we thought we had lost my father and we were homeless, we went to the kibbutz and the kibbutz took care of us.

The first stop of the convoy was in Tel Aviv, which means "Spring Hill" in Hebrew. It was one of the largest cities in Palestine. I didn't care about going sightseeing. All I wanted was a good night's sleep and to be ready for the next day's trip, but Mother wanted to show me the city. This was the first time that I had been in Tel Aviv. We ate in a café off Dizengoff Street. I couldn't finish the meal and I fell asleep. The next morning we had some time before the convoy was scheduled to start up again, and we got a ride to Be'er Sheva which, in Hebrew, means "Well of Seven." Jews and Arabs were living together, and the city reminded me of my hometown. We went to the market and we saw Bedouins and ate some Arabic food. It should all have been an adventure but I wasn't happy; I was dying to see my father.

Next day we arrived in Egypt in Al-Arish. It was Thursday. That was the day, when the *souq*, the Arab outdoor market, was held in the oldest part of town. You could see children running naked in the market. They looked three to five years old. The Bedouins came in from the desert on camels or on foot. The women were veiled and sold embroidered dresses they had made. With the money they earned they bought gold bracelets. You could judge the wealth of the women by how many gold bracelets they wore. The men sold camel saddles and domestic animals like dogs, cats, chickens and goats.

I really felt good hustling the Bedouins for honey candies. Even though they were Arabs, they spoke Hebrew. They quoted me a price for the candy, but I didn't want to pay that much. I asked if I could try the candy and if I liked it, I would pay them their price. They let me taste them and then, when I was supposed to pay them, I told them that I didn't like them. They knew that if I didn't buy them, they would have to throw them away, so they let me have them at my price. I had learned this technique from my Arab friend, Ali.

After taking a good night's sleep in a cheap hotel and having a good breakfast, we were ready to face Cairo. My heart was pounding, the blood was flowing. All I heard was "Cairo." That was where my father was. I was breathing hard. I could feel that my mother was nervous. I started to prepare myself to face my father. I was afraid I would vomit from nervousness, so I didn't eat for several hours. I combed my hair and I wore clean clothes. My mother combed her hair and put on some makeup. She really looked great.

Cairo is a cosmopolitan city. It is absolutely huge and very congested. Millions of people live together there. I couldn't believe how big the city was and how many skyscrapers were there. I was all excited seeing the Nile river.

Finally, we reached the veteran's hospital. It was a huge brick building, maybe six or seven floors tall and a block or two blocks wide. It was fenced and had a large gate. The driver wished us luck and told us that he hoped we would find my father in relatively good health. My mother tried to tip him, but he didn't accept the tip. He told her to keep her money, that Cairo was a very expensive city.

We went to admissions and asked the nurse where we could find Dolf Modena. She checked her records and told us that she didn't have anybody by that name. My mother almost fainted. After spending four days traveling to Cairo we felt as if somebody had played a joke on us. However, before we became completely hysterical, the admissions clerk told us that there were about four hundred patients whose records were not up to date and, if we wanted, we could look through the hospital for him.

There were huge rooms filled with army cots all lined up in rows that held wounded soldiers. They were moaning and crying and I could feel their pain. Some of the solders were screaming and yelling for help. My mother was impatient, asking me if I'd found him, as if I could recognize him better than she. I didn't know where to start looking for him.

"Mom, what will he look like?" I asked her.

"He is your father. When you see him you will know," my mother replied.

We started our journey through the hospital. The smell was of ether, and the sights of amputees and horrible wounds was just too much for me. Without warning, I vomited on the floor and I cried. I was angry at my mother and I asked her, "Why didn't you leave me in the kibbutz? Why did you bring me here to see this horror?" I felt that I was *zevel* again–garbage. I felt dirty and I didn't want to go near the wounded soldiers.

I started searching for my father. I yelled *Aba*, father, in Hebrew, "Aba, Aba, Aba," as loud as I could. To someone else it must have sounded like a squeaking voice or like when you're slaughtering a chicken. I was pleading, "Aba, Aba, Aba." The more I yelled the more I felt that I was doing my job. My mother told me to stop shouting and be considerate about the wounded soldiers. I didn't care. I wanted my father.

Some of the patients asked me for water and, although I was afraid of getting close to them, I brought it to them. I felt that I had become a servant and I hated being there. I wanted to find my father and leave this horrible place. I saw some soldiers bleeding. Why do I have to see this? I asked myself. There were rows and rows of helpless solders, lying and begging for help. I didn't know what to do. The floors were dirty and the walls were dirty. The doctors and nurses were overworked and I was yelling, calling my father's name, "Dolf, where are you?"

Nobody replied. I felt so lonely without my father. I couldn't cry anymore; there weren't any tears left. I couldn't talk, there wasn't any voice left.

All I wanted was my father. "Where is he?" I asked God.

After spending four hours searching for my father I was hungry and tired. We went to the cafeteria and I helped myself to a hot dog and French fries. In spite of everything I was able to eat for the first time that day.

My mother went again to the admissions office and started barking at the clerk. "I know that my husband is here. He sent us a telegram, and this has to be the place he told us about. Where is he?" she said. The clerk was offended by my mother's yelling and she called a security guard to have her removed from the premises.

We were lucky that the security guard was a Jewish *sabra* (the natives of Palestine/Israel are called *sabra*, which is the fruit of the cactus, sweet inside and hard outside) and when he learned that we were also from a kibbutz he told us that he would help us find my father. Together, we checked the records and this time we looked for the last name, Modena, which is what we should have done at the beginning. We found out that he was registered under the name Abraham Modena, which was his Hebrew name.

Once we found his name, we asked the clerk if we could see him. She told us, "Yes," and a guard accompanied us to his room. I was so nervous. I wondered if he would remember me, if he would be happy to see me. We reached his bed I saw a strange, older-looking man, sleeping. I asked Mother, "Is this my father?"

Mother started to cry and was choking.

Conflicting emotions flooded through me, and all I could do was to keep repeating, "Is this my father…?"

# Chapter Seventeen, My Father

When my mother and I finally located my father in the hospital in Cairo and I saw him lying in the hospital bed, I was shocked. The man I expected to see wasn't there. I remembered him as a husky man, full of life, with a bubbly personality. When he had left us for the army two years ago he was handsome, athletic, one hundred fifty pounds, five feet four inches tall; a middle-aged man, with black hair that was well trimmed and had not a trace of gray, and clear brown eyes. He was always spotless. Even though he worked hard, he always looked like he had just gotten out of the shower. He didn't have an ounce of fat on his body. He used to do between three to five hundred pushups a day. I always envied him. He was an excellent athlete; he played soccer, skied and swam.

The man my mother said was my father was lying in his bed, helpless. He looked tired and as though he needed maybe a year of sleep. He had long uncombed gray hair, and an untrimmed beard and mustache. He was skin and bones and probably weighed no more than ninety pounds. He was a living corpse. The scariest part of him was his eyes. They were blank–no emotions, and I felt this man couldn't be my father.

My mother was holding back her tears. I knew that any moment she would start crying. She gently woke my father, kissed him and said, "Hello." My father just lay on his bed, speechless. I wondered if he recognized us. He was just staring at us. He didn't show any emotions and it was so sad seeing a grown-up so hopeless.

My mother tried to comb his hair and tried to make him presentable. I was sick to my stomach seeing my father in this condition. I was angry at seeing him this way and didn't know what to do with myself. I didn't want to be there. There was a chair and I sat down. I put my hands under my thighs, placing the palms on the chair, and I began to swing my legs.

My mother told me, "Alex, kiss your father."

I was angry and I told her, "He isn't my father, don't make me kiss him."

"Alex, I am begging you; he is your father."

"Mom, he isn't."

"Alex, he is very sick, and he has suffered a lot."

"Mom, we saw him, now let's go home," I begged.

"Alex, I am not leaving your father. I am going to take good care of him."

"Mom, why didn't you leave me in the kibbutz? I am a little boy and why did you let me see this horrible place?" I was crying on my mother's shoulder.

My mother said, "Maybe I shouldn't have brought you, Alex, but I was afraid to travel alone. We have a big job to do and you are here to help me."

"Mom, I can hug him but I am not going to kiss him."

I hugged him, and for the first time I saw some emotion. He was crying and I could hear his breathing. I wondered if he was aware of his surroundings.

Before we found him I was afraid of the unknown and I was in denial. I hadn't seen him for two years. I had grown and become older and wiser. But my father had aged terribly; he looked old and withdrawn. I bargained with God, "Please, God, keep my father alive." Then I said, "Mom, let's go." I was nagging her.

She told me, "Alex, you have to behave yourself." I was sitting on a wooden chair swinging my legs, not thinking about anything. I only saw the wall of dry and pitted wood. Then Mother gave me some papers and crayons and told me, "Alex, you ought to make some beautiful drawing so you can cheer your father." I didn't feel like drawing; the place was sad and gray.

The day was long and our emotions were high. Neither I nor my mother could take it anymore so we went to our room without eating. We were so tired we just wanted to go to bed and face a new day. It didn't take long to fall asleep in one of the rooms in the hospital. I slept with my mother in the same bed.

The following day we got up early. After showering, dressing and eating breakfast we went to see my father. He was sitting up in his bed, already washed and dressed. A Polish nurse named Irene was feeding him hot cereal. He was so weak that he couldn't feed himself. Once again I asked my mother, "Mom, are you sure he is my father?"

"Alex, don't worry. As soon as I cut his hair and shave him you will see his birthmark on his upper lip and you will recognize him."

I watched Irene feed him hot cereal. My mother asked Irene, in Polish, if she could feed him. Irene was happy to be replaced My mother told my father to open his mouth so she could shovel food. You could see that my father wasn't hungry and my mother had to feed him very slowly. He didn't show any emotions; you could tell him to do anything and he did it. It was sad and painful. My mother told me to talk to my father, to tell him what I did at home. I couldn't talk to him. I still didn't think it was my father. My father would never have let my mother feed him. He was the one who fed us.

After an hour of feeding him the bowl of hot cereal, my father fell asleep. My mother told me, "Alex, stay with your father. If he wakes up I want him to see a friendly face. I am going to see the doctor and ask him about Father's condition." She left me without hearing me say a word. I watched my father. He was snoring and moving restlessly in his sleep.

All of sudden I had to go to the bathroom. I had to pee. I wondered why I didn't tell my mother to let me go first to the bathroom and then she could go. I crossed my legs and had a hard time controlling myself. I knew that I should wait. I was praying that my mother would come soon so I could leave my father. I pretended that I was a soldier protecting the army base. If I leave, I thought, the enemy could take the base and I didn't want that. Finally my mother returned and I ran to the bathroom.

When I returned, I told her that I loved the father I had known, but not this weakling man. I felt sorry for him and I wondered if he had a wife and a child. Mother told me, "Seek out the best in each day, and everything around you." I heard her words but they had no meaning for me. I wondered why we had to cater to this man and thought, if we have patience maybe the army would find my real father?

The man in the bed was silent and he didn't thank my mother for feeding him. He didn't thank her either for taking him to the bathroom. He was sweating and my mother wiped his brow. The nurse, Irene, took his temperature and pulse and he remained motionless. I started to resent him because I was jealous; he was getting all the attention.

I tried calling him by name. "Dolf, Dolf," but he didn't reply.

It was lunchtime and my mother fed him applesauce. I was bored, and I didn't know what to do with myself. None of the other wounded soldiers seemed in better shape than my father. They had to be fed, then washed and taken to the bathroom.

I asked my mother, "Can I feed him?"

She gave me the plate, with applesauce and a spoon, and told me, "Be my guest." I fed him very slowly. All of a sudden we switched roles, I was the adult and my father was a child. He finished the bowl of applesauce and fell asleep. Mother and I went to the cafeteria for lunch.

Mother couldn't finish her turkey sandwich, and told me, "After lunch I will shave your father's mustache and beard and prove to you that he is your father."

"Mom, what happens if you find out that he isn't my father?"

"He is your father, Alex–I know."

I couldn't finish my lunch either, and I didn't want to look at the man in the bed. I was tired and I wanted a nap. It was very hot and the fans were working hard. There was a breeze of hot air and I felt as though the heat wouldn't let me breathe.

Before she left for the hospital room, Mother confessed her doubt to me: "If this man isn't your father I will die. I am so tired of looking for him." She left me in the cafeteria and went to see him. She had a mission to do.

I felt terrible. I was tormenting her because I was jealous. As far back as I could remember, my mother had never shown any emotion toward me; it was always my father who wasn't afraid to kiss me in public and show affection toward me. I went to our room and I took a nap. I slept two or three hours. When I woke up I didn't want to go to see my father. I didn't want to be disappointed. Finally, I got up and I went to see my father. I saw my mother sleeping on a chair next to him and he still had his long hair and was unshaved. I knew that my mother was afraid to cut his hair and shave him, in case she had made a terrible mistake.

Irene was my father's nurse. She was Polish and had left Poland in 1939 and had gone to Russia. In 1943 she had joined the Polish-British Army. Her husband and two kids also joined the Polish-British army but they stayed in Palestine. Irene spoke Polish, Russian, English and Hebrew. She had learned Hebrew while she was staying in Palestine.

I asked Irene, "When are you going to cut his hair and shave him?"

She replied, "Don't you like him the way he is?"

I said, "No."

Irene looked at me and said, "We are going to give him a bath and we are going to cut his hair and shave him tomorrow. You are going to see a new man."

I felt relief. Maybe tomorrow he would start to talk and we would find out who the mysterious man was. Irene brought dinner and asked if I would like to feed him. It was mashed potatoes and carrots. It looked like baby food. He also had a glass of milk. I told Irene that I would feed him. My mother was still asleep. I knew that she needed to rest. I started feeding my father, playing a stupid game. I told him, "Open, open." He opened his mouth and swallowed some spoons of mashed potatoes and carrots and then he closed his mouth and didn't want to eat. I told him, "Eat for Alex." He opened his mouth and ate some more, than he closed his mouth again. I told him, "Eat for Laura, my mother." He ate more. Than I told him to eat for X, Y, and Z. Maybe he was humoring me or just following orders, and in no time he finished his dinner.

Mother woke up, kissed my father and we went to the cafeteria for dinner. We had chicken and rice, and ice cream. I took my mother's arm and I asked her, "What happens if we find out that he isn't my father?"

"Alex, we got his dog tag, and that is how we identified him."

"Mom, somebody could have switched the tag and pretended to be Dad," I told her.

"Alex, when you look at him don't you see any resemblance?"

"No, Mom," I said.

We finished our meal and we went to bed. Mother couldn't sleep. In spite of her assurances to me, I felt that she was wondering if that man was really her husband. She got up and went to his ward and sat next to his bed. She couldn't wait until morning.

Next morning I got up and I didn't see my mother in the room. I ran barefoot and topless to my father's ward and saw my mother asleep in a chair next to the man. Then I saw the nurse with a tray of food. I asked her, "How long does it take to get back to normal?"

Irene replied, "Sometimes it is quick, sometimes never." She started feeding him. I woke my mother and we went back to our room. We showered, got dressed, ate breakfast and went to see the man who was supposed to be my father.

I told Mother, "Mom, Irene told me that he might be in this condition forever."

My mother told me, "Alex, even though Irene is an excellent nurse and she is keeping us informed about Dad, she is wrong. Dad is going to be okay."

My father had three nurses who rotated every eight hours. They came to check on my father, mother and me. The doctors and nurses in these wards worked very hard. They were polite, courteous and well-informed. They were happy that we were helping them. When other wounded soldiers arrived they often weren't able to communicate with the staff, and the staff didn't have a chance to get to know the patients' personalities. With my father it was a different story. We told the doctors and nurses everything we knew about him. Very few soldiers had members of their families with them.

I started to draw. I wanted to show Ali how the hospital was. I drew stacks of beds and soldiers lying in them. When the grown-ups saw my drawings they were polite but it was apparent they didn't think much of them. But I didn't give up, I decided to work harder on my drawings.

After we had been at the hospital for almost a week we ran out of money, and Mother got the idea to ask them if they would hire her. It turned out they were in need of trained nurses and they were very happy to accommodate her. My mother took charge of ten patients, and one of them was my father. She ordered a bubble bath for him and a barber. This time we were going to find out who he was.

My father seemed to enjoy the bubble bath. The barber cut his hair and my father didn't show any emotions, but when the barber started to shave him he became hysterical and tried to fight off the barber. He was afraid of the razor. Mother spoke calmingly to him and gave him some sedative, and after a while he let the barber shave him.

Mother and I watched, and I asked her, "What side is his birthmark on?" My mother was suddenly confused, and she told the barber to shave the wrong side. I was impatient, I was dying to see the birthmark. After a few moments that seemed to be hours I saw the birthmark on the left side of his lips. My mother couldn't help herself; she started screaming, "Dolf, Alex and I are here and we will take good care of you."

I started to cry. Now I knew I really had a father. Mother hugged me and was crying also. Other staff members that were nearby hugged us and were smiling and laughing with us. They knew how difficult it had been for us.

Days six, seven, and eight were the same. My father didn't show any emotions nor did he speak to us. He ate, slept and went to the bathroom. My mother discovered that the hospital had an Olympic-size swimming pool. She knew that my father loved to go swimming. We took him to the swimming pool. He seemed happy in the water. He wore a bathing suit and a lifejacket. It was the best therapy he got. I noticed that when my father and I walked to the swimming pool he was limping. The doctor informed us that when my father was captured his leg had broken and it had never healed properly. Now the doctor must break it again and try to heal it properly.

I continued drawing even though I wasn't satisfied with my first picture. Grown-ups never understood anything by themselves, and it was tiresome to explain my drawing to them. For my first picture I used black and white crayons and combined them to make gray. I drew a stack of beds and soldiers. For my second, third and fourth drawings I drew the same picture but used different colors. The grown-ups started to compliment them.

Day nine. They operated on my father's leg. When he woke up from the anesthesia he spoke to my mother for the first time, "Lola, it hurts." My mother and I couldn't believe that he recognized her!

That night my mother slept in the same bed with him. He still didn't talk much but my mother comforted him.

She told him how much she loved him and how much she missed him. I was jealous. I slept in our room.

Day ten. My father was searching for me. When he saw me he asked Mother, "Who is this?"

My mother told him, "It is your son, Alex."

He was angry and he told her, "This isn't my son."

Next to his bed he had a dresser. He opened the drawer and he had a picture of me when I was five years old. He showed the picture to my mother and he told her, "This is my son, Alex."

I cried and I took the crumbled, dirty picture of myself and told my father, "This is me, Alex." I couldn't understand why he rejected me. Irene came to my rescue and comforted me.

"Give him time," she said. My mother didn't even notice the incident; as always she was self-absorbed.

I asked her, "Will you come to lunch with me?"

She replied; "No, I am going to eat with Dad."

Irene saw what happened and said, "Alex, I know a nice place outside the hospital and I will treat you to pita falafel."

I wiped my tears and I went with Irene for lunch. I was angry and I found myself pouring out my heart to Irene, tearfully describing my feeling and how painful it was to be forgotten by a parent. "Mother hardly notices me now that she has found Father, and he doesn't even know that I'm here." I started to cry. Irene told me that she had a son the same age as me. She told me that he was in the army station in Palestine. She asked me, "Would you like to meet him?"

I replied, "Yes, I want to meet a soldier the same age as me."

Day eleven. My father complained to me that he had a lot of pain. He asked if I could call the nurse to help him. The nurse explained to me that he was already heavily sedated. I was angry with the nurse and I told her, "Please give him something for the pain." My mother couldn't help him either. The doctors and nurses thought that if they didn't give him so many painkilling drugs he would remember more and come out of his depression faster.

In order to cheer him up I drew the sun. I drew an orange circle and yellow lines crossing the circle. It was pretty good. It was the only entertainment I had, drawing pictures and talking to them. I wondered if, back home, Ali saw the same sunset that I did. I asked my father, "Are you sad?" He didn't reply. "Look, Dad, I drew a picture of the sun and I hope it will cheer you up." He still didn't reply. There was a moment of complete silence, and then he fell asleep.

Day twelve. My father started to show some emotion toward me. In the morning when he woke up he asked me to help him to get dressed and help him to wash up. He seemed to enjoy eating with me and Mom. He hugged me and tickled me. I enjoyed laughing with him after crying for so many days. We started to feel that we were a family once more. He gained some weight and didn't complain about his pain. He still didn't tell us about his captivity. The doctors told us not to press him. Eventually, they said, he would tell us when he felt comfortable.

Days thirteen, fourteen, and fifteen. My father remained stable. Since my mother was busy with other patients, she wasn't able to take him to the swimming pool, and he missed it. He loved to go swimming. He started to bond with the other patients. Some of them were from Israel so I was able to talk to them. They used swear words and they swore in English since Hebrew was a newly-revived language and there weren't any Hebrew swear words. I quickly learned the English swear words, but I didn't know what they meant.

Day sixteen was a lousy day. My mother lost two of her patients. Even though they didn't communicate with us, seeing them every day I got accustomed to them. My father was depressed from seeing his roommates' deaths. He stopped eating and didn't want to leave his bed. My mother moved him to another ward where the patients were healthier.

Days seventeen, eighteen and nineteen. He started to improve. He actually enjoyed the other patients' company and started to enjoy the radio, music, news and was addicted to radio soap operas. My mother knew how to speed my father's recovery; she hugged him and kissed him and praised him. I didn't care what she did as long as I saw my father improving.

There were flowers beside each bedside table. My job was to get a sprinkling can of fresh water and tend the flowers. I was happy to see the fresh flowers, but when they died I was sad. I guess I was very sensitive.

Day twenty. My father started to bond with the other Jewish patients and told them that once he went home he would come to see them in Palestine. I spent most of the day with my father, helping him to walk.

Day twenty-one. This was a good day. We saw a rabbi and we went to the chapel to pray. The doctors removed my father's cast and everything looked good.

Days twenty-two and twenty-three. My father saw some Italian and German prisoners. He got upset. I thought he recognized some of them and I wished he would start to tell us what had happened to him. He became deaf and mute once again.

Day twenty-four. The doctors informed us that my father was dismissed and could go home any time. But we stayed in the veteran's hospital for another six days.

I felt that I owned the place. I played chess, checkers, dominoes and cards with those patients who were able. Even though I only spoke Hebrew, we were able to communicate. I found out that the hospital also had a children's ward and they had patients from Palestine who spoke only Hebrew. The children were very sick and it depressed me. I would rather be with the adults because I was the center of attention.

Finally it was time to leave Cairo. My father was assigned an army jeep driver who took us back to Palestine. On the way to Palestine we stopped at Al-Arish, Egypt. Once again we went to the Bedouin market. I couldn't believe what I saw. They had oranges from Jaffa, dates and almonds from Gaza, watches, pocket knives, clocks from Switzerland, radios from the United-States. The Bedouins found dead soldiers, both British and German, and took their clothes and weapons to sell. You could buy uniforms and weapons to your heart's desire. My parents bought a radio and I bought some watches, for myself and Ali.

On the third day when we stopped at our kibbutz, everybody was happy to see my father. They treated him like a hero. We found out he had been in captivity for two hundred and fifty-two days–but he still refused to talk about it.

# Chapter Eighteen, 1943

The year was 1943 and I was happy to be leaving the kibbutz. I was the only kid who had been to Egypt from my kibbutz. I couldn't converse with my classmates; they were in their narrow-minded world, bickering about their games of marbles, who won or who lost the marbles. The loser was sad because he didn't have any marbles to play and the winner was also sad because he didn't have anyone to challenge him. I wished that it was my world, too, but seeing the wounded and dying soldiers in Cairo had changed my world.

Cairo, the capital city of Egypt, seemed like a fabulous place to live. Coming from a small town and a kibbutz, it was just like night and day. Seeing the pyramids, the minarets, the domes, the mosques, the Sphinx and the Nile river made a big impression on me. I had read the book "The Arabian Nights" and in Cairo the stories had come alive, seeing the bazaars, the men in turbans, crafty servants and enigmatic veiled women in long robes.

When people asked me about Cairo, I told them about the sad experiences I had observing injury, pain and suffering. I didn't tell them that Irene, the Polish nurse, took me to the zoo, where for the first time in my life I saw living animals like lions, tigers, giraffes, zebras, monkeys, coyotes, birds and reptiles. The zoo was also a beautiful botanical garden and was located near the west bank of the Nile. It was within walking distance of the veteran's hospital. The first time that I saw the lions freely wandering on an island off the Nile I was afraid and I asked Irene if the lions could jump out and kill us. Irene assured me that it was safe. I saw animals that in their natural environment were now extinct. Among these were mountain goats, rams, Egyptian gazelles and herons. My favorite cages were the monkey cages. I could spend all day watching them.

Irene even bought me my first book. It was in Arabic, and I wanted to share the book with Ali. It was an animal book illustrated in color. The animals looked real and I enjoyed it. Ali and his sisters owned some books since they had to purchase their school textbooks. Ali inherited his books from his older sister and had to keep his books spotless since he had to give them to his younger sister. At the Jewish school we didn't have to buy our textbooks; they let us borrow them.

In Cairo, when Irene and I were walking from the zoo to the hospital, we saw a young boy selling matches. He was courteous and charming. Irene gave him some coins but he wouldn't take them unless Irene took some match boxes. He wasn't a beggar, he was very proud person. I wondered if Ali and I had to work to support our families, would we sell match boxes instead of going to school?

I had come from a kibbutz of two hundred people and had lived in a small town of a few thousand people, and then I went to a city that had millions and millions of people. At first I was afraid but then I got used to it. Goats, camels and donkeys were running on the street. People were everywhere and that was what I enjoyed the most about Cairo. It was an exciting city and it left an indelible impression on me.

Back in the kibbutz I was sick and tired of listening to the same questions over and over again. "Had my father killed any Germans or Italians?" My answer was, "No."

"Did he have a gun, and why didn't he kill the enemy?"

The answer was, "Yes, he had a gun, but he didn't have a chance to fight with the enemy."

"Why is he called a hero?"

"Because although he was tortured he helped keep the morale of the Allied prisoners of war high; otherwise, several would have committed suicide."

Nobody was impressed.

I couldn't wait to leave the kibbutz. Even though the kids didn't tease me there and it was a safe place, I was eager to leave. I knew that going back to the town was for me; the excitement of going shopping, hustling with the merchants, going to the cinema, seeing shows, riding on the bus and eating at restaurants. That was my life. In the kibbutz I felt like a prisoner.

After returning from Cairo with my father, we stayed in the kibbutz for four days. On the last day, after breakfast, somebody gave us a ride to town. I was looking forward to seeing Ali and going to school. I knew that I was in the third grade and Ali was in the fourth grade, but I didn't care what grade I was in as long as I had my father.

After we arrived at our house, my father had a hard time climbing the stairs. The forty-four steps took him almost an hour to climb. Every time he climbed a step he had to rest. When he reached the second floor he was sweating and I had a chair and a glass of water ready for him. When he reached the third floor Mother greeted him and he took a big breath of air and smiled. He said, "I made it!" Then he went to bed and slept until the next morning.

The following morning I went to school. I picked up Ali's gang–Ali and his two sisters. I gave Ali the watch that I had bought for him in Egypt. Neither one of us knew how to tell time but we were proud to wear our watches, even though we walked to school barefoot. We acted like big shots. In contrast to when I had returned to the kibbutz, everybody at school was happy to see me. Even though I had left them almost a year ago, it was like I never left. Several of the Arab boys who had been to Egypt asked me what I did in Cairo; if I had gone to the zoo and if I had seen the pyramids. I really enjoyed talking to them. They spoke my language. They were more mature than the kids in the kibbutz. They were already smoking, playing cards for money and knew how to survive in their world.

After staying in bed for a week and being cared for from head to toe by my mother and I, my father told us that it was a good day and that he would soon be able to go to work. He started to gain weight and was able to move around the room without any help. He still had a cast on his leg from the hospital and was looking forward to removing it. He already had gone downstairs to the store and bought the newspaper. I helped him to climb the stairs back to our apartment.

Since Father slept during the day he had a hard time sleeping at night. He was afraid of the dark and had nightmares. Gradually, he began to talk about his army experiences.

In 1942, he had joined the British army at the age of thirty-eight, which was pretty old. The reason why the army accepted him was because the British were at war and they needed able bodies to fight for them. Father was stationed in Cairo. He spent most of his days guarding the army base there. When he was off duty he visited the museums in Cairo. In July they sent him to fight the Italians and Germans. At first, my father didn't want to tell us what happened to him after that, but once he started talking about his captivity we couldn't stop him.

"The desert is a place of real fear; no roads, no trees, no houses for miles. I felt that I was completely lost. At night when there was no moon, without a compass, if I left my trench it took me two hours to find my way only 400 yards."

I nodded my head and I asked him, "Did you have any sandstorms?"

He told me, "Alex, the sand penetrated my food, my clothes, my hair and every part of my body."

"Dad, did you have any water to wash yourself?"

"Water was the most precious of all commodities. It was worth more than diamonds and gold. The water was rationed. We got a gallon a day and we used it for drinking, washing ourselves and washing our clothes. The biggest crime we committed was stealing extra water from our water trucks."

At this point Father began to tremble.

"Dad, do you want a glass of water? We don't have to ration water here," I said.

He grabbed the glass of water and was drinking it very slowly. Some dark memories must have affected him because all of a sudden he was quiet and didn't talk to us. My mother and I didn't want to pressure him.

At that time I was busy going to school and playing with my friend, Ali, while my mother was starting her manufacturing of clothes. She got raw material from the army and hired women to sew the army uniforms for her. She had learned to sew and make clothes at the kibbutz. Most of her workers were Arab women. Ali's mother helped her find workers and supervised the work.

A few weeks later, they removed the cast from my father's leg and he was able to walk freely. He started to laugh, and I felt that I had gotten my old father back. He started to tell us more about his life in the desert.

"You can see miles and miles of sand. You can see jeeps and tanks stuck in the sand. You see rocks where the bloodiest fighting took place and you find corpses rotting in the sun and smothered in black swarms of flies. The flies enjoy any particle of blood from a scratch on your body. They infected the soldiers. It wasn't enough that we had to fight the Italians and Germans; we also had to fight flies and mosquitoes. We got bowel diseases, malaria, sand fly fever and typhoid."

❧

It was a Saturday afternoon and my father had invited some of his veteran friends who had served with him in El Alamein, Egypt. They had all been prisoners of war in the same camp. They were three guys, all younger than my father, and their names were Moses, David and Ari. My father could have taken them to a coffee shop but decided to be a host in our small apartment. My mother made some sandwiches and lemonade.

They hadn't arrived yet, and Ali and I were in the apartment, waiting to see and hear some war stories. I told Ali that when they come we should be quiet and not ask any questions; I thought that way they would feel at home and they would be more likely to tell us some good, bloody stories. We were at the balcony watching the traffic and waiting patiently for the three guys. Ali asked me if they spoke Arabic or only Hebrew. I told him that I didn't know because I had never met them.

Finally we saw three men walking to our house, wearing army uniforms. I had a sudden scary thought, and I hoped that my father wasn't planning to join them and leave us in order to fight again.

When you saw Moses you couldn't help liking him. He was short, husky and he looked and acted like a lovable hooligan. Ari and David were tall and slim and didn't talk very much. Moses did most of the talking. When my father opened the door and let them in Moses yelled, "How are you, you son of a bitch?" Then he grabbed Ali and me and started to play-wrestle with us. My father told him to quit clowning, and started serving the food.

Moses told us how great my father was. "I remember when I met your father in the desert, ten or twenty miles from El Alamein, a small town in Egypt that is 80 miles from Alexandria. He was a tough guy and during the Battle of El Alamein he helped all of us to maintain high morale when we were captured and taken to a prisoner of war camp. Dolf was tortured and left hanging upside-down all night to teach the rest of us a lesson. In the morning he was still alive, and when the Germans discovered that he could speak German and Italian, as well as English and Hebrew, they decided to use him as an interpreter and took him back to our camp at night.

"Our evening meal, the only one that we were given all day, consisted of a potato or two and some thin, cold soup.

"In June of 1942, Rommel, who is known as the Desert Fox, launched an offensive from Tobruk, Libya, to take control of North Africa. It had been tried before, but this time the Germans and the Italians were successful. They had many tanks and they won. However, in October of 1942, General Montgomery and the Allied forces swooped down on him and drove him back. Half a year later we were released from the POW camp. All told, 80,000 soldiers died in that campaign! We are lucky to be here with you today."

Ali, impatient, started to ask questions. "Were you afraid of the German and the Italian soldiers? How did they capture you? How many Germans did you kill?"

My father told Ali to be quiet, but Moses told my father to let the kids ask questions. "That's the only way they are going to learn."

I begged my father to let Moses tell us one story about the war.

Moses began with, "All four of us were in the infantry division. We all walked behind the tanks, and what the tanks didn't do we had to finish by killing or capturing the enemy. The day started at six-thirty, before the sun was rising. The stars faded, the vault became suffused with changing hues, shapes solidified and all movement had to cease because the enemy was near. They were just a short distance from us. I wondered if we had gotten lost or, during the night, they had moved closer to us. We heard them talking in Italian, wondering what they were going to have for breakfast. Our sergeant ordered us to attack and to start shooting at the enemy unmercifully. He told us it was us or them, to kill before they killed us. So we attacked them by surprise. That day we killed many and captured several hundred Italian soldiers.

"We noticed that in their camp they had eaten better than us. They had fresh tomatoes and wine. We never saw fresh vegetables or wine." Moses paused to grab some sandwiches and started to eat.

My father started to tell us his part of the story. "Since I spoke Italian, German, Hebrew and English, I was busy. Most of the Italian soldiers that we captured were country kids who hardly had any education. They had joined the army because they didn't have any skills and unemployment was high. They sure didn't care who was their master as long as we fed and clothed them. Toward midday the battle was over and we were stuck with several hundred prisoners. In the afternoon the hot air was stifling, and we felt like we were suffocating. It was so hot we began to hallucinate and see mirages. An hour or two before sundown a sandstorm started, and at night the temperature dropped from one hundred degrees Fahrenheit to fifty or forty degrees."

David started to talk. "Is that place what the Germans and Italians came to conquer? Forget it, it isn't worth it."

My father, looking at us one by one, said, "We had to stop them. Otherwise they would have reached Palestine and killed us all. We were lucky that we stopped them. Now we will win the war."

Ari described how as soon as they captured the Italian soldiers, the Bedouins appeared from nowhere and started to ransack the Italian camp. "Children as young as three or four years old started to pick up guns, food, clothes and anything we weren't fast enough to pick up ourselves. Our officers did nothing to stop them. They were just like ants carrying their goods to their goatskin tents and camels, and they refused to let us inspect them."

David said, "I wonder if they collaborated with the enemy and hid them from us. It was just like a feast. They felt that it was easy for them to take the goods, like an adult taking candies from a baby."

My father finished by saying, "We saw the goods at El Alamein's market. The Bedouins made a killing."

It was getting late. My father's friends finished all the food, said goodbye and promised to come to visit him again. Ali and I also left the apartment since we noticed that my father was dozing. We started to play army. Ali was the enemy and I pretended to capture him. He pretended to escape and I tried to recapture him. We played for hours until my mother called me for dinner. It was a great day.

# Chapter Nineteen, POW

Ali, myself, and twelve other boys, both Jews and Arabs, pretended to be in the army. We started to march. Left, right, left, right, we marched around our neighborhood block. Ali and I were the leaders. Ali was the leader because he had a whistle and a helmet. I knew the drills and I also had a helmet. We halted and initiated movements from the position of attention, a military movement my father taught me. At first we walked without arms, but later on I gave them some broken broomsticks. We pretended that the sticks were rifles, or swords or spears. We did some exercises like completing a run-and-walk one time around the block. Then from a starting line, we ran 30 feet to another line where there were two blocks of wood. We picked up one block, returned, set it down, and ran back for the other block, and returned it to the starting line. We did push-ups and sit-ups. When we finished we started to play the game of war.

We ran and hid from each other. We crawled and pretended that the opposing team, the enemy, was shooting at us. "Ra-ta-ta, ra-ta-ta." Ali screamed, "Alex, I got you!"

I replied, "You didn't!"

"Yes, I did!" Once again Ali was screaming, "Ra-ta-ta, ra-ta-ta!"

Ali had a group of six boys with him, and so did I. I pretended to be in the British Army and Ali was in the German Army. Each one of us had our own toy weapons. I had pistols, machine guns and pretend hand grenades. We both were hiding behind different buildings. The purpose of the game was to surprise and capture the opponent. Ali screamed once again, "ra-ta-ta-ta-ta." Alex, you're dead!"

I screamed back, "I'm not! You're crazy!"

Ali shouted, "Follow the rules, Alex. I caught you and I killed you. Pretend that you are dead."

"Ali, I'm not dead," I answered. "You tried to shoot me and you missed, but I had a hand grenade and I blew you and your whole group up and I am the winner."

Ali was laughing. "Alex," he said, "You are dead. Ask Mohamed. He will tell you that we won the battle."

"Ali, I'm not dead!" I yelled back.

"Alex, I'm invulnerable and I'm bulletproof! Nothing ever happens to me!" Ali shouted.

"Ali, I'm the winner, and don't you ever forget that! All the weapons are mine and if you're not playing my way, give me back my toy weapons." Ali and the rest of his group dropped the toys and were leaving me. I was laughing at them. "Poor losers!" I screamed at them. "For once we are going to play my way and, Ali, keep dreaming that you are invulnerable."

We were playing war. Our rules were that we had to play in our neighborhood which consisted of one block of twelve buildings. There were four buildings in front of the block, four in the back and two each on each side of the block. All twelve buildings were the same. They consisted of three stories of different size apartments and a courtyard. They had been mass produced by the Turks, who dominated Palestine until World War I. The only difference in the buildings were their colors: blue, pink, gray and white.

Clothes were hanging on the balconies, on the roofs, and in the back yards. We could hide in the back yards of any of the buildings.

In the war game, at first I captured three of Ali's soldiers and I had to sacrifice two of my best soldiers for guarding the prisoners. Ali and I knew that we shouldn't hide inside the buildings. Once we entered a building we couldn't get out of without becoming an easy target. On this day, Ali and his group were surrounded by us and had lost. He knew he lost so he screamed that he killed me. Ali was a poor loser.

Mohamed told me, "I'm sick and tired of playing that stupid game. Let's go eat some watermelon."

I told him, "I don't want to eat with poor losers, and Ali should know that." I picked up the toys and I was ready to take them to my apartment. Ali stopped me. "I don't like the way you play," said Ali.

"You know we killed you and you should be honest about your death." Right at that moment I suddenly felt that my absent father was in trouble. I felt a strange, cold breeze across my back and no one else did. I was sure something bad had happened. Maybe he was dead or captured. I pushed Ali out of the way and went home and I put the toys in the toy box.

Several minutes later, I heard the ice truck parking in front of our house. Ali came to my door and said, "Alex, come get some ice with me. It's a very hot day and it will cool us, since we have been in such a strong battle." I was still angry and I told Ali that I had no appetite for ice and I told him to go away. All of a sudden, I saw some army jeeps with British soldiers and I ran outside, begging the soldiers for gum. I didn't share my loot with Ali. He didn't care, since both of us got a large amount of gum.

Ali couldn't admit that he had lost the war game but he wanted to make peace with me. He asked me, "Would you like to go to the movie, Alex?" We walked to the theater and we both snuck in and saw a free movie. At the movie I told Ali that I was hungry. Ali went to the concession counter and picked up some popcorn from the floor and filled a paper bag and brought it to me. We were eating the popcorn with gusto. When we left the theater, our war was over and we were friends again. Ali put his arm around my shoulders and we walked home as though nothing had happened.

<hr />

One evening my father was feeling relaxed, and he started telling us more about the war.

Tat-a-rat-a-tat-tat, boom, boom, boom. This wasn't a child's game, this was the real thing. I realized that my father couldn't stop fighting and tell the Germans to stop the game. He couldn't yell that he had killed this guy or that guy; soldiers were really alive or they were dead.

The Germans were attacking all over. They were vastly superior to the Italian army. They brought new tanks and antitank guns. The Germans were winning in Europe and the British had suffered heavy defeats in Africa.

My father was in an infantry battalion, which consisted of 450 men. He was in a rifle company that usually took the brunt of casualties. They were fighting on open land in the desert. Nothing was growing and you couldn't see any sign of life, but there was actually plenty of life in the desert: lizards, mice, scorpions, snakes, coyotes and gazelles. My father wished he was a snake or a scorpion hiding in the desert sand, but those animals also had to take their chances in order to survive. Finally my father and his buddies saw the enemy face to face.

After two major assaults by the Germans the battalion was too weak to successfully defend for another. The sun was hot and after fighting for sixteen hours without food and water, the British soldiers gave up. When the Germans traded guns for water most of the British stopped fighting. My father was surprised that his battalion gave up and didn't fight. But they were frightened and they had run out of ammunition and food. They were surrounded, and his captain decided to save lives and surrender instead of fighting.

Early in the morning tanks and troops rolled into my father's camp. That's how he was captured. Father told me that rarely did the Germans take prisoners but this time, instead of killing them, they took some British prisoners; maybe because they saw that the British had been holding a few hundred Italian prisoners without harming them. The Germans freed the Italian prisoners and their role changed; now they were guarding the British.

My father and his colleagues were under the mercy of the Germans and the Italian ex-prisoners. The Germans started to interrogate the British soldiers and shot the Jewish soldiers in cold blood. My father didn't have a chance; he knew that the Germans were going to kill him. He wished that he had poison so he could kill himself instead of being killed. He wished that he had a hand grenade and could place the grenade under his body so that the pin would stay open and kill as many Germans as he could, but the Italian prisoners knew him and they were going to deliver him to their captain and claim that he was a deserter.

When the Germans interrogated him, all my father said was his name, rank and his serial number. When they found out that his name was "Modena," which is a town in Italy, they accused him of being a deserter. They tortured him. They hung him naked upside-down, tied his feet to a wooden pole and left him there all day long.

It was hot and he was sweating and the blazing sun was burning down on him. The sun was doing its job and it was uncertain if he would be able to survive the heat and severe sunburn.

At night as soon as darkness came, the temperature fell to zero. He was crying and praying to God to give him strength to survive this ordeal. He thought if he died they would give his body to the coyotes. When he begged for water they urinated on him. He was so thirsty that he swallowed the German soldiers' urine. They hit him and beat him and broke his leg. Then, after all the torture, they discovered from the other soldiers that he could speak Italian, German and English, so they cut him down and decided to use him as an interpreter. That is how his life was saved.

My father also told us more about how Bedouin appeared from nowhere and started to ransack the camp. He could see that they cooperated with the enemy. They had radios and they had talked to the Germans, reporting to them where we were and what we were doing.

The British captain realized how stupid they had been to trust the Bedouin.. The reason why the Bedouin helped the Germans was that they wanted to become independent from the British and hoped the Germans would help them to accomplish this. The Germans used them to guard the prisoners while they went to fight. My father could see children aged ten or eleven years old, both boys and girls, with machine guns pointed at us. He wondered if I was capable of holding a gun at the age of ten and guarding prisoners. The Bedouin kids couldn't read and write but they knew how to use modern weapons like rifles and machine guns.

Life in the desert was very hard and the Bedouin kids had to collect the camels', donkeys' and goats' manure. They used them as fuel to cook their food. The children had no toys; when they played, they played with real knives and guns.

Strangely enough, very few Italians could speak German and very few Germans could speak Italian. Since both armies were together they needed interpreters. My father was lucky that he could speak, read and write Italian, German and English. He was given an office and started to work there. The Italians were gentle but the Germans were mean. They didn't trust him and hit him and beat him often.

Life as a prisoner was hard because the Germans were bored. They used the prisoners for entertainment. They decided to have spectacle events, torturing the prisoners, just like in the gladiator days of the Roman Empire. The Bedouin lent the Germans their camels. They tied prisoners by a rope to the camels and then forced the camels to run with the prisoners chasing the camels. The prisoners usually fell quickly and the camels pulled them across the hot sand. As they were pulled across the sand they would scream as their skin was torn from their body and their bones were broken. Very few prisoners survived this torture. If by some stroke of luck a prisoner did survive, the Germans would reward them with an extra ration of water.

My father suffered hunger, verbal abuse and physical abuse for two hundred and fifty-two days. When New Zealanders finally rescued the soldiers in his POW camp, he was in terrible condition. My father told me that the only thing that kept him alive was thinking about my mother and me. He had managed to keep a picture of me; I was four or five years old, standing in front of a garden, smiling and wearing polka-dot overalls, a solid shirt, shoes and socks. Every night before he went to sleep he looked at and talked to the picture. He never complained to the picture, only telling me the good things that happened to him. The extra ration of food he got was because he was the interpreter. When the Bedouin kids left goat meat on the sand he was able to steal it and eat it, and when the Italian soldiers brought him a fan, he was able to work in slightly cooler air. Sometimes he was able to listen to the radio, and it was a treat. Even watching the desert spiders fighting for ants was an amusement for him.

In spite of the terrible suffering he had experienced, my father told us, "Wouldn't it be nice if after the war I went to Germany or Italy and made friends with the enemy and we all lived in peace and harmony?"

# Chapter Twenty, The Shoes

I remember the year was 1945, World War II was almost over and I had just turned ten years old. It was springtime and the days were getting longer and warmer. It was the nicest time to visit my country. The temperature was 50 to 73 degrees Fahrenheit.

When I went to school I wore shorts and a t-shirt. I didn't wear secondhand clothes anymore; now my mother made my clothes. Besides sewing army clothes, my mother was sewing clothes for different department stores. I was able to choose the cream of the crop. I still wore secondhand shoes or I went barefoot. When I went to school barefoot I felt free, and when I wore shoes I felt that I was tied to the floor and I wasn't able to move freely.

In the summer my feet were hard as a rock from walking barefoot on the hot road, and in the winter I walked in the mud. I remember that since kindergarten, the teacher greeted us with a bucket and water and washed our feet. It took a whole hour to clean the mud between our toes and to dry and warm all our feet. I was happy that I wasted school time and didn't have to study so hard, but my teacher was smarter and he used that time to help us memorize poems.

Sometimes I would get splinters in my feet. My mother would take a sewing needle and sterilize it with the flame of a match and poke my feet. I didn't scream; I was used to it, and besides, my mother would scold me and tell me not to walk barefoot. I didn't care as long as Ali kept me company.

At that time of year the cherry trees had blossomed. There were rows and rows of cherry trees in our neighborhood. The trees gave us shade, beauty and fruit. They produced lovely clusters of small white and pink blossoms. Ali and I loved to go under the trees and shake them until the petals of the flowers fell on us. We collected the petals and sold them to the beauty parlor. With the money we made we bought candies. The beauty parlor made eau de cologne with the flower petals. I loved the smell of the cherry blossoms.

It was my tenth birthday and my mother baked me a cake that I brought to school. Everybody sang me "Happy Birthday." The only present that I wanted was a pair of brown leather shoes. I'd never had a pair of new shoes. While other children dreamed that their parents would buy them watches, bicycles, toys, or jewelry, I was dreaming that my parents would take me to the childrens' shoe store and buy me a pair of brown leather shoes. Before this, a pair of new shoes were beyond my dreams. In my mind new shoes meant that we weren't poor anymore. Both my parents were now working and we were able to have three meals a day.

The shoe store was named *Pill*, which, in Hebrew, translates to "elephant." I remembered when Ali's mother had bought shoes for his sisters Lylla and Nadine . *Pill* was a factory shoe store and it looked like an amusement park. In the center of the store was a large elephant which had a slide. You climbed a ladder which was the back of the elephant and in the front was the slide. I used to love to climb the elephant and slide down. I felt that I was in Africa or India riding elephants.

There were several elephants that you had to put a coin in to have a ride. Ali's mother always treated us to an elephant ride. The salespeople always treated us to a toy. Even though Ali and I never bought new shoes, we always bought used ones or got a pair free. We got coloring books and crayons or yo-yos or stuffed animals from the store clerks. Ali and I used to beg for remnants of leftover pieces of leather. We made bracelets, sling shots and other toys; Ali was very artistic and creative. Whatever we made we enjoyed.

Finally the day arrived when my parents took me to the Pill Shoe Factory. I knew this was the day that I was going to wear a brand new pair of shoes. My parents usually bought used shoes a size or two larger, but this time the salesperson would measure my foot and I would be able to try as many new shoes as I wanted. "Isn't it great to own my own new shoes?" I thought, "and once I get the shoes I'll be able to keep the shoebox."

The box had pictures of elephants–wasn't that great? Once a month they had a raffle. They raffled a book about elephants in Africa. I had never owned a book and I wished I could win this beautiful book. I could read it and enjoy the beautiful colored pictures.

I used to love to go to the bookstore and the owner would let me browse the books. Before I was able to touch the books I washed my hands. I tried to save my money so I would be able to buy a book, but hunger won and instead I bought food. Ali never cared about books and never went with me to the bookstore.

At the Pill store, the friendly saleslady approached us and asked, "What kind of shoes do you want?"

I was speechless at first. Then I said, "Brown leather shoes."

She showed me several models. I asked her, "Can I try them?"

"Of course you can try. Take your time, I want you to be happy with the shoes."

"Mom, Dad, did you hear what she said?"

"Yes, Alex," my father said.

I tried maybe ten to twelve pairs of shoes. Once I chose a pair I kissed my parents and kissed my shoes. I looked so happy with the new shoes. I couldn't believe that I had gotten a new pair of new shoes.

The saleslady asked me, "Do you want to wear them?"

I looked at my parents and asked them, "May I?"

My father said, "Go ahead, Alex, they are yours."

Tears were in my eyes. New shoes were a very emotional thing for me.

The following day I went to school wearing the new shoes. I knew that now, nobody would call me *zevel*, garbage. I wore new clothes and new shoes. It rained and I didn't want to dirty them, so I walked barefoot and I carried the shoes to school. My feet were hard as a rock since most of the days I walked barefoot. Nobody told me that I had to wear my shoes. I didn't realize that in half a year I would outgrow them. The shoes looked so nice and smelled so good that I didn't want to damage them.

When I came home from school I put the new shoes in the shoe box. I didn't go outside to play with Ali. I was busy opening and closing the shoebox and looking at my new shoes. They were my treasure. I didn't want to wear them–they were just like the desserts that I saved to eat later. When "later" arrived, the dessert had often spoiled. I hopeed this didn't happen to my new shoes.

There was a kid in our school name Boris. He was a poor Russian-Jewish immigrant who had started school only a few months ago. He was older and taller than Ali and me. He was dressed in rags and old torn tennis shoes without laces. He had curly, dirty blond hair and large black eyes. Everybody at school called him "Curly." He hated that name and he told us that he would shave his hair. Then everybody told him that we were going to call him "Baldy." He hardly had any friends since he was what they called a "juvenile delinquent" in those days. Ali and I kept away from him. We saw that he carried a switchblade and everybody at school was afraid to report on him.

Every morning Boris would stand silently in the same spot by the school fence. He would frighten the younger kids. I knew he hated me because I always hung out with the Arab kids. One morning I arrived at school by myself. I saw Boris standing at the school fence as always. I was an easy target. He grabbed me and told me to take my shoes off and give them to him. I obeyed like a servant. He cut the shoes apart with his knife and told me that people like me don't deserve new shoes.

When he finished cutting the shoes he dropped them on the floor. I took the torn shoes home. I was too ashamed to tell my parents. I put them in the shoebox and I buried them. I didn't cry. The shoes had lasted three months and two days.

# Chapter Twenty-One, The Arab Wedding

I remember when Lylla was a little girl, even though she was older than me. We were children and we lived in a special place because it was the place where Lylla, Ali and Nadine had been born and had learned to walk, talk and had grown to young adulthood.

The apartment that Lylla lived in had four rooms, each with a different personality. The family room, where the family gathered, ate, worked and prayed, had a wall that was painted with Arabic prayers from the Koran. There were three bedrooms: the master bedroom for the parents, one room for the girls and another room for Ali. The parents got the largest room and we couldn't run in or play in their room. The girls' room was dark but Ali's room had a large window and was sunny.

We had space enough to run in the rest of the apartment and play "tag" and army games. Lylla was a good runner and she always tagged us. Her younger sister Nadine, Ali and I were her little domain. Lylla felt good about herself; she seemed to have no fear, no tension and no problems. Lylla once told me, "There is something wonderful about being a little girl, something warm and comfortable. I love to play dress-up and pretend to make a meal." She was alive, always laughing, and if her brother or sister or I got hurt she comforted us. When we walked to school she held our hands. She, Ali and I sang together in Arabic and Hebrew.

Lylla was aware that she was the oldest of us three children, and that meant she was in some ways responsible for us. Sometimes she came to our classroom and checked on our work. She would often hug us and tell us that we had done a good job.

She always wore an *abeyya*, a long dress. Actually, she wore seven dresses, one on top of the other. In generations past, Arabs lived in nomadic tribes and were always ready to pack and leave. It was also the custom and the seven dresses represented the days of the week. Lylla wore them until they were old and torn and then she gave them to her younger sister.

Lylla's hair was long and black. She never cut her hair; there was only that one time when the school nurse had found lice in her hair at school and then they shaved her. She cried and lamented that she looked like a boy. Ali and I teased her. They had shaved our hair also and we told her she should dress like a boy. Ali owned pantaloons and a shirt and suggested she wear them until her hair grew. But Lylla didn't want to dress like a boy; instead she wore a scarf and covered her shaved head.

My mother told her, "You are lucky not to be an orthodox Jewish woman, because the night before she gets married she shaves her hair and makes a wig and wears it for the rest of her life."

Lylla replied, "At least she has a wig to cover her head."

My mother comforted Lylla, "In no time the hair will grow and you are going to be a beautiful girl."

Lylla had a beautiful face and great, dark eyes. She was a good kid and did everything to please her parents. She knew that sooner or later her parents would arrange her marriage to an older man, but now she could play some silly games with us.

At school she learned how to sew, to crochet, to cook and clean house. She was a good housekeeper. She helped her mother clean the house, wash the dishes and take care of her brother and sister.

Lylla was very religious. She was a devoted Muslim and she tried to make me feel guilty because I wasn't a Muslim.

When Lylla was nine or ten years old, one night she knocked at our door, wearing a nightgown full of blood. She was white as a ghost. When my parents opened the door Lylla fainted, but then recovered. She was bleeding heavily from between her legs. My mother washed her and tried to stop the bleeding. My parents knew that if they didn't take her to the hospital she would die.

My mother, being a nurse and working as a midwife, knew the procedure to which young Muslim girls were subjected when they reached puberty. It was called female circumcision, and it was practiced in Palestine in those days, even though it was against the law. To many Arabs, traditions were more important than the penalty or punishment that they might receive under the law.

My father took her to the hospital. Lylla was pale and exhausted and she had lost a lot of blood.

I wondered who had stabbed her and who was trying to kill her. I was crying and afraid that somebody might try to kill me, too. I wondered why Lylla left her apartment and hadn't asked her parents for help. I thought that maybe her parents tried to kill her. I wondered what she could have done to deserve that treatment.

My mother stayed at the bedside with Lylla. My father informed Lylla's parents where she was. Ali, Nadine and I went to see Lylla at the hospital. Her mother was too ashamed to face Lylla. Her father didn't come to see her, either. They believed that if she was not circumcised she would never make a good wife and they already had made a deal with an older man that when she reached the age of fifteen she would marry him.

Lylla's mother hadn't told Lylla what was in store for her–either the circumcision or the marriage. Her parents believed that Lylla wouldn't be able to get married unless she was circumcised, so she hired a gypsy woman to do the operation. The gypsy didn't have any tools to perform the operation, so she used a piece of broken glass from a bottle as a knife.

The gypsy undressed her and Lylla's mother held her while the gypsy performed the operation. As soon as she cut her she sewed her with a sewing needle and thread used to make dresses. It was very painful and Lylla wasn't prepared. Lylla's mother paid the woman and she left after the operation.

At the hospital, my mother asked Lylla, "How do you feel?"

Lylla cried and answered, "It hurts."

"I will give you a pain killer," my mother said, holding Lylla's hand, but for some reason she didn't want it.

"Lylla, do you know what happened to you?"

"No, I don't know, but it hurt a lot."

"Lylla, what your mother did to you is against the law and she could be arrested."

"I don't want my mother to be arrested." Lylla said.

"Did she ever talk to you about that part of your body?"

"Yes, she told me if my *kouss* (Arabic for vagina and clitoris) wasn't cut it would grow into a full-sized penis."

"Did she tell you she was planning on having it done?"

"No. Are Jewish women cut?"

"No," my mother replied.

"I used to touch between my legs and it felt good. Will it still feel good?"

"Not as much," my mother said.

"Will I be able to have any babies?" Lylla asked.

"Yes. You can have as many as you want."

Lylla's sister Nadine was there and she was crying. Lylla saw her and said, "If my mother touches Nadine I will kill her."

Later, Lylla's mother told her how the same thing had happened to her when she was a young girl. Her mother had come to her bedroom one night when she was fast asleep and had held her tight while a gypsy circumcised her. The pain was excruciating. All the time that the gypsy operated on her she tried to scream but her mother had gagged her.

Lylla's mother told her that one day Lylla would be grateful "You will do the same thing to your daughter. Don't hate me."

This was how I found out about female circumcision. I already knew about male circumcision, and of course I had no memory of my own. Male circumcision had been explained in a way that made it seem a positive and proud custom, but Lylla's circumcision seemed terribly wrong to me. The tradition of female circumcision has been passed on from generation to generation, and in many countries the practice is still commonly performed today.

Lylla stayed in the hospital several days until she felt better, then my mother took her home. My mother was angry and told Lylla's mother if she ever did it again they would report her to the authorities and she would go to jail; Palestine was under British domain and female circumcision was against the law.

Until Lylla lost her childhood those were happy days. She stopped laughing and didn't tickle me anymore. Now she was serious; she had become a woman and I wasn't allowed to go to her room anymore. Lylla was only ten years old and in my eyes she was still a little girl. I wished she could still play with us. This story is one event which still stays in my mind, seeing Lylla wearing a bloody nightgown.

When I told Ali what I had seen, Ali just laughed..

A few weeks later after the circumcision, Lylla's mother summoned her. I was with them at the time. One of the butcher's wives had come to their apartment and brought some jewels. Her mother told her, "Pick any piece that you want." Lylla picked some pearl earrings and asked, "Are these for me?" The woman told her, "Yes, these are yours." Lylla hadn't had her ears pierced. The woman took a hammer and a nail and pierced Lylla's ears on the spot. I saw it and I almost fainted. Nadine saw it, too, and said that she didn't want to pierce her ears. Lylla didn't know who had given her the earrings or why, and her mother didn't tell.

From time to time when Lylla had gone to the butcher's store she had felt uncomfortable there. She told her parents that the butcher was looking at her like a piece of meat. Her parents told her that three years ago, when she was twelve years old, they had made a deal with the butcher that she would marry him now.

Marriage with Muslims was not a private arrangement between individuals, but a legal contract between families. When she was told, Lylla cried, without speaking or moving. Then she deliberately scraped her head on a nail on the side of the door until it bled. Her mother scolded her, "Do you wish to disgrace the name of your father and destroy your poor mother? You are lucky that somebody wants to marry you."

Lylla pondered how she could avoid the marriage, and constantly prayed that it would not happen. She shared her thoughts with my mother rather than her own. When she became a woman and had her first period she had no idea what had happened to her. Her mother hadn't told her anything, and when she started bleeding she thought that she was dying. My mother reassured her that she was okay and told her that she was growing up normally.

Her future husband, the butcher, was expanding his house and he was adding another bedroom, kitchen and a bathroom. Lylla was going to be his fourth wife. He had many children and some of them were older than Lylla and in the same school. Even before the marriage they teased her and called her "Mother."

I thought that Lylla was the cleverest, the most beautiful, the most perceptive human being that I knew. By the time she was fifteen she was, to me, the perfect bride. Ali and I worked and raised money for the wedding. People hired us for odd jobs. With every bit of money that we made we bought gold bracelets. Ali and I went to the Jewish people's field and collected charity corn, and then baked and sold it on the street. We had a challenge, to help the family complete Lylla's dowry. It would be a terrible disgrace to Lylla's parents if they sent her to her husband like a pauper.

Just before the wedding Lylla and her mother went to visit her new home. She told my mother, "I didn't know how beautiful the room was furnished. I grew excited and I asked my future husband if this room was mine. When he told me that it was all mine and gave me a document of ownership to prove it I got excited and my spirits were lifted."

Lylla's future husband was fifty-five years old, while her own father was forty years old and her mother thirty years old. Ali and I were then ten years old and Nadine nine years old.

World War II had just ended and many people were getting married. Lylla's father had a hard time renting wedding rooms at a hotel, but the butcher, Lylla's future husband, supplied meat to the restaurants at the major hotels and was able to get some rooms for the wedding.

You could see our neighborhood become more alive, and the pawnshop was busy a week before the wedding. Because the owner, Ibraim, had refused to return my mother's bike even though he knew it had been stolen from her, I had vowed never to set foot in there again. But everyone else did. Everyone was asking each other what they were going to wear. The pawnshop owner was ready; it was like a museum, and you could find men's suits from Europe and women's fancy dresses that had been worn in another life. Their owners wore them to weddings, jobs, etc., and when the owners needed money they would pawn them. The pawnshop owner would dust off the clothes and he would put them on display.

He offered three deals: you could redeem your own pawned clothes, buy somebody else's old clothes or rent them. It was unbelievable how much he was charging the public for these old clothes, but most of the people in our neighborhood were poor and the pawnshop was the best that we could do.

There were glass displays where you could find jewelry; somebody's pawned earrings or bracelets or rings were available for rent. People felt guilty renting a piece of jewelry, knowing the previous owner of the jewelry, and wearing it to the wedding where everyone could see.

The shop was busy because everybody was negotiating. Our parents got new shoes for Ali and me, and rented suits for us. We looked great. Our parents told us not to wear the shoes or the suits before the wedding. We knew that our parents could not afford to buy us new suits and they had scraped their last few pennies together to buy us shoes. Nadine and her mother got new dresses; Lylla's husband-to-be bought them the new outfits. The butcher felt he didn't have to impress Ali and Nadine, however, and they didn't get new clothes from the groom. My mother made Lylla three dresses that she wore for the wedding.

Lylla's greatest fear wasn't her husband or her wedding; it was not giving birth to boys. The butcher's three other wives had given birth only to girls. His first wife told Lylla about her own wedding; the noise, the food, the bustle and hennaed hands and feet. Henna is a reddish-brown dye obtained from leaves of the henna plant and used to paint designs on the bride's hands and feet.

Ten months after her wedding, his first wife gave birth to a girl, and after that she had two more girls. He wasn't happy with that and he got himself a second wife. The same story repeated itself. His third wife also had four girls. Everybody thought that he was cursed. Lylla prayed to Allah that she would break the curse.

Lylla's wedding festivities took three days and three nights. The first day the groom came to the bride's parent's house and brought a roasted kid goat. The only ones that were invited to the wedding were the immediate family, like the butcher's parents, the butcher and his three wives. Lylla had her parents, grandparents and her brother and sister. They exchanged rings and signed pre-marriage agreements.

He would divorce her if she didn't have any children or if she gave birth only to girls. She was his last hope. Lylla was happy because her own family's position would improve with a relatively wealthy husband; as it was, her father barely made a living as a taxi driver and he had to pay rent for the taxi, since he didn't own it.

The second day Lylla gathered with all her friends in a hotel where the women painted their hands and feet with henna. The women told her jokes and entertained her. Ali and I were there also; I was like a member of the family.

The food on the first and second days was great, but the best was coming on the third wedding night. The women painted flowers and birds on Lylla's hands and feet. I drew several Stars of David on my hands. Ali drew swastikas on his hands and feet. What a contrast!

The third night was the actual wedding. Everybody was dressed to kill. Lylla wore one of the dresses my mother had made and the butcher's three other wives had embroidered it with silver and gold thread. She wore jewelry and a crown. Lylla walked in her wedding dress and jewelry between rows of bright candles, with rich scents wafting in the air, to the grand saloon where she found throngs of women waiting for her, as was the custom on the third wedding night. This was her night. She was the queen and everybody was going to admire her.

Lylla sat down on the bridal throne, surrounded with yellow and orange marigolds and flickering candles. Little girls threw rose petals on the ground and we boys tried to catch them. Lylla looked at us with anger, and we knew that we were going to be scolded for fooling around at this important moment. I told Ali, "Be good, this is your sister's wedding."

The band came and belly dancers started to entertain us. Lylla wore a veil of silver thread over her head. The bridegroom entered the room and ceremoniously led her to another room where the marriage was consummated. After an hour the bride and groom came back to the party and everyone cheered. They were all laughing and singing. The men were dancing by themselves and the women the same. The drums were beating and everybody was intoxicated, not by drinking alcohol but by dancing and singing.

The couple was escorted to a side of the room where the guests came and brought presents. There was a photographer who took pictures of the bride and groom and the family. Meanwhile, the rest of the guests were served sandwiches, cold meat, cheese, fruit and sweets.

There were jugs of fruit juice and pots of coffee and tea–no alcohol, for this was a Muslim feast. There were several belly dancers who danced in front of the bride and groom. The groom, after watching the dancers gyrate their plump hips and bosoms, joined them. Lylla was embarrassed and she asked her mother, "What shall I do?" Her mother replied, "Nothing. He can do what he wants because it is a man's world."

After the belly dancers a comedian delivered some jokes. I didn't understand him since he spoke in Arabic and Ali didn't want to translate it for me. At the beginning of the night Ali was happy, but later his mood changed and he was crying. He told me, "I lost my sister, and we aren't going to live in the same house ever again." I tried to console him by telling him that I would give him my soccer ball, because I knew that he had always wanted it.

Immediately after the comedian there appeared several women singers. They sang in French, English, Arabic and Hebrew. By now the party was in full swing, with everyone continuing to sing and dance. At last, in the dawn hours, the bride and groom cut the cake, everyone had a piece and the guests began to leave.

The room was now filthy. People had spilled drinks on the floor and dropped food. The waiters hadn't cleaned up or picked up the dirty dishes yet. A few hours ago the room had looked so luxurious and now it looked like a dump.

Those were the happy days and I wished they would never end. But there was a happy ending for Lylla. She was smart and the only one of the butcher's wives that could read and write. Lylla was his favorite, especially when, after three years, she gave birth to two boys.

## Chapter Twenty-Two, Curfew

How can you tell a freedom fighter from a terrorist? I guess it all depends on whose side you are on. The year was 1946 and the Jews were struggling against the British. Illegal immigration of Jews into Palestine had actually begun before the Second World War. Beginning with Churchill's White Paper of 1922, which sought to maintain good relations with Arab countries, the British limited the entry of Jews into the Palestine Mandate. With the inauguration of this policy, Jews began entering the country illegally to escape the oppression they had experienced throughout Europe.

After Hitler's rise to power, illegal immigration started to grow faster. The MacDonald White Paper of May, 1939, had set a total quota of 75,000 Jewish immigrants for the following five years. With the promulgation of this White Paper, the Zionist leadership in Palestine declared illegal immigration the primary means for opening the gates of *Eretz Yisrael*, the Nation of Israel. In 1939 alone, ships brought more than 15,000 illegal immigrants to Palestine.

The British took stringent measures to block the path of refugees; to contain illegal Jewish immigrants who had fled certain death in Europe, they chose to send some refugees to detention camps in Palestine; others were exiled to Cyprus and to Mauritius, a British colony in the Indian Ocean, near Africa.

Both my parents were illegal immigrants. My mother came from Poland and my father came from Italy. They both came on the same ship, but at different times. According to British law my birth in Palestine gave them legal citizenship.

From time to time Jews would attack the British soldiers, fighting against actions that the British were using to control immigration. The British called them terrorists but the Jews called them freedom fighters.

The Jewish illegal immigrants were all Holocaust victims and after surviving the concentration camps they had no homes left to go back to. Eretz Yisrael were the magic words, and knowing that they could go to a Jewish state gave them the courage to go on living.

The Jews tried to humiliate the British. They would blow up their lorries and steal their weapons. One of those incidents involved Ali and me. One day on our way to school, Ali and I saw a dead body. At first we only saw a pair of legs blocking the gate of an apartment house. When we reached the dead body we were surrounded by British soldiers. Even though we didn't speak English we knew what the soldiers were shouting at us: "Hands up! Hands up, quickly, do what we tell you!"

We were only children, eleven years old, but in reality we were only six or seven years younger than those young soldiers. Ali and I couldn't understand the sudden change; they used to play soccer with us and give us gum. We didn't say a word when we saw that they pointed their guns at us. Ali started to cry but I was calm, because my father worked for the British Army and I was familiar with them. I hated to see Ali crying. He was gagging. He tried to swallow his own saliva but he couldn't. I heard a funny sound that came from his mouth, like the sounds of dying soldiers in the hospital in Cairo. I thought that I should slap him so he would control himself. I suddenly realized that Ali wasn't a tough guy, he was really a *sabra*–tough on the outside, but soft on the inside, like the sabra cactus fruit.

Ali suddenly felt the urge to wet his pants, so he took down his pants and urinated in the street. The British soldiers laughed at him, and the tension eased.

They frisked us and then they walked us to school. When we arrived there were more soldiers at school. They were searching every room at school. My classroom was in the shape of a rectangle. The main door faced a large glass window facing the court. The desks were arranged in the room in the shape of the letter "u." Every table consisted of two desks and between each two desks was an ink container. Sometimes when we hit the desks we spilled ink on them and then we spent hours cleaning our desks.

Ali went to his classroom without saying a word. I was worried about the British soldiers and I thought that I would never see Ali or my parents again. When I reached my class I saw my classmates crying and praying. Our teacher was also crying. When they entered our classroom the British soldiers, perhaps to show that they were in charge, hit our desks and spilled ink on them. I told my teacher that I was not staying after school to clean my desk. Let the British soldiers clean it since they made this mess. That was when I started to hate them.

I noticed that my teacher seemed lost and didn't know what to do with us. I asked her, "Can we draw what we saw in the street today and write about this?"

The teacher replied, "Yes, Alex, that is a good idea."

The class calmed down and all the kids were working at their desks. Then she asked each one of us to come to the blackboard and tell her what we experienced. Very few of us were able to talk, we were so frightened. We had never seen soldiers in our school with weapons before. They looked like giants with their khaki uniforms and weapons, and they were mean. I told myself that if I wanted to survive I must be smart. I should win them over if I wanted to live. I shouldn't cry, I should smile and show them that I wasn't afraid of them. I shouldn't talk back to them and I should follow their orders–whatever they were–in order to stay alive.

At three o'clock school was over and the British soldiers informed us that after five o'clock we must stay at home. Their newly imposed curfew would start at five o'clock and end the following week. If the soldiers found anybody on the street they would shoot to kill. The first thing that I did when I left school was to run to the grocery store. The whole neighborhood was in the store. Everybody was pushing and grabbing anything that they could pick up. The store was chaotic and it didn't take long to empty the shelves. I picked some lemons, fruits, bread and some canned goods. I knew that if we didn't eat citrus we were going to be sick. I made sure that we had some food to eat in the house.

I wondered where my parents were. At first I was angry that they weren't taking better care of me, but the longer I waited for them, the more I worried. But then I realized that my mother was in her dress factory, trying to make a living for the family, and my father was a clerk in the British army, the same army that was here harassing us.

I guessed that I was the only one available in our family to prepare for the curfew. Ali, on the other hand, had his mother and sisters that went to the store and got food for the whole family.

The clock struck five o'clock and curfew time started. The streets were empty except for British soldiers patrolling the streets in jeeps. They put up barriers and there was no way that anyone could escape from that area. Later on, they put old tires on the roads, and when they lifted the curfew we had a feast burning those tires. The black smoke in the sky and the smell of the rubber was intolerable. I guess we did more damage to ourselves than to the British.

During the curfew loudspeakers were shouting in English, Hebrew and Arabic, "Stay home, anybody on the street will be shot." It was lucky for us that my parents made it home safely before the curfew began. I was a nervous wreck, waiting for them and not knowing if they would arrive.

When they came, my parents and I stayed in the house. The first few days I rested, but then I became restless and I had to see Ali. We lived in the same apartment building so we were able to visit each other, when our parents allowed it, without going outside.

The British soldiers went from house to house checking for terrorists and illegal immigrants. It felt to me that we were not in a free country, but instead were in wartime Germany where the Germans were hunting Jews so they could kill them. The British checked every apartment and pulled the men out of the houses. I was astonished when they picked up my father, knowing that he was working for the British army. When I saw my father pushed into a cattle truck, I thought that would be the end of him. I saw Ali's father also taken away in the same truck with my father. Neither Ali nor I were crying. Before, we were afraid of the soldiers, but now we wanted to hit them when we saw how cruel they were to our parents; when they came near us and tried to be friendly, we spat on them. We believed by doing that we showed them that nobody could mess with us.

Terrible things came to my mind. I thought the British were going to kill the men first and then the women who were no longer protected by their men, and later they would take the children. We were not armed and I thought it would be easy to gather us up and get rid of us.

My father was away for two days, but Ali's father remained in jail longer. Ali's family waited patiently, but the later it got the more anxious they became. They tried to dismiss their worried thoughts. "Father is sure to come back," they told themselves. He was kept for two weeks because he was a taxi driver and the British thought that he was transporting terrorists and illegal immigrants. When Ali's father came back, although he looked like he had been through an ordeal, he told us that they had not tortured him. He had been held in a camp surrounded by wire fencing and he had been able to wander around. They fed him three meals a day, but waiting for the unknown was, by itself, a form of torture. Several times they interrogated him. The interrogator was an Arab that shouted at him. Instead of hating the British, who had put him there, he hated our countryman, who had sold himself to the British.

We had several curfews during the year. We were getting used to it. While the curfews were on, they lifted them every two or three days for a few hours. During that time the farmers were able to bring food to the city. Ali and I took the opportunity and became businessmen. Ali knew a fifteen-year-old Arab boy who was selling milk. He had a wagon and a few metal crates full of bottles of milk. The boy was more interested in smoking a water pipe full of hashish than selling his milk, and Ali offered him a deal that he would sell the milk for him. We took advantage of the situation and we sold milk at triple the normal price. When the break of the curfew ended we still were peddling milk through the neighborhood. We took a chance and stayed out. We could have been shot, but we didn't care; we had a business, and we were attending to it.

When Ali and I went back to school we found out that the British had arrested some Russian-Jewish kids that went to our school. They were older than Ali and me and the crime that they had committed was scattering anti-British leaflets. They were sentenced to a year in jail

Many people took advantage of the curfew by raising the prices of their goods. Ali and I were two of those people. Although we were only eleven years old, we traded merchandise like shrewd, experienced businessmen and we made sure that our families were well fed. If you ask me if I hated this time of my life, I'd say "No." It was full of excitement and adventure. Although we were Arab and Jew, Ali and I worked well together when mutual trust was necessary. The money we made we split equally. Though Ali, having a larger family than me, needed more, he told me, "We both took chances and worked the same, so we should get paid the same."

The excitement of being a target gradually died down. What were the British doing here? Neither Arabs nor Jews wanted them here. The British soldiers spent most of their time at the army base, and when they got free time they spent most of it in saloons, drinking cognac and beer, and watching burlesque shows. We thought they could have been more useful helping to build the country. They could have picked up shovels and made roads or planted trees, and years later they could return to see what they had done. But they had no investment in or concern for our land, and couldn't wait to go home.

❦

It doesn't matter which side you are on, the wounds of war affect you. We were both affected. The British soldiers went from being our heroes during WW II to being our enemies, and we were fighting for our freedom and the right to live peacefully in our land. When the British finally left and ceased being our enemies, then we gained a new enemy–the Arabs.

# Chapter Twenty-Three, Stolen Childhood

I met Irene when I was in Cairo, Egypt, in the year 1943 when I was only eight years old. She was the nurse who took care of my father in the military hospital. Irene and I bonded right away. She told me that I reminded her of her son Patrick. Patrick was the same age as me and was in the Polish-British Army that was stationed in Palestine. It may seem very strange to the reader that an eight-year-old child was in the army, but I will explain how that happened very shortly.

Irene told me that Patrick was very smart. He spoke Polish, Russian, English, Hebrew and Arabic. The reason that Patrick was in the army was because in 1942 her husband joined the British Army and the family was able to join him. Patrick got a free education and when he graduated from school, he would have to serve in the army for four years.

Because Irene was a nurse, she was stationed at the veteran's hospital in Cairo. I couldn't wait to meet Patrick. I really wanted to meet a kid who spoke so many languages. At first I was jealous of Patrick, a kid who was in the army, wearing an army uniform and actually learning to use weapons. Ali and I would have loved to change places with him. But sadly to say, everything that shines is not gold and I can say the same thing about Patrick and his army experience.

After my father recovered from his injuries, we moved back to our home in the city. Irene and Patrick came to visit us in our apartment, and even though Patrick was my age he was a head taller than both Ali and me. He had curly blond hair and sad green eyes.

My mother and father invited Irene and Patrick for tea. My parents set the table with delicious pastries and my mother made some cabbage rolls. Patrick was very polite and he acted like a gentleman. Ali was with us, and he and I, knowing the territory, were a little mischievous.

Patrick told us that he was born in a little village in Poland not too far from the Russian border. In 1940, just when the Germans were trying to eliminate all the Jews in Europe, the Russians were doing the same thing to many of the prominent citizens of Poland, to Jews, Gypsies, Ukrainians and anyone else that didn't meet their ideal of the master race.

Patrick said, "I was only five years old, ready to start school, when my father got a wagon and carried our family's clothes and food on our trek to Russia. There we lived just like slaves for two years. I was lucky that I didn't get typhus and die, but many members of my family got sick and were lost.

"In 1942, Poland signed a treaty with Russia and we were able to leave. We were able to join the Polish-British Army as a family unit but we became separated; my parents were sent to Egypt and I was sent to school, first in India and then in Palestine."

I noticed that Patrick talked like a robot when he told us this story, as though he was repeating the words but could not think for himself. When Ali and I were gobbling the meat and cabbage rolls, Patrick could not decide what to eat. He asked his mother, "Which cabbage roll should I eat, the meat or the vegetable?" I was surprised that Patrick was so dependent on his mother and was so well-behaved. If somebody invited me to such a party, I would attack the cake and cookies before anything else, but Patrick waited until my mother served him a piece of cake. He asked his mother, "Can I eat the cake?" Once his mother gave him permission, he gobbled the cake, just like he was in the army and could not attack the enemy until he got an order to do so.

Patrick told us that the first year that he was in Russia, his family was starving to death. It was very, very, cold, and his parents sold the extra clothes and goods that they had brought from Poland in order to buy what little food was available. He told me that one day in winter some older kids stole his shoes and he walked barefoot on the snow and almost got frostbite. Luckily, a Polish woman brought him to his parents and they wrapped his feet in rags to provide what little protection they could.

When he was in Russia he had to speak Russian. Polish and Russian are very similar languages, they are Balto-Slavic languages. Patrick sometimes mixed both languages and if he used Polish words the teacher and the other Russian people beat him up. He told me that they had lived in a "co-op" where two families lived in one room. There was no privacy; the room was divided with a sheet. They all slept on the floor together and that's the way they stayed warm.

Patrick continued telling his story. "My parents were sent to the forest as woodcutters, and I joined the elderly, the sick and other children to cut wood for fuel with a handsaw. I was always hungry and cold. The Russians constantly beat us and told us that we didn't deserve to live in this world. When I was at the Russian co-op camp, I never knew if I would see my parents again. In the morning a cattle truck took my parents to the woods and in the evening brought them back. Sometimes my mother had food for us and I provided wood for the fire. I was so wretched I tried to kill myself several times. I don't know what kept me alive."

Ali and I were luckier. Even though we were always hungry, we had the love of our parents and the love of each other.

One day my mother invited Patrick for lunch and she made baked potatoes. Patrick didn't eat them. He told us that when he was in Russia, sometimes his parents didn't get paid for their labor. They didn't have any food so they had to go to the field to steal potatoes. If they got caught they would end in jail. He was still scared of potatoes and that was why he couldn't eat them.

Patrick told us that not all Russians were bad. He remembered Easter Sunday in Poland when they had always celebrated it by eating good food. In Russia, Easter arrived and his family ran out of food. "There was nothing to eat in our house," said Patrick. "The other family that we shared the room with were in the same boat. We consisted of three people; my father, mother and I. The other family consisted of four people; mother, father and two girls almost the same age as me. I told the girls, 'Let's do some begging among the natives.' We were very shy but hunger overcame our shyness.

"We went from house to house to beg for food. At one house we entered a back yard and saw a local woman baking buns. We were standing in the corner inhaling the smell of the baking, hoping to be noticed. The woman collected the puffed-up buns and gave us a basketful of buns. We ran home and we felt that this was heaven."

Patrick asked me and Ali, "Do you know what a curse is?" I replied, "I don't know what you are talking about. I never heard this word." Ali hadn't either. Patrick then told us a story of how a curse saved his life. He said, "I remember when I was five years old and I was living in Poland, in a large apartment house, on the third floor. I was staying with my grandmother, my aunt, and eight cousins. The men were in the Polish Army and there was nobody at home to protect us." He went on to say, "I remember that every day there was an air raid and we had to go down the stairs to the basement. Because we were on the top floor, we were usually the last ones to get there, and sometimes the shelter was full and we couldn't get in. My mother begged the landlord to change our apartment from the third floor to the first floor. On the first floor was an older couple, and from the third floor it wouldn't take them as long as it did us to reach the shelter because we were thirteen people and they were only two. When the couple heard that we wanted to exchange apartments with them, they cursed us. They said, "If you move to this apartment, you will drop dead." Being superstitious, my grandmother dropped her request to exchange apartments. One day either there was no air raid warning or we didn't hear it, and the Germans bombed our building. Part of the building collapsed, sparing the third floor but crushing all the occupants on the first floor. So the curse turned on the couple who had made it and it killed them. That's why I believe in the power of curses."

That was what Patrick believed. Now Ali and I understood what curses were. I thought that the curse was not directed to the older couple, but that it was an indirect curse–one that applied to whoever was in the apartment at the time.

Patrick's parents were sent to Egypt. His mother was a nurse and his father was in charge of a supply detail in the Polish-British army. Patrick was sent first to India and then to Palestine and his base was not too far from us.

In 1946 Patrick and I became friends. I had a chance to see the army camp where he was staying. It had an elementary and secondary school. The teachers were army officers. The purpose of the school was to produce future officers. Sometimes I brought Ali to visit Patrick. Patrick was always stiff; he never laughed and didn't seem happy, while Ali and I had a ball at the camp. We pretended we were soldiers running around the trenches, and we did the obstacle course. My favorite part was swinging from a rope from tree to tree pretending to be Tarzan. Patrick was very tense. He told us that this was serious and not a game. We were laughing and told him, "Don't be so square. Loosen up and have fun."

Patrick told us most of the kids on the base were Polish. They were called cadets, and after six hours of academic study and military exercises, they were free to do whatever they wanted. Some of the kids played soccer and others read books, but others did absolutely nothing, not even their homework. Those kids had been moved from country to country and did not even remember their Polish homeland. The adult soldiers on the base often mistreated them, and they had become apathetic. "Poland" was not a magic word for them, not like "Eretz Israel" was for the Jews.

He told us there were always guards on duty 24 hours a day and they really couldn't get far without being noticed. The guards kept the cadets' weapons locked up and when the cadets took rifle practice, they were always given one-on-one instruction and watched carefully.

The buildings in the camp were temporary shacks. There were eight to ten kids living in each shack. The beds were folding cots and were easy to move from place to place. The toilet was a hole in the ground and, boy, he told us, did it smell bad! The showers were temporary showers without privacy. Patrick was in the boys' section of the camp. There was a girls' section farther away. The boys were not allowed to mingle with the girls. There was hardly any social life. There was always order and discipline and the instructors told the kids that they were lucky to be alive and that they must sacrifice for the Polish fatherland.

There was a brick building where the cadets ate and went to school. Next to the brick building was a water tower. When we visited the base, Ali and I enjoyed going swimming in the water tower. At first I was afraid to climb up to the water tower, but later

I got used to it. Now that I am older I realize that Patrick was living in a kind of military orphanage. He had been removed from his home and family and been placed in this or other camps without hope of ever seeing his parents again. He missed the love and security of his parents. He never knew where his next home would be.

Patrick told me that Ali and I were lucky. We knew that Palestine was our home. He didn't know if he would ever see Poland again.

Patrick wondered how long it had been since his parents were sent to Egypt. Why had his parents allowed the army to separate them, or why had the army done so? Those questions were always in Patrick's mind and, later, when he and his parents were reunited their answer to his questions was always the same: "It was because of the war, and we are lucky to be alive."

He also told us that many kids in the camp knew their mothers only from old passport photographs and that was why he carried his mother's picture in his pants. In my own case I had asked my mother for her picture because I was afraid if we were separated, at least I would have her picture. She had given me a small picture of her with my dad.

In 1947 the British dismantled the Polish army bases and Patrick was reunited with his parents. I saw him leaving the camp. He was told that he was going to live in England and then he would try to go to the United States. Once he left I lost touch with him again and I forgot about him.

In the year 2002 I went to an adult education school in San Francisco, taking a photography class. Among the students in the class I noticed that there was an older man who was looking at me. He looked strangely familiar, a ghost-like figure from the past. For all his age he had a babyish face and curly gray hair and green eyes. He seemed an entire foot taller than me; I am 5 feet, five inches, and he looked about six feet, five inches. I overheard him talking and I noticed that he had an accent. I couldn't place it, but I knew from the way that he acted that he was not an American. He was dressed very neatly, with a suit and tie, and I wondered why he was so tense. I, on the other hand, wore Levis and a t-shirt. What a contrast!

This class was for retired people, and the time that we took the class was from ten in the morning to twelve noon. It was more a social event for me than an academic experience. Finally, at ten minutes after ten, the teacher arrived and took the roll, and I heard the name Patrick so-and-so. I asked myself, "Could this man possibly be the Patrick I knew from Palestine, the Polish boy in the British army?" The teacher called my name, "Alejandro Modena." I heard Patrick talking to an older woman. He said, "I think I know this man," referring to me. "I knew somebody with the same last name but his name was not Alejandro, it was Alex or Alexander. What shall I do?"

The woman, who I later learned was his wife, told him that during the break he should approach me and ask me a question in Hebrew.

Patrick, just as when he was a boy, had to have the okay from his wife before he approached me. Once she nodded her head, he asked me, out of the blue, *"Ata madaber evrit?"* Do you speak Hebrew?"

I answered him in English, "Why do you want to know?"

He replied, "You look like somebody that I knew in Palestine, but his name was not Alejandro." I laughed and hugged him and I told him, "Patrick, this is me, Alex!"

We couldn't control ourselves. We both were very emotional. We were crying, but the break was very short and we had to return to the classroom. I had to leave the class early because I had a ride and I didn't want my driver to wait for me, so I didn't have a chance to talk more with him. The following week I went to the class early because I was eager to find Patrick and talk with him. I was going to invite him to my house. But neither Patrick nor his wife came to the class. I called information and I asked for his phone number but they told me that it was unlisted. Mine is also unlisted, so I guess that it was not meant for us to connect further after all those years.

Before I had left that first class, Patrick told me that from England he had come to the United States at the age of eighteen. He was a retired engineer and he had two grown-up daughters. I asked myself why he hadn't returned or wanted to contact me. I guess that I reminded him of the past, which was a terrible time in his life, and he hadn't wanted to remember it.

On the other hand, even though we were poor, and except for a difficult time when my father was away, I had loving parents who took care of me.

# Chapter Twenty-Four, The Jewish Wedding

Rita, our former tenant, was getting married. When we were living in the kibbutz, we subleased our apartment to her. She invited somewhere between five to seven hundred people to her wedding. She couldn't afford such a big wedding but her future husband told her that the Lord would help them. They had chosen our kibbutz for the wedding ceremony and reception. The kibbutz had two hundred residents and they were all invited to the wedding; both old and young adults, children, toddlers and babies. One hundred Arabs were also invited, including sixty people in Ali's family. Ali's father, mother and his younger sister, Nadine, made four. Lylla's husband, three wives and ten children made fourteen. Ali's uncles, aunts and cousins made sixty people altogether. It seemed to me that anybody who heard about it came to the wedding ceremony. Most of the guests gave Rita money as wedding gifts so she was able to pay for the wedding expenses. The kibbutz supplied the food, entertainment and the dining room, which was big enough to accommodate all the guests.

Many of the wedding invitations were handwritten; the kids in the kibbutz did them. They used crayons, pencils and pens, and decorated the invitations individually and wrote some quotations from the Bible, such as "And the Lord God said: it is not good for man to be alone. I will make him a helper to match him…" (Gen. 2:18). The invitations were written in Hebrew, English or Arabic. Ali and I helped to hand-deliver the written invitations. If we had mailed them the cost of the stamps would have been very expensive.

We felt that the whole community took part in this wedding. Most of the invitations were actually not written but delivered mouth to mouth. If Rita saw someone that she knew, she asked them, "What are you going to do this Tuesday?" If they answered, "Nothing," she would then ask them, "Would you like to come to my wedding?" Then they would ask her if they could bring their boyfriends or their families. Rita would tell them, "Be my guest."

The kibbutz had a band and they rehearsed day and night because if people liked them they would hire them outside the kibbutz and they would make a good income. Ali had some Arab friends who could play the drums, so Rita hired them also.

Rita, who was a belly dancer, had met her future husband, Moses, at a bar. He was a bartender and he didn't mind that Rita worked at the same bar with him. Both Rita and Moses were immigrants from Morocco who had come to Palestine at an early age. They could hardly read and write, but they were always happy, laughing and telling jokes to each other.

Rita and Moses chose their wedding day to be Tuesday because the Bible repeats the words *ki tov* ("And God knew that it was good," Genesis 1:10-12) in referring to the third day of Creation, and Tuesday is the third day of the week. Even though they were working days the guests took two days off.

Ali and his family lived in our apartment house, and whenever Ali had seen Rita he had always flirted with her. He would tell her, "Wait a few more years and I will marry you, Rita." Rita would brush his hair and tell him, "Ali, you are so handsome you will be a killer, every girl will want you."

Ali would reply, "Rita, I don't want anybody but you." Ali and I were only twelve years old, but while I was thinking about soccer and basketball, Ali was thinking about girls.

Ali had told me that Rita was attracted to him and that she had used any number of excuses to see him. I told him he was crazy. He told me that he had felt her breasts, and that they were nice and soft. He asked me, "Did you ever feel a woman's breast beside your mother's?" I was embarrassed and told him to stop it.

"Alex, listen. I saw Rita belly-dancing and I put some money in the top of her costume and I felt her breast," Ali told me.

I told Ali, "I don't think her husband, Moses, will let her do that again," and I left him.

As it drew closer to the wedding, there was a special feeling in the air. Everybody knew that Moses loved Rita and Rita loved Moses. At the kibbutz everybody was decorating the dining room. They made paper flowers of tissue papers. They made paper chains of construction papers. They wrote on the wall, "Moses loves Rita, and Rita loves Moses." When we mentioned their names we were all excited and happy.

My parents hadn't had a great wedding; they had gone to city hall and gotten their marriage license. They promised each other that one day they were going to have a big wedding. It was very important to have a great wedding. Although my mother hadn't had a big wedding herself, she made Rita's wedding dress. My mother tried the dress on, herself, several times and was daydreaming. She asked us, "Don't I look beautiful, just like a bride?"

My father blushed and tears were running. He felt ashamed that he and my mother had not had a decent wedding. Every girl dreams to have an elaborate wedding. Every girl wants her parents to give her away. Every girl wants a nice ring. If things were normal my mother would have brought my father and his family to Poland and they would have had a great wedding. But things turned out differently, thanks to Hitler and his thugs.

Ali's sister, Lylla, had mixed feelings about Rita's wedding; she envied her. She knew that Rita was in love while she hadn't been. She told Rita, "You are lucky because you are going to marry the man you love, while I married a man who is taking care of my parents and the rest of the family."

Rita replied, "You have a man that loves you and you have two boys."

Lylla told her, "He doesn't love me, because I am only an object or a trophy that he shows around."

Rita looking at Lylla and said, "Yes, I'm lucky, but are you sure he doesn't love you? Look at the beautiful ring he gave you. Every girl dreams about her wedding ring. That ring began as a dream and now is a reality. The ring one day will pass down to your daughter, if you have one."

Lylla was crying and said, "He has four wives and he still goes to the whorehouse; what kind of a man is he?"

Rita replied, "He is just a foolish man, and please don't spoil my wedding."

Lylla was sobbing, "He used to beat me when I didn't get pregnant. When I got my period I used to hide it from him."

"Lylla, why are you telling me this?" asked Rita.

"Maybe because I am envious of you, and because I don't want Moses to hit you and abuse you," Lylla said.

"I don't think he will do that. Why didn't you tell your parents that your husband was hitting you?"

"I cannot. If I complained to my parents they would kill me."

Rita looked at Lylla and said, "Now I remember when you all of a sudden wore a veil and covered your face when you were working at the butcher shop. He had probably hit you then"

"Yes, he did, and I cannot do anything about it. I am an Arab woman and I don't have any voice."

Rita told her, "Lylla, you are living in Palestine where there are laws, and you do have a voice."

Lylla looked at Rita and changed the subject. "You can spot it right away. Is he cruel to animals? My husband kicked the dogs and hated to feed them."

"No, Moses is very kind to our kitten. Sometimes I am even jealous of the way he treats the pet."

"Does he constantly criticize or say cruel, hurtful things to you?" Lylla said.

"No, he writes me poetry and he tells me how much he loves me, even though he can hardly read and write."

Lylla said, "Even though I am the only one who can read and write, my husband constantly tells me that I am stupid. His mood swings go from sweet to violent in minutes."

Rita put her arm around Lylla and told her she understood, and that she felt very sorry for her. Then she reassured Lylla that Moses was kind and would be the perfect husband. They both looked at each other, face to face, and, without saying a word, wished each other the best. Even though Lylla was younger than Rita, in many ways she was more mature and experienced. She had given birth to two children, and Rita was a child in her eyes.

In Palestine a wedding was the moment of exultation. Every member of the kibbutz wanted to get married or have another wedding. The kids pretended to get married; they played dress-up and make believe. I was happy that I was going to be able to stuff my stomach, especially since my parents had helped pay for the wedding.

I remembered not so long ago when Ali and I had gone to bed hungry. It was so hot that we had slept on the roof. Somebody had left a mattress up there, so we had laid on the mattress and we tried to fall asleep, but we couldn't. We were hungry; our stomachs would growl, and we looked at the sky and watched the stars and pretended that the stars were noodle soup. We opened our mouths and swallowed the stars. We pretended we ate many stars, but we were still hungry.

I remembered the many nights I didn't have any dinner when my mother and I lived in the city, because we didn't have any food. The cabinets were empty, only a few cups and plates were there. If the grocery man would throw away some overripe bananas I would eat them with the skins on. I had to fill my stomach. Sometimes I was so hungry that I repeatedly opened and closed the cabinet doors looking for food. The answer was always the same: "None." My mother would tell me to stop banging the cabinet doors. I would tell her that I was hungry. "Alex, go to sleep, tomorrow I will get you some food."

I was angry and I yelled at her, "I want it now."

My mother was crying and told me, "Maybe you can lick my tears and your stomach will be full." I was hungry and I was thinking about food. Even though I was seven years old I still sucked my thumb. The thumb comforted me. I felt that by sucking the saliva it would help fulfill my hunger. While I was sucking my thumb I would fall asleep.

A week before the wedding, at our temple on Saturday morning we celebrated *aufruf*, which is a Yiddish word that means calling up Moses, the groom-to-be, to read the blessings before and after one of the sections of the Torah reading. Then the groom presents his bride-to-be to the community. Rita and Moses went to the stage holding hands. Rita presented Moses a *kippah*, also called a *yarmulke*, a head covering worn by men inside the sanctuary as a sign of respect; and a *talit*. A *talit* is a prayer shawl, which is a garment to hold the *tzitziot* which are the fringes of the shawl. The fringes are said to represent the 613 commandments in the Torah. The *talit* was white with blue stripes. Blue was a favorite color of Jews because the Mediterranean sea was blue.

Moses draped the *talit* around his shoulders. Even though Rita and Moses were *Sephardic* Jews, that is Jews from North Africa or Spain, they took the European customs. Moses looked very pleased with the presents. He looked surprised when Rita had given him the *kippah* and *talit*. He told her, "I didn't expect these beautiful gifts."

Rita couldn't control herself and kissed him and looked embarrassed. When the groom finished reading the blessing we threw candies at the bride and groom. This was but one of many customs designed to wish the couple fertility. I was holding the candies as though they were my last meal. I put them in my pocket and I forgot to take them out; over the next hour they melted and soiled my slacks. Moses caught some candies and acted like a kid, throwing candies back at us and trying to hit Ali.

After the evening service we had a feast. Everybody brought food. We had both Jewish and Arabic food. Moses was surrounded by his male friends and Rita was surrounded by female friends. Ali and I, being kids, were able to mix with both groups. We checked the food in both groups and discovered it was the same.

Moses and Rita parted because now they weren't allowed to see each other until the wedding day. The only reason that Ali and I had come to the morning service was to stuff ourselves. We weren't paying any attention to the prayers, only looking at the food, and when the service was over we raced to the food table. Our conversation was only about the food; what we ate, what we liked and what we didn't like. There was chopped liver on a silver plate. It is said, "A taste of chopped liver brings a memory." The lady who made the chopped liver told us to remember this event and if we liked her chopped liver she would make it for the wedding. Deviled eggs were on a tray. I thought to race Ali and see who could eat the most eggs but there were so many delicious foods that I didn't think it was worth it. There were dates and figs, which I enjoyed. There were many different *kugels*, some sweet, some savory, but all were loaves of noodles made with lots of butter, sugar and eggs. I had a hard time deciding which one to eat. Cakes, cookies, candies and chocolates were also plentiful. There were stacks of pita bread, both round and flat. The pita bread was torn and dipped into the salads and eaten with our fingers. There was *tahini, hummus* and *falafel*. Tahini is made from eggplant, hummus is made with crushed garbanzo beans and falafel are like small meatballs but are made with grains.

In between stuffing ourselves, Ali and I became messengers. Rita told me how much she loved Moses and I would run and give the message to Moses. Moses would recite poetry to Rita, and Ali had to learn it by heart and recite it to Rita. Sometimes Moses and Rita would tip us for the service.

Rita couldn't wait to get married; she had to see and talk to Moses. When Ali brought her a message she would start to cry, and told us, "I have to see Moses." I heard the plaintive words, "I must see him," and they made me sad. I wondered why people who love each other have to be separated. I thought it was a stupid custom. To ease Rita's anguish, my mother made sure that she was busy before the wedding.

The wedding day, Tuesday, the third day of the week and the third day of Creation, finally arrived. Moses wore a navy blue suit and a black hat. His father and brothers also wore blue suits. I finally got to see Rita in her wedding dress. She was beautiful; being in love had done something to her face. Her dress was a long, white, beaded satin gown. She was covered from head to toe, with matching satin shoes. She wore a veil and a golden crown. She was a little nervous because she was afraid she would drop the crown, even though it was pinned to her hair very firmly. The crown was heavy and she mumbled to herself, "I know that I'm a queen, but do I really need a crown to prove it? I can't wait for this ceremony to be over so I can put the crown away and start dancing."

Rita and Moses had hired a photographer, a cousin of Moses, who was instructed to be as unobtrusive as possible. He was considered almost an integral part of the wedding party, with all the associated rights and privileges.

Under her veil, Rita had hidden a cheat-sheet. It contained all of the prayers that she had to recite, those prayers that consisted of wishes for a good life. She prayed for fertility and also that they would be able to earn a living; and the most important thing of all, they prayed for good health. The gold crown had been rented from our neighborhood pawnshop.

Moses was clean-shaven but had nicked himself with the razor that morning. But the tiny bandage on his cheek could not take away from the look of joy that he displayed. And even though the ceremony was solemn, he could hardly help grinning from ear to ear as he looked at his lovely bride.

Moses' grandmother handed him the wedding ring to give to his future wife. In the Jewish religion when the groom gives the bride a ring he is not "buying her;" rather, he is changing her status from that of a single woman to that of a married one.

"The ring is a circle of life that has no beginning or end. There are three points in the circle of life: birth, marriage and death. Since marriage is the point where a new generation is about to begin it is a key point in the cycle." That was what the rabbi told us at the wedding ceremony. He also said, "The ring may be silver or gold. Gold is usually used because it is considered to be the most noble of metals. It may also be silver because silver represents love, while gold represents strength. It is written: 'The world is built on love. Since the bride and groom are building a new world of love, silver may also be used.'"

Several guests noticed that Rita seemed uncomfortable with the heavy crown. Rita said to them, "It is heavy, and I hope I will be able to wear it the whole day and night."

"Are you nervous?" one of the guests asked Rita.

"No! I'm not. I am only thinking about pleasant things." But everyone could see that she was very tense.

The dining room was divided into three sections: The groom's room, the bride's room and the room where the wedding would actually take place. The wedding room was full of flowers; marigolds, gladiolus, dahlias and tulips. The kibbutz grew flowers and sold them, so they were able to provide them for the wedding room, and it looked spectacular.

When the guests arrived they found the groom in one room, sitting at a table with a group of rabbis. The rabbis helped Moses to write the *ketubah*, which is the marriage contract. The rabbis came from both the bride's and the groom's families, and they negotiated the details of the contract.

In the next room, Rita was sitting on her throne, an elevated platform big enough to hold the bride, her mother and the rest of the females from Rita's family. All the guests were greeting her and tried to cheer her up.

Moses, with the rabbis, was writing and signing the *ketubah*. It was written in Aramaic. I wondered why, since nobody spoke Aramaic. The rabbi explained to us that Aramaic had been the official language of all Jewish legal documents since ancient times. The *ketubah* spelled out the legal obligations of the husband to the wife, should he die or divorce her. The wife's obligations to her husband were not written in the *ketubah*; they were always taken for granted. But the wife's first duties were to bear children and stand by her husband in all things.

Here is the actual translation of a *ketubah* from the Aramaic.

*On the _____ day of the week, the _____ day of the month _____ in the year _____ since the creation of the world, according to the reckoning which we are accustomed to use here _____ in _____. Now _____ son of _____ of the family _____ said to _____ daughter of _____ of the family _____: Be thou my wife according to the law of Moses and of Israel, and I will work for thee, honor, provide for and support thee in accordance with the practice of Jewish husbands, who work for their wives, honor, provide for and support them in truth. And I will set aside for thee _____ silver zuz, which belong to thee according to Rabbinic law, and thy food, clothing and other necessary benefits which a husband is obligated to provide; and I will live with thee in accordance with the requirements prescribed for each husband.*

*And _____ consented and became his wife. Her belongings that she brought from her family's home, in silver, gold, valuables, clothing and household furnishings, all this _____ the said groom accepted in the sum of silver pieces, adding from himself another _____ pieces, making a total of _____ hundred silver pieces. And thus said _____ the groom: I take upon myself, and my heirs after me, the surety of this ketubah, of the dowry and of the additional sum, so that all this shall be paid from the best part of my property, real and personal, that I now possess or may hereafter acquire. All my property, even the mantle on my shoulders, shall be mortgaged for the security of this ketubah and of the dowry and of the addition made thereto, during my lifetime and after my lifetime from this day forever.*

*And the surety for all the obligations of this ketubah, dowry and the additional sum has been assumed by _____ the groom, with the full obligation dictated by all documents of ketubot and additional sums due every daughter of Israel, executed in accordance with the enactment of our sages, of blessed memory. It is not to be regarded as an indecisive contractual obligation nor as a stereotyped form.*

*And we have completed the act of acquisition from _____ son of _____ the bridegroom, for _____ daughter of _____ this _____, for all that which is stated and explained above, by an instrument legally fit to establish a transaction. And everything is valid and established.*

*Witness*
*Witness*

Once the *ketubah* was signed, both mothers witnessed it. The mothers had to break a porcelain plate. This custom symbolizes happiness. The pieces of the broken plate were given to the bride and then after the wedding the bride would make jewelries from the broken plate and give them to the bridesmaids.

The wedding ceremony started in the late afternoon. There was still daylight and when we saw Rita sitting on her throne, her shadow was bigger than she was. Ali and I raced our shadows. It made me mad when my shadow shrank and I knew that very soon the lights would be turned on and we wouldn't see our shadows.

When the wedding ceremony started we were all sitting and waiting for the bride and groom and the rest of the members of their families to parade in front of the *chupa*. A *chupa* is a wedding canopy. It is made of silk or velvet and it is supported by four firm poles. All around the *chupa* we saw beautiful vases of flowers. The *talit* shawl that Rita gave Moses, when fully spread out, was large enough to cover the *chupa*.

The families paraded in the hall and stopped in front the *chupa*. The only ones that were actually under the *chupa* were the officiating rabbi and the bride and groom. The bride walked around the groom seven times, while her mother held her train and provided the crucial service of counting. The reason for the walkaround was to protect her husband from demons.

The rabbi started the ceremony by blessing the wine. He asked the groom and the bride to drink from the same cup because they came from different households, and this symbolized the making of a new household.

Moses presented the rabbi with the ring, and two of his friends acted as witnesses. The rabbi showed the witnesses the ring so they could determine if it met the minimum requirement of value. It must be worth at least one *pruta* (a coin of very small value). The ring was a silver ring of modest value. Since Moses could not afford to buy Rita an expensive ring, he gave her his grandmother's ring. Rita knew that in a few years Moses would get her a diamond ring, as he had promised.

Moses was then asked if the ring belonged to him and whether it met the value requirements. He replied, "Yes." Rita then lifted her veil in order to see the ring without interference.

Moses then recited the espousal formula, which is: *Harei at m'kudeshet li b'taba zo K'dat Moshe v'Yisrael*, which means "Behold, you are sanctified to me with this ring in accordance with the laws of Moses and Israel."

Before he placed the ring on Rita's finger, Moses asked himself, "Am I doing the right thing by marrying Rita? Am I going to be able to support her? I know that my parents want a grandson and they are pressuring me, but is that what I want?"

And Rita asked herself? "Am I doing the right thing? My parents are pressuring me to produce children, but is this man the right one for me?"

In spite of these unanswered questions, Moses then placed the ring on Rita's index finger so she could show it to the witnesses. Rita would transfer the ring it to her ring finger after the ceremony. Then she replaced her veil.

After the ring ceremony, the rabbi read the *ketubah*. The purpose of that was to show that the document was there, had been signed, and that the nuptial ceremony could begin.

The blessing over the second glass of wine was followed by six more blessings. After the Seven Benedictions were recited, a glass was placed on the floor and Moses, the groom, stepped on it and broke it. The breaking of the glass signified that, as it will take a million years to put the glass back together, so will the marriage last that long.

The ceremony was over and everybody was yelling *Mazel Tov!* Congratulations! Then the dancing began. The men were dancing with each other and trying to entertain the groom. The women were dancing with the other women and trying to entertain the bride.

My father lifted me onto his shoulders so I could have a better view of the entertainers. I felt great being up there, just like a king. I knew that my father had a bad leg. He had gotten hurt in the war, but now he wanted to show everybody that he was still strong and able to lift his son. Ali's father did the same with him, and Ali and I wrestled each other while we were atop our fathers' shoulders, each trying to knock the other one off, but only for fun.

The men got a chair and placed the groom in it. Then they lifted him, in the men's section of the room. The women did the same with the bride in the women's section of the room. Moses was holding a napkin and he threw it across the room to Rita. They reached toward each other and pretended they were holding hands.

Each set of parents were bragging about their child. The groom's parents told everybody how lucky Rita was to find such a nice, kind guy that would be a good provider, and Rita's parents told everybody what a fine, healthy young woman Rita was and that she would bear him many fine, healthy children.

I don't remember when the wedding ended because I was tired and I went to sleep outside on the grass with Ali and many other children from the kibbutz. The following morning I saw that the room was a mess and nobody had had the energy or the strength to clean it and make us breakfast, but we helped ourselves to the leftover food.

I wasn't happy or sad over the wedding, except that I had really enjoyed stuffing myself. But later in the day I saw that my parents were happy, and that pleased me and I soon became as happy as they were.

# Chapter Twenty-Five, Blood Brothers

What I wanted most was a day to be the center of attention. Being thirteen years old I was going to celebrate my *Bar Mitzvah*. I wanted everybody to praise me, to tell me what a great job I did and to get a standing ovation; to tell me how handsome I was in my new outfit–I was wearing a custom-made navy-blue suit. The local tailor had sewn the suit. He gave me several fittings and treated me as an adult. I still wore short pants, along with a white shirt, a tie and a jacket.

This was the day that I would be called to read the Torah and I would be accepted as an adult Jewish man. I wanted everybody in the temple to shake hands with me so I could be the talk of the town. Maybe my relatives from Europe or the United States would come to my *Bar Mitzvah*. Everybody would say that they had been to many *Bar Mitzvah* but this one was the best; the way he performed was one in a million. He was not a son of a *rabbi* but he knew how to perform just like a rabbi.

A month ago, Ali had been the center of attention for his circumcision. Everybody praised him and congratulated him and told him how brave he was. He had been brave and, like me, he had prepared himself for a year prior to his circumcision. In Islamic tradition, his parents had a choice to circumcise him just like the Jews at eight days, or at three years, five years, seven years or thirteen years. His parents had chosen the age of thirteen, since it was traditionally the most popular and his parents wanted to be sure that Ali wanted to be circumcised.

Every day, after school, Ali went to the mosque and studied the Koran. He had to memorize God's ninety-nine names in Arabic. After his time at the Mosque, Ali met me at the synagogue where I was studying for my *Bar Mitzvah*. I wasn't a scholar. At the age of twelve I started studying for my *Bar Mitzvah*. I already knew how to read, write and understand Hebrew since it was the only language I spoke. Just as the Koran is written in Arabic, the Jewish Bible is written in Hebrew. I went to study for my *Bar Mitzvah* on Sunday, Tuesday and Thursday, while Ali had Koran classes on Monday, Wednesday and Friday. We finished school at three o'clock in the afternoon and at four o'clock we went to study at our religious schools. Ali followed me just like a puppy to my *Bar Mitzvah* studies, as I followed him for his.

I wasn't interested in my religious studies. I preferred to play soccer or army games. My rabbi was a short, stocky man who wore glasses and dressed in a black suit. He never scolded me when I came late to the class, but three times a week he came to the park to take me and some other boys to study. He would ask me, "Did you score?" If I replied, "No, I didn't," he told me, "You score when you learn the Torah!"

We started the lesson by reviewing what we had learned from last week's lesson. My mind was not on the lesson; it was on the soccer game. I wondered if my soccer replacement, a younger kid who had been hanging around the field hoping for a chance to get into the game, did as good or better than I did.

As the days passed and the weeks and months flew by, I was almost ready for my *Bar Mitzvah* in spite of my lack of concentration. But first, I must tell you about Ali's experience.

It was Friday, and the mosque was crowded with worshipers. People were everywhere, pouring in and out of the mosque. There were dark-eyed girls wearing colorful dresses and head scarves. There were old and young men wearing turbans and dazzling white cotton robes. Ali was dressed in a white robe, called a *galabiyah*. He was hanging out with several other boys who were going to be circumcised in the mosque. We were all gathering in the men's section of the mosque. Lylla and Nadine wore new dresses. Lylla brought her husband and two boys to the ceremony. Her husband brought candies and small figures made of dyed ice-sugar. One of the figures was a soccer player and I wanted it. As Ali's closest friend I was the guest of honor, and I knew that the guest of honor gets the first choice of gifts, so I asked Ali to get it for me. Being my friend, he grabbed the candy figure and gave it to me. I was smiling, not only because I had gotten the candy I wanted, but because of the close bond between us.

Women were allowed to be in the mosque behind the men, or they were outside preparing the food for the celebration. The table had white tablecloths decorated with flowers and delicious food. They had cakes and cookies made from honey and peanuts, or honey and sunflower seeds, and *baklava*, the delicious Middle Eastern dessert made from pastry, pistachios, honey and lemon.

When the actual ceremony of circumcision took place, the boys, under the direction of their leader, engaged in a ritual of chanting "God is great, God is Great, God is great" and swaying, designed to produce a hypnotic sense of union with God. Ali seemed in a trance. He looked hypnotized. He had told me earlier that he was not afraid. For months he had taken cigarettes and burned himself. He did this to prepare himself for the pain of circumcision. The pain of circumcision was less than the pain of burning himself, he thought. It was very important for his family that he not show weakness of any kind, and if he did, his family would be dishonored.

Just like Abraham had circumcised himself and his son using a stone knife, the same tool was used on Ali by an older member of the mosque. Both Ali's father and grandfather held him and made sure that he didn't move. Ali didn't shed a tear, keeping the pain inside, but I knew it hurt him a lot.

When I saw the ceremony I almost fainted. I thought that it was barbaric and savage. A week later, when Ali was healed, we went to the park and we urinated. Ali tried to shoot his urine farther than me and he told me that he didn't have a "broken dick" anymore and now he wasn't ashamed to show it. At that age, the possibility of a broken dick meant a lot to a young boy.

Now that Ali was circumcised and he didn't have to go to the mosque every day, we had time to concentrate on my *Bar Mitzvah*. Ali pressured me to do well in my ceremony. When we walked to school in the morning he would sing part of the ceremony "Hine ma tov uma n aim Shevet achim gam yachad." (Behold, how good and how pleasant it is for family to dwell together in unity.) Ali had a beautiful voice and he really enjoyed learning my service and prayers for my *Bar Mitzvah*. As the day got closer and closer, I got serious and didn't play any more soccer after school. I studied hard and my grades improved from Cs and Bs to As.

After my last lesson, the rabbi shook my hand and told me that tomorrow was to be my big day. I wasn't afraid because I knew that if I forgot something Ali would bail me out, just like in the theater when an actor forgot his lines. He knew my part of the service better than I did and would prompt me if I failed. I was very dependent on Ali. Sometimes I wondered if he would have been a better Jew than a Muslim.

Finally my big day was here. Before the ceremony my father gave me a *talit*, a prayer shawl. I performed the ceremony with flying colors. My parents were very proud of me and told me that had earned the celebration that we had at the temple, that I had earned the challah, wine, gefilte fish, chopped liver and herring with every word that I had sung at the service.

Shortly after that, Ali and I decided to become blood brothers. It was Ali's idea. We knew that we were growing up and each one of us would go a different path very soon. Ali was afraid that I would forget him because, in three years, when I was scheduled to graduate, I probably would leave our town to study in a bigger city, while he, when he finished elementary school, would look for a job. He was afraid that once we were apart we would no longer have so many things to share.

Ali took his pocket knife and pricked his thumb. I saw blood running. I hesitated, but I didn't want to lose face, so I also pricked my thumb. We tied both our thumbs together with a bandage and swore to be "Blood Brothers" for the rest of our lives. This bonding made the next events even more confusing and devastating than they were.

# Chapter Twenty-Six, Hatred

The year was 1948, a few months before Israel became an independent nation. I was thirteen years old and during the eight years that I had lived in this neighborhood, at the beginning the majority of the population was Arab. Now the Jewish immigrants from Russia and Poland who had flooded in were in the majority. Before, you saw girls wearing long dresses and *hijabs* (female scarves) and the boys wearing robes and *kaffias* (male head scarves). Now you could hardly see them

I saw many Jew and Arab real estate agents poking their noses into our neighborhood. They were pressuring us to move out of the neighborhood. There was a panic. Everybody was leaving the neighborhood, especially the Arab families. These real estate agents spread rumors that it wasn't safe for the Arabs to live in our neighborhood anymore.

There was a shortage of buildings. Nobody was building houses and large numbers of immigrants wanted to live in our city. The real estate agents made a lot of money charging new tenants for their services. I saw several Jewish immigrants knocking at Ali's door, asking his parents if they were going to leave. The immigrants wore shabby-looking clothes; they had mended their torn clothes until there was no more cloth left to mend. Their kids were in the same boat. But at school their poverty and the difficult conditions did not detract from their desire and will to learn. They were the best students in our school.

Our public school also had changed. When I first came to the city the school had a Jewish side and an Arab side, which was bigger. The Arab side had two classes for every grade. The Jewish side had one class for each grade. The grades were kindergarten through eight. Now I noticed that the Jewish classes had increased in size and some of the grades had three classes. The Arab side, on the other hand, had dwindled to hardly one class per grade. Also, the Arab school had more boys than girls, while the Jewish side was more or less even, girls and boys.

The Arabs didn't force their daughters to go to school; they would rather that the girls stayed at home helping their mother take care of the household. Ali's sisters were an exception. Their parents wanted them to be educated. Lylla was already eighteen years old and had two children, while Nadine was ten years old and in the fourth grade. She was planning to go to college and wanted to be a doctor or a lawyer. Realizing these changes made me sad. I enjoyed going to school with both groups of people. We had good Jews and bad ones, and there were good Arabs and bad ones also.

I noticed Ali was not as friendly toward me as he had been before. We didn't go to school together as we used to do. It really hurt me a lot, and I wondered if it also hurt Ali, being apart from me. I knew Ali as well as I knew the palm of my hand. I knew his moods and actions. He was my blood brother. We had mixed our blood and had sworn that we would take care of each other. Now all of a sudden I felt that Ali was apart from me. One day I cornered Ali at school and I asked him "Why aren't we going to school together anymore?"

Ali didn't face me and replied, "I don't know."

"Can we go to school together tomorrow?" I asked.

Ali replied, "No. Salim, Kamil and Sarah said they don't want to walk with you. "

"Why?" I asked.

Ali wasn't even looking at me when he said, "I don't know."

"Ali, have I changed? Do I have leprosy?"

"Alex, I don't have time to talk to you. I have to go to work at the butcher store," and he walked away.

At school the Arabs used to roam around the playground and mix with the Jewish kids. Now they had isolated themselves; they didn't mix with us. Their parents took them to school and picked them up after school, or even stayed with them during school hours. None of the Arab kids walked to school by themselves; they were always in a group. It was apparent that they were afraid of the

Russian and Polish immigrants. The immigrant kids acted like hooligans. They were used to pogroms, and what the Russians had done to them in Europe, they were now doing to the Arabs. They attacked the Arab kids and took their food. Before, both Jewish and Arabs kids used the slide and swings together; now I noticed only the immigrant kids used the equipment. The Arab kids were bunched together in the corners of the school. The Jewish kids were running around the playground as if they owned the grounds.

I particularly remember one incident. There was a Russian immigrant boy, thirteen years old, the kid that used to hit Ali and me. He was a bully named Boris. When I saw him I was afraid of him and I didn't want to irritate him. I don't know where Boris got his meanness or badness. I don't know if he was a concentration camp survivor or just a World War II survivor. I don't know if his parents mistreated him. All I know was that he was a big kid for his age and he was full of hate. He carried a switchblade and everybody at school was afraid to report him. I didn't do anything to provoke him to hit me, but he resented that I was with the Arab kids.

Once I saw him mutilating some birds. He saw me and warned me he would do the same to me. I thought if I ignored him he would leave me alone. Ali was a different story; he decided to take care of Boris. Ali had been taking self defense classes and boxing. He was an excellent fighter. I could see that Ali was looking for revenge. He was just waiting for the opportunity to fight with Boris. He hated being a scapegoat and he hated seeing me hurt. He never forgot what Boris had done to my new leather shoes; he had cut my new shoes apart with his knife and told me that people like me don't deserve new shoes.

One day Boris approached Ali and told Ali to bow to him. Ali ignored him. Boris kicked Ali and told him to bow to him. I was with Ali and I told Ali to bow to him. Then Boris kicked me and told me to mind my own business. Ali got angry and attacked Boris. Ali was smaller and younger than Boris, but he kicked him in the groin, bit his stomach and was able to get Boris' arm bent backwards until it broke. It was just like David and Goliath. Boris was crying; nobody at school had ever hurt him before. Ali yelled at him, "That will teach you never to fight an Arab." I was speechless. I couldn't believe the hate that Ali carried. Was it just concern for me that generated that hatred?

Before Ali started drifting away we had always supported each other in everything we did. My mother used to cut Ali's and my hair. We had no money to pay a barber, so my mom took care of our hair. She put a soup plate around our heads and cut our hair outside the plate. We looked awful. After this experience we had to shave our heads. Finally, Ali and I got our hair cut by a barber, but that cost money, and we didn't have any. The barber allowed us to pay for our haircuts with food. The price of the haircut was one egg. We didn't have any, so we stole the eggs and we carried them to the barber. Our excuse for stealing the eggs was that our appearance was important so we could get a job; and once we got a job, we told ourselves, we would repay the grocery man.

At the beginning, the price of a haircut was one egg. As time passed, the price increased to two eggs. We still were able to steal them, but by the time it reached four eggs our standard of living had improved and we didn't have to steal any more eggs.

We weren't the only ones that paid the barber with eggs for a haircut. There were younger children from neighboring villages who were embarrassed by their haircuts and who walked four to five kilometers to the barbershop, carrying eggs in their pockets for payment. When Ali and I saw them walking to the barbershop we pushed them and made sure that they cracked their eggs. Once we saw the yoke of the egg running down their legs, we laughed at them. Those poor kids not only didn't get a haircut but had soiled legs and pants and were crying. We city kids didn't have a good relationship with the kids from the villages and the kibbutz because we felt that we were superior to them.

I really envied the two kids who were sons of Ibraim the pawnbroker. At the age of three they had raised enough money to get haircuts for the rest of their lives. When Jewish boys reached the age of three they got their first haircut. One time one of Ibraim's sons was to get a haircut at his orthodox Jewish birthday party. There were balloons, sausages similar to hot dogs, coleslaw, potato salad and a big birthday cake. The birthday cake was studded with jellybeans and decorated with brightly colored frosting. Ali and I couldn't believe the amount of food that was there. We were hungry and couldn't wait to start eating. In the middle of the room on top of a table was a chair where Ibraim's son was sitting. We were all to observe his first ritual haircut, known in Hebrew as *upsheren*.

Ibraim formally asked his son, "Are you ready for your first haircut?"

The son replied enthusiastically, "Yes."

Before Ibraim's son's hair was cut he explained it to us: "The Torah compares man to the trees of the field. Since the branches of a tree are not cut during its first three years, so a boy's hair is not cut until his third birthday."

Ali told me, "He is lucky waiting till the age of three for a haircut, because I don't like to have my hair cut every month."

Ibraim gave his son a lollipop and a *tzedakah* box, which is a box for children to put some of their money for charity. Then he told us, "Each person who cuts the hair is expected to give my son something to deposit in the box." He was the first one to snip a lock from the head of his son, and deposited some coins in the box. The rest of the guests did the same thing.

At that time of year it was hot, and I remember that every Friday the ice man delivered a block of ice for the iceboxes in the neighborhood. Ali and I watched him and when he left the truck, we told the other kids that the coast was clear and then we ransacked the truck of all its small pieces of ice. I think that the iceman knew what we were doing because he never locked the truck. We usually had an ice fight but we never hurt anybody.

Sometimes we used an ice pick and we made our own cones of ice chunks.

Ali had been my right-hand man for my *Bar Mitzvah*. He knew the Hebrew songs better than I did. He had a beautiful voice and he pronounced the words better than me. In turn, I had supported Ali through his ritual circumcision at the age of thirteen and at his sister's wedding. All the holidays, both Jewish and Muslim, we had observed together.

Now Ali was very cold toward me. He informed me that in the month of March his family was going to move to the Arab section of the city. He hated that idea. I saw tears in his eyes, but he was holding them back. I knew that when I left he would cry; he didn't want to embarrass himself by crying in front of me. We both were considered to be men, he by being circumcised, and I by celebrating my *Bar Mitzvah.*

If you walked into his apartment you would notice that the walls were decorated with hand-painted calligraphy from the Koran. He asked me, sarcastically, "Will a Jew live in this room praising Allah?"

I replied, "I did."

I helped him pack his things and I watched him leaving the apartment. He told me, "This is not fair. I was born in this building and so was my mother and my aunts and uncles, and now this has become a Jewish house. Those Syrian bastards sold this house to a Jew."

Tears were in both our eyes; we couldn't help it. We hugged and promised to visit each other. I told him that my parents were sending me to live in a kibbutz and I hoped he would come to visit me. He didn't answer. Seeing the apartment vacant was very painful for him. He kicked the door and left like a homeless refugee, just like the Jews in Europe when the Germans took their homes and possessions. They left because they were being harassed and they did not feel safe in their own home.

Ali's family's horse and buggy was filled with their possessions. They were going to live with his sister and brother-in-law, the butcher, in a three bedroom house.

The next day a Jewish family moved into the apartment. My mother greeted them and gave them a dish of salt, a loaf of bread and a bottle of wine. Those three items symbolized that they would never be poor and would be very happy in their new apartment. I thought that my mother was a kiss-up. She believed it was better to have a Jewish family in the building instead of an Arab family. I didn't care for the newcomers; I missed Ali. Nobody was going to replace Ali.

The new family had four children; two were about my age and in the same grade. My mother said to me, "Alex, please take them to school and make them feel at home."

I replied, "You cannot make me, and I am not going to do this." I was a nasty kid.

"Alex, they are refugees and they suffered a lot; please be nice to them."

"Mom, I hate them. They shouldn't live here. This is Ali's apartment and don't you forget this." Next morning I didn't go to school. I didn't want to walk to school with the new kids. I hated them; and besides, they were poor and wore mended, torn clothes, a reminder of what I, myself, had been.

The neighborhood had changed completely. Once there was a mosque, where Ali and I prayed to God. When they had stolen my mother's bike and my mother had lost her job I had prayed to God in all the ways I knew, and I felt like a Muslim, a Catholic and a Jew at the same time.

Ali had studied the Koran in that mosque and I had kept him company. When Ali and the other Arabs left the neighborhood, the city council tore down the mosque and made a grocery store, a dental office, and a small synagogue.

No wonder Ali resented me. Even before he and his family left, he had asked me, "When are you going to kick us out of the city and make this a Jewish city?"

I told him, "Things change. You have to accept change as a natural part of life."

Ali asked, "Would you like to be in my shoes?"

I replied, "I don't know."

He left, and I didn't have a chance to remind him about our blood oath.

I knew that I didn't have any control over what was happening to our city, and Ali and me. I wish I could stop the clock and return to when Ali and I lived in the same building and were happy. One day my parents heard a rumor that the Iraqis were coming to attack us and they sent me to the kibbutz for safekeeping that very same night.

# Chapter Twenty-Seven, Heaven or Hell

Kite flying was a very popular activity for boys in the town where we lived .I remember when Ali and I made our first kite. We were probably six or seven years old. After that we did it every year. Because my parents were working it was a good substitute instead of us running on the street unsupervised. We took activities like arts and crafts after our regular school day, and we were all excited because this was the first "useful" project that we did. We usually drew pictures or colored with stencils, but this time we made kites. At first the kites looked crudely made but as the years passed they looked better and flew better. They looked professional and we could sell them at stores. Besides arts and crafts, the school offered sports like soccer, basketball and many others. Ali and I usually played sports, but making kites was an exception because it produced something, instead of just making us sweat.

We used bamboo sticks, glue, string and colored tissue paper. We joined three bamboo sticks together in a criss-cross, placed one stick over each other stick, and tied them with a string. Next we outlined the kite frame and covered it with tissue paper. We glued the paper to the string, dried it, and then we were ready to fly our kite.

We were told never to use metal in making a kite because it might attract lightning, nor to fly during a thunderstorm. We were also taught never to fly a kite near telephone or high-voltage wires because we could be killed.

Ali and I believed that we could communicate with the dead while flying our kites, because we thought our kites could reach heaven. It was heartbreaking when we accidentally let our kites fly away from us, but we knew that they were carrying a message to our loved ones. While flying our kites we would take a piece of paper, write on it, put a hole in the piece of paper and slid the paper on the string that held the kite. It was amazing how the paper flew along the string all the way up to the kite. Sometimes, during kite competitions, we put razor blades on the string and they also flew up to the kite, but this was dangerous because the razor blades could destroy our own kite as well.

Unknown to me at the time, my cousins were in the Auschwitz concentration camp, but I thought that my cousins were in Poland and that when my kite got loose and flew away it would somehow find them and tell them about me. Ali, whose goal was to go to the holy city, Mecca, thought that when his kite flew away it went there and that the kite would have magical powers that would protect him from the hooligans who lined the road to Mecca. We both had big dreams.

It was always by the end of autumn when the rainy season started that we lost our kites. We knew that the wind would help fly our kites but the heavy rain would drop them. We took chances in the rain and the risk excited us.

We knew the year by its holidays and not by the seasons. In Palestine we didn't have four seasons, only two: the rainy season, from January to March, and the hot season, in June, July, and August.

We were able to play all year round outside since the weather was never cold, and our favorite toys were kites. There were many kite-flying competitions and the rules were simple: the kite that stayed in the air longest won. We tried to win by destroying our opponents' kites.

Each kite carried a razor blade on its bamboo sticks and we tried to manipulate our kite to hit our opponent's kite with its sharp blade. We also tried to outmaneuver the other kites by teasing them and forcing them to be in turmoil until their kites fell. Winning for us was heaven; losing was hell.

I wondered if Ali and I both went to heaven would we meet there? Are the Jewish and Muslim heavens the same? For me, heaven was the home of God and you lived there forever, in a beautiful house. The walls were of marble and on the walls were written The Ten Commandments. Even as a young child I usually could remember them all:

"I am the Lord thy God.

Thou shalt have no other gods before Me.

Thou shalt not make unto thee a graven image.

Thou shalt not take the name of the Lord thy God in vain.

Remember the Sabbath day, to keep it holy.

Honor thy father and thy mother.

Thou shalt not murder.

Thou shalt not commit adultery.

Thou shalt not steal.

Thou shalt not bear false witness.

Thou shalt not covet."

Ali knew the version of the Ten Commandments from the Muslim scripture, the Koran, which were similar.

Some of my classmates made kites and wrote the Ten Commandments on them, and when we had kite fights we were afraid to hurt those kites. But they were not afraid to hurt our kites. I guess since they were not very skillful in flying their kites they needed help, and by covering the kites with the Ten Commandments they thought that they got extra help from God.

I believed that the marble house of heaven was surrounded by beautiful gardens, and both wild and tame animals all lived in the same place. My whole family would be there. I visualized a line of kites there also. They all looked new; after all, they were in heaven. I thought that the old and the broken kites were in Hell.

Ali was a devoted Muslim. He prayed five times a day. We used to play soccer and when Ali was losing he would shout, "Alex! It is time to pray to Allah. Stop the game."

I replied, "No way. We're still hot and if we stop the game we will lose."

"Alex," Ali said again, "I have to pray. You know that all Muslims pray five times a day. We are going to pray to Allah."

"Okay, Ali," I said, "but do it fast." Ali and his friends prayed for a few minutes. I thought they were just resting. When they finished praying it seemed to me that Allah helped them, and Ali scored. I wondered if the prayer helped Ali or if I and my team had just cooled off.

Once he won the game Ali was very cocky and I couldn't stand being with him. He said to me, "You see. Praying to Allah helped us win the game. Now let's go home."

I really hated myself for being so gullible; when Ali was winning we never stopped the game and prayed to Allah.

Islam means "Submission." Those who submit to the teachings of Islam are called Muslims. Ali tried to observe his religion to the best of his ability. He followed the Five Important Rules:

Believe in Allah, and Mohammed, His Prophet;

Pray five times each day;

Be kind to the poor and give alms;

Keep the Fasts during the Month of Fasts;

And make the yearly pilgrimage to Mecca, the Holy City, if possible.

When Ali went to school he took his rosary with him. The rosary was of ninety-nine beads for the "Ninety-Nine Most Beautiful Names of God." As he walked he slipped the rosary through his fingers, murmuring a name for each bead. If he forgot one name in the right order he was angry with himself. I used to help him to recite the names of God.

But returning to our kite flying, it became apparent that Ali and I were better kite *fighters* than kite *makers*. Some flaw or other in our design always spelled its doom. Our parents never bought us any kites, we had to earn them. A kite seller sold his kites and spools of string on the street. We helped the kite seller to sell his kites by going from house to house, and we brought him customers who bought the kites. We spent one entire summer in this adventure and received a kite from him in return. The reason the kite-maker was eager to deal with us was because he knew that we were excellent kite fliers, and that if we won the competition with one of his kites, everybody would want to buy them. When we won he would trade us our winning kite for a new one. We didn't mind since the new kite was the talk of the town.

I remembered the story Ali's grandfather had told us about how when he was a kid and had fallen in love with a girl he had been able to control his kite so that it dropped on his girlfriend's balcony.

The day of the kite flying competition was like a holiday. It was one of my favorite days since it didn't involve religion and anybody could participate. People gathered on the sidewalks and roofs to cheer for the kids, but neither Ali's or my parents were there–they were busy working.

The streets were filled with kite fliers. Ali and I flew our kite together. One of us did the actual flying and the other fed string from the spool as needed and kept a sharp lookout for what the other kites were doing. This time I was flying the kite and a strong wind came up and downed many of the other kites, but ours stayed up as if by magical power. Everybody was trying to gain position to cut his opponents' lines.

I was making some mistakes and Ali was chiding me for them, but we were still in the contest. The spectators were cheering wildly. Several people were betting; some for us and some against us, but we didn't care. We eliminated several kites out of the race. My hands were bleeding from the string cutting them, but I didn't care.

Our strategy was to let our kite fly very high, then pull it down suddenly and surprise our opponents by cutting their kites with the razor blade that was on our kite. We had made sure that our razor blade was sharp. We couldn't believe that no one noticed our strategy and tried to copy it. I wished that my parents could see us winning the race.

It took a lot of skill and cooperation to win. Ali and I worked very well together. One person could not handle the kite by himself and four eyes were better than two eyes. While I was manipulating the kite, Ali made sure that no one would surprise us. If someone came close, he warned me and told me how to move the kite away, either lower or higher, to avoid the enemy kite. Although we were young we understood the wind currents and how to maneuver the kite quickly. Ali checked the wind direction by throwing sand and watching the way it moved. We made sure that the sun didn't hit our eyes and blind us like it was doing to several of our opponents.

Now there were only five kites left. Last year's winner had a beautiful, shiny blue kite. and he was doing a lot of damage to the other kites. I tried to avoid him because I knew that he was older and very skillful. But in spite of all the competition we appeared to be close to winning. And then for some reason, Ali's facial expression became very hard and his eyes seemed to change from dark to blazing black. He hit me so hard on my arms that were holding the string that I let the kite go. Then he brought our kite down and deliberately crashed it!

I was astonished. It had taken me completely by surprise. I was too shocked to react. Why had Ali done this? Had he secretly bet on someone else? Was he under pressure to let another kid win? Had he begun his personal war of Muslims against Jews? I didn't say a word. I took the broken kite and went home. The kite didn't deserve to be in Hell, it had done its job well.

That was a long, long time ago, and I still don't know why that happened. To this day I enjoy flying kites, but not in competition, just for pleasure of seeing them in the sky.

# Chapter Twenty-Eight, Wounded

The story in this chapter describes a dramatic turning point in my life. It is also a story of how Jews and Arabs lived together peacefully in Palestine in the years of 1940 to 1948. The words "Jew" or "Muslim" never came between us. We were united. We celebrated the holidays together, and for us as kids food was more important than the meaning of the holiday.

When we fasted for Yom Kippur or Ramadan it was little different than our daily experience. We were always hungry and the reason why we were sure to go to school was to get a free meal.

My parents wanted me to grow up to be a decent person and so did Ali's parents want the same for him. If there was not a war in 1948, although we would most likely have gone in different directions after high school, we both would probably have gotten married and lived in the same community, watching television and melding the two religions into one.

Now, Jewish-Arab tensions were rising, but why did this happen to me?

In those days when you entered a hospital it always smelled like ether. Ether is a light, volatile, flammable liquid used chiefly as a solvent and anesthetic. When you are the young patient and you cannot run away from your hospital room and its smell, lying in a hospital bed, restrained, with intravenous tubes feeding you and a catheter for your urine, and being unsure of how you got there–it is all very scary.

A hospital is supposed to be quiet because the patients need rest. This hospital was noisy. The nurses didn't tiptoe quietly down the hall way., and every time they dropped something it sounded like an explosion. The nurses chattered constantly with each other.

You could hear the wheelchairs squeaking. When nurse's aides rolled the food cart you could hear them chattering.

I wondered why I was lying in a hospital bed. What was a thirteen-year-old boy doing in the hospital?

I heard sobbing at my bedside. My mother was crying. I sensed she was angry at my father. She was yelling at him, "You and your big idea, sending your son to the kibbutz." I wondered what was going on. I heard her again saying, "Dolf, we are a family and Alex should have stayed with us even if the Iraqis were trying to kill us."

I wasn't sure what had happened to me. I wasn't hungry, only thirsty and tired, and all I wanted was to sleep. I closed my eyes. All I heard was my mother, Laura, sobbing. Through a fog I heard her asking me in German, the language that I hated, "Is anything hurting you?" I wished she would shut up and leave me alone. Why couldn't they leave me alone? I wished that I could turn around and wouldn't have to see them.

My father, Dolf, told my mother to let me sleep. He kissed me on the front of my head. I felt some tears wetting my face. "Laura, the boy needs his rest."

I slept for twenty-four hours. I woke up and again wondered what had happened to me. I didn't know what was hurting me. All I knew was that now I was in pain. I felt that my whole body was on fire. I couldn't concentrate. I was anxious to find out what was going on. There was blood on the sheets. My arm was hurting me and it frightened me. I could hear noises but I couldn't comprehend what they were. I felt as if someone was pulling my arm and I asked him to let go.

My mother was there again, tugging gently on my arm. She asked me, "Are you hungry?"

I twisted my eyes toward her. The light was bothering me. I didn't know if it was daylight or night light. I asked my mother, "What happened to me? Am I going to die?" At first my mother didn't reply. My father was there, too. I knew that he would tell me.

"Alex, are you hurting?" my mother asked me.

I started to cry. I knew now that I had gotten hurt. They had wrapped me tight just like a baby in a blanket. They didn't want me to move my hands. I learned my right arm had pieces of shrapnel in it. My right hand, both my knees and my face were also injured. My nose was itching and I couldn't scratch it. I wondered, "What happened? Why me?" I was restless and I started wrestling with the blanket. I was getting red from the effort.

I screamed, "Mom! Get me out of here. I don't want to be here." I was scared for my life. I was depressed and feeling lonesome and rotten. "Mom, scratch my nose!" I yelled.

My mother asked me in German, "Where?"

I yelled at her, "Don't speak German! Speak only Hebrew! We are in Israel, not in Germany."

Again I asked my parents if I was going to die. My parents reassured me that everything was going to be okay.

The year was 1948 and the month was March. Only a month ago had been my *Bar Mitzvah*. Well, at least I can die now, knowing I'd become a man, I told myself. But I didn't want to die, especially not in the hospital where, thirteen years ago, I was born. I wondered if it smelled this bad back then. I just wanted to sleep and to be refreshed to face the world.

I slept and slept and slept.

The name of the hospital was *Hadassah*. Hadassah is the Hebrew name of Queen Esther, whose story is told in the Old Testament book that bears her name.

Later that afternoon my anesthesia wore off completely. I was in terrible pain. Even though they were feeding me intravenously I was terribly thirsty. I thought I could drink a whole five gallon bottle of water. I was sweating profusely. The more I sweated the more I felt thirsty. I heard my mother asking the doctor when I would be able to take a bath. I had been in the hospital since Friday night–two days. I had a very high fever and it didn't look like the wounds were healing. I was talking and talking and not making any sense. Sometime I spoke when I was asleep. Strangely enough, I spoke in German. This was the language I hated and this was the first language that I had learned at home. You are not born hating but you learn to hate.

I remembered school. Only two weeks ago I had moved from city school to the kibbutz school. I was in the sixth grade and I thought that we city kids were ahead of those who came from the farm. I hadn't been doing my schoolwork and had been fighting with my classmates. They called me an "Arab lover." I wished Ali was with me to help me fight those kibbutzniks. My parents and teachers had warned me about my behavior and told me if I didn't shape up I would be sorry. I was afraid that I would be punished at school for not doing the assignments. I was delirious and I asked myself, "Is this what happens to kids who don't do their homework?"

This was the fourth day that I had been in the hospital. My mother slapped my face lightly and spoke to me, once again in German. "Are you okay?" I thought, can't she see that I was in agony? I wished I could cover my ears and not listen to her. I heard my mother and father whispering and mentioning Ali's name. "Ali, Ali, Ali," is what I heard my mother and father saying. "How could Ali do this?" "Why did Ali do that?" My parents were angry every time they mentioned Ali's name.

I knew that my body was broken and people were trying to repair it. I heard the doctors saying that there was shrapnel in my stomach and they couldn't operate until the fever went down.

<hr />

Ali and I had been inseparable for eight years. I had met Ali when I was five years old, back in 1940. Ali was my best friend. We were kids who did everything together, and no history, ethnicity, society or religion was going to change that. I was Jewish and he was Muslim, and nothing was ever going to change that, either. Nothing!

We lived in the same building. Jews and Arabs lived in the same buildings in my town. Our building was three floors tall. Each floor had one apartment that consisted of three bedrooms, a kitchen, bathroom, hallway and a balcony. On the first floor lived a Jewish family: father, mother and three adult kids. Ali's family lived on the second floor: father, mother and three children–Ali, Lylla and Nadine. Ali's father was a taxi driver and his mother a housewife. On the third floor I lived with my parents in one room. There was another family that shared our balcony, bathroom and kitchen. They were older.

When we moved to the building I was five years old. Ali was also five years old. He and I went to the same school. He went to the Arab section of the school and was taught in Arabic and was also learning Hebrew. I went to the Jewish section but was only taught in Hebrew. Even though at first we couldn't speak the same language we became good friends. We were inseparable. We used to play hide and seek, cops and robbers, and cowboys and Indians. I was blond with green gray eyes and light skin. Ali was dark with black hair and black eyes.

World War II had started. We were always hungry and searching for food. Ali, older boys from the neighborhood and I went to fields to gather food. If it was a Jewish person's field they left ten percent of the field for the poor people to gather the crop, as prescribed in the Bible in the book of Ruth. If it was an Arab field they chased you away.

Even with the constant hunger and poverty, in 1940 through 1945, the days of picking crops were the happiest days of my life. Jew and Arab boys worked together. I remembered when I helped to pick corn. The corn plants were six to seven feet tall and Ali and I were only four feet tall. We removed the corn by hand. We bent the plants and removed the husks. The older boys helped us to pick the corn. My mother and Ali's mother and the girls worked together in Ali's family kitchen, making corn bread, pita and falafel. Usually pita was made of wheat flour but we substituted corn flour.

Ali and I picked onions, tomatoes, cucumbers and fruit. We usually ate while we picked the crops; we were so hungry that once we filled our bellies we often had stomachache, diarrhea and we vomited. We still ate the crops. We didn't wash the cucumbers or the tomatoes; we ate them with dirt. We were hungry. We were really hungry. Our parents cried when they couldn't feed us.

When we were older we baked corn and sold it on the street. With the money we made we bought meat. Ali and I were breadwinners. I remember I felt like I was always starving until the age of ten. For many years the only meal I had was lunch at school. My mother sent me to school hungry. I couldn't concentrate at school. I couldn't wait for lunch. It didn't matter how bad the food was–when you are hungry you eat it. Ali was in the same boat.

We used to love to eat olives. We ate the skin and kept sucking the juice from the pits. We held the pits in our mouths for hours.

When I was thirteen years old, in 1948, my parents sent me away to the kibbutz. More and more Jewish immigrants were moving to our town, and the Arabs were leaving. Was I so naïve and preoccupied with my own life that I didn't see the Arab-Jewish war was coming?

When Ali left the apartment house he told me; "I never thought that I would leave the place that I was born, the place my parents and grandparents lived." He was angry and sad. He told me, "You foreigners pushed us away from our city. All those properties used to belong to Arabs. Now you bought them and you charge high rent and we can't afford them."

Ali showed me the Arab cemetery where his grandparents were buried. We used to play hide and seek, or cowboys and Indians or cops and robbers there. Life was beautiful when both Arabs and Jews lived together. We had so much to offer each other.

My parents had sent me to the kibbutz thinking that it would be safer living there than in the city. They were afraid that the Arab-Jewish war would start and both sides would kill each other. At that time, the British were still keeping the peace in Israel.

Being the new kid at the kibbutz school, I was an easy target for teasing. I remember when the kibbutzniks had come to our city school, poorly dressed, we had teased them; but the roles were now switched. I was now a minority. I had already had some fistfights. I hated to share my kibbutz room with two girls and a boy. At home I had slept with my parents. At the kibbutz I was bashful and I didn't want to change clothes or shower in front of the girls or boys. But I enjoyed eating at the kibbutz. For breakfast we had half a hard boiled egg, cheese, bread and juice. For lunch the same; and for dinner soup, salad and bread and butter.

Also, I got a job at the kibbutz working in the kitchen serving food, washing dishes, and cleaning the dining room. I couldn't help comparing myself with Ali. At home, Ali never did any work. He was the male and his sisters did all the work. They cleaned his room, they washed his clothes and fed him. The girls were trained for marriage as soon as they reached puberty. The boys were trained to be the breadwinner.

Ali's hair was cut short, free and uncombed. His sisters' hair was long, never cut, and the ends of it were in rubber bands. My hair was cut as short as Ali's, but was combed. Ali went out into the street to play without asking his parents' permission; the girls always stayed at home. Ali was dressed in shorts and was topless; his sisters were covered from head to toe.

Now back at the hospital, in the same room with me, I was surprised to see that two kids from my kibbutz were also wounded. They were my roommates, Dona and Ada. Ada was like a sister. When I was born we had lived in the same kibbutz and my mother had breast-fed Ada. I was jealous when I saw how many get well cards, flowers and candy the girls got and I didn't get any. I wondered why. I thought it was that I was going to die and people didn't want to spend any money on me since I wouldn't be able to enjoy the cards and candies. I wondered if I was going to heaven. Do Jews and Arabs go to the same heaven? Would I be in the same heaven as my pet calf, Black? When Black was born, my father was able to pick up the newborn calf. Every day the calf gained a few pounds and my father was still able to pick up the calf. I had wondered if my father would be able to lift a full-grown steer, but Black didn't live that long. I knew that my father was able to lift me when I was a baby. Was he able to lift me now, since I was already a teenager? Would he be able to lift me when I was an adult? I'd never find out if I died now. Those were the kinds of thoughts I was thinking, while lying there.

Almost a week passed and I was finally healing. Ada was the first one to tell me about the explosion, and that Ali had tried to kill us. I didn't believe her. I told her that I was going to prove to her that she was wrong. I asked her, "Is my roommate, Amos, okay?" She told me he was okay. When the explosion had occurred he was in the bathroom. She told me, "Remember, it was Friday night and we had a dance in the dining room."

"Yes, I remember," I told her, and without stopping I said, "I remember we roasted marshmallows at the fireplace."

"We had a good time dancing the Hora and some other Israeli dances," Ada said.

"At nine o'clock we went to bed," I said.

Ada started to cry and asked me, "Did you tell Ali where you were staying?"

I answered, "Yes, I told him to come to visit me."

"He did, with a grenade," Ada said.

"We found out that the Kibbutz wasn't protected from intruders," Dona added. "Ali penetrated the kibbutz and poisoned two of our dogs. Then he waited until we were asleep and tried to kill us. Lucky for us that he pulled the safety pin and didn't hold the lever and blew himself up instead. He was only ten feet away from our room. Fragments of the grenade hit our window and broke the glass and hit us."

"Ali did this!" Ada said, once again.

I didn't believe her. I was very curious to find out how Ada and Dona found out that Ali tried to kill us. I asked them, "Who told you that Ali tried to kill us?"

Ada replied, "My parents told me, and they don't lie."

With every breath of air I took I justified that Ali was innocent. I told her that Ali was my blood brother. We had known we would soon be going our separate ways, so just a few weeks ago before we parted we had cut each other's thumbs and mixed the blood and promised to die for each other. In my heart, I felt that Ali and I would always be together in spirit, if not in body. I thought that once Ali and I mixed our blood, the good in me would go to Ali and the strong in him would come to me.

At that time, March, 1948, there had been no signs of killing between Arabs and Jews in our town.

Ada laughed and didn't take me seriously. I told her that when we were little, one day we had gone to the beach. I was drowning and Ali called for help and saved my life. I told her that Ali had given me a Swiss army knife for my *Bar Mitzvah*. She told me he probably stole it. I knew in my heart she was right.

———

I was crying. I couldn't believe what my friends and parents had told me. I felt like choking. This was the first time in my life that somebody had tried to kill me because I was a Jew.

I remembered during World War II when Ali and I chased after jeeps of the British soldiers, begging for gum. Once we got the Chiclets we shared them. We chewed the gum and then we washed it and chewed it from mouth to mouth. This was our treasure, a piece of gum that we shared.

There were so many good times I recalled. I remembered secretly feeding Ali on his fasting holiday, Ramadan. Maybe it was wrong, but we were only children and I thought that Ali wouldn't last without food. I remembered at Passover how the Jews left bread outside their houses because on Passover all leavened bread must be removed from the home. Ali and I collected it. He had a wooden wagon and we filled it with bread.

Ali celebrated all the Jewish holidays with me. When I studied for my *Bar Mitzvah*, Ali knew the words better than I did.

At the age of eleven, in 1946, we both joined youth organizations. They were just like boy scouts. Ali took boxing, judo and self-defense. In my youth organization we took cooking, planting trees and trying to beautify our city. When I was about to fight with another boy I tried to talk him out of fighting. In contrast, Ali enjoyed using his hands. I remembered his concern for me after Boris, the bully, had cut up my first pair of new shoes and had hit me. Both Ali and I were afraid of him. Ali trained to have revenge on the boy. Years later Ali had a fight with him and broke his arm, and when the boy started to cry Ali told him that would teach him never to fight with an Arab.

I wondered what made Ali try to kill me. It had been on a Friday night about nine-thirty or ten o'clock when I heard a loud blast. My bedroom window broke and broken glass was over me. I felt shrapnel hit me and I started to bleed and then I fainted.

Earlier that night we had celebrated the Sabbath. We had greeted it in the traditional way, like a groom greets a bride. After lighting the candles and blessing the bread and wine we'd had a special meal. We had all worn our best clothes and then we danced. We had danced Israeli dances like the Hora. We'd all had a good time. For dessert we'd had cookies and punch, and later when we went to bed a chocolate bar had been waiting for us. Up to then it was a great evening.

⚜

After spending a week and a half in the hospital with Ada and Dona, I was able to return to my dorm at the kibbutz. When I was sleeping I didn't have to face the consequences of my naiveté. Was I naïve? Should I have anticipated such an act? I remembered how he had stopped going to school with me, and how he had resented having to move. But did Ali ever give me any hint of what he was going to do? Until today, I still wonder. If Ali had been successful he could have killed several of us.

After the explosion, the kibbutzniks had found Ali's body and had seen the broken beads from his rosary scattered around the area. When I was better I tried to recover the beads but I never found all ninety-nine. I wanted to reconstruct the rosary and give it to Ali's family, but my mother took the beads and threw them in the garbage.

When I was mostly well, a few months later, I went with a bouquet of flowers to the Arab cemetery. I went to Ali's grave to place the flowers. On his grave I saw his picture and on it was written in Arabic "A young solder who died for Palestine, 1948." I was crying. When Ali had taken me to the Arab cemetery I had noticed only graves of old people or babies. Now I noticed several graves of young people my age. I was still very naïve when I entered the cemetery. The cemetery was filled with Arab visitors. All their eyes were on me. I could feel they were hostile. I saw some of the kids collecting stones and that they were getting ready to throw them at me. I was lucky there were some British soldiers there, and they took me home and told my parents to keep me out of there.

I never hated Ali. He was my blood brother. We shared our youth together. We grew up together. We shared hunger and ceremonial rites of aging together. It is still hard to believe that my "brother" would try to kill me. At that time I didn't realize how much that incident affected me. But it did, and I have spent all the rest of my life still wondering how Ali could have changed from blood brother to my attempted assassin so quickly, and at the power of ethnic hatred.

Even today, I still sleep in my room with a light on.

# Chapter Twenty-Nine, Cuba

It was May of 1948 and I was thirteen years old and in Havana. I had never been on an island before, and it was hard for me to correctly pronounce the name Cuba in Spanish. I had to pinch myself to find out if it was true that I was alive and living thousands of miles away from Palestine.

My parents took me to Cuba because they believed history was going to repeat itself. My father had left Italy to escape Mussolini and my mother had left Poland to escape Hitler, and now they were leaving Palestine to escape the war with the Arabs. They took me to Cuba after I was wounded by my best friend's suicide mission. My mother said, "You are the only child we have. We don't want to lose you." Having family in the United States, my parents thought that we could pack and move there, but it was harder than we thought. Both my parents had been born in Europe and there was a quota for new immigrants to get to the United States. But Cuba was selling visas and trying to bring immigrants to their island.

All they had been able to acquire in fifteen years of living in Palestine was a condominium apartment which was the result of very hard work and a sum of money my father received from the British army for back pay during his captivity.

We never lived in that condominium. Using the skills she had learned making uniforms for the army, my mother used it as a factory to manufacture dresses. My parents were able to sell the apartment and we got ten thousand dollars for it, which covered the costs of the Cuban visa and the flight.

We left Palestine on May 13 and our first stop was Athens, Greece, where we spent the night. The following day, we landed in Prague, Czechoslovakia, with a plane full of Jewish Palestinians who had been sent there to train to be pilots and to fight in the war against the Arabs. From there we flew to Amsterdam, where we had a chance to spend a few days. My parents and I acted just like tourists. We went to the museum, to the parks and the zoo. I had a chance to become friends with Dutch kids because I was a good soccer player and they accepted me with open arms. I didn't have to speak their language, only score goals for my team.

From Amsterdam we flew to Curacao which is an island in the Caribbean, off of Venezuela. All I remember about that place was that it was very hot, and I took five or six showers a day. Then we flew to Havana, Cuba.

We landed with five hundred dollars in our pockets and three suitcases, containing the minimum necessities. We couldn't speak the language, had no job and couldn't get one because we had to be citizens of Cuba, which took five years. We could have asked my mother's family in the United States to help us, but my parents were too proud. But because we were Jews, the Jewish community helped us to get settled down. The first thing they did was to welcome us to the community and they invited us to their homes.

One Jewish family became our best friends. My parents became friendly with the adults and the children became my friends. We joined a temple where my parents became active. The members helped us to find an apartment house, furniture and a maid, and made sure that we didn't starve. They brought us food and made sure that I dressed properly.

In Palestine, I had worn shorts everywhere, but in Cuba, even though it was hot, all the boys wore long pants. The members also bought what was to me the extravagant purchase of six pairs of new shoes, which I treasured. I shined them every morning and then chose the ones I would wear that day.

With the help of the Jewish community, my parents opened a women's clothing factory. Before the factory opened, no one in Cuba had been able to buy finished dresses. They had to buy material and find a dressmaker to sew their dresses. My parents' first customer was Sears Roebuck. My parents didn't have money to buy raw material but Sears had a large inventory of raw material that they hadn't been able to sell. They got together, Sears supplied the raw material and my parents supplied the finished products. It was very successful. It was the first time in history that people in Cuba were able to buy ready-made, finished garments that were made in Cuba. Before that, if you wanted to buy finished products in the stores they were all made in the United States and were very expensive. In addition, the American-styled clothes didn't look good on the Cuban people. Most of the young Cuban girls were slim with big hips and small waists, while the American girls were taller and a little heavier. When a Cuban woman bought an American dress, she had to shorten the skirt and widen the hips, while making the waist smaller. It wasn't worth the trouble to buy an American dress, while my parents made well-fitting clothing for Cubans. It was a pleasure for the Cuban woman to go into a store and buy a dress without having to have it tailored. Well-fitting, good quality and lower prices–that's why my parents were so successful.

In Havana I started school at the Hebrew Academy, where I was one of the oldest kids. The school was kindergarten to sixth grade. I knew Hebrew and Yiddish. Yiddish is the traditional language of Eastern European Jews and it is based on German with the addition of Hebrew, Aramaic and Slavic terms. At school I also studied Spanish and English.

The school was located in one of the suburbs of Havana, Vedado. It was an old building not too far from my house, so I was able to walk to it. The building had twelve rooms, a large kitchen, dining room, four bathrooms and a large backyard. The backyard was full of gym equipment and I enjoyed climbing on the monkey bars.

Most of the teachers were elderly women who enjoyed teaching and who spoiled us. They hugged us and rewarded us when we did a good job. They looked like loving grandmothers. They wanted us to succeed and most of the students went on to do well in high school and college.

School was their life and when they taught a kid to read or to write his name, they gleamed. They were never negative, always positive, and we tried very hard to please them. But at the Hebrew academy I had some conflicts with authority. We had to wear a uniform. In the public schools in Havana, the boys wore khaki pants and shirt and the girls wore a khaki skirt and blouse. At the private school which I attended, I wore navy blue pants, a white shirt, and a navy blue tie. On the pocket of the shirt was a Star of David surrounded by the words *Academia Hebrea*, or Hebrew Academy. I did not want to wear a Star of David on my clothing. I remembered the stories about my mother's family in the Holocaust in Poland, where the Jews were forced to wear white armbands with a blue Star of David until they were led off to the trains and certain death. I refused to wear such a sign. I felt that at any moment, the Gestapo would somehow find me and come to take me to the gas chamber. At the age of thirteen I was determined to question authority and never agree to rules that I truly believed were pointless, arbitrary or could cause me harm.

The principal asked me, "Aren't you proud to be a Jew? Look across the street at the children in the Catholic school, wearing a red cross on the pockets of their shirts."

I answered, "I wonder how so many Jews could have walked off to their certain deaths. Now I know. We have so many Holocaust survivors here in our school, and I am the only one who is refusing to wear the Star of David."

The principal told me that we must obey the rules of the school, otherwise we would have chaos at school. But I couldn't agree, and I went home and I told my parents I felt that we had not learned anything from the Holocaust if we were still required to publicly identify ourselves as Jews.

I went to school wearing the same navy blue pants and tie but a white shirt without the Star of David. I was able to convince the other boys at school not to wear the Star of David. I could not believe what I had created. Almost immediately, almost everybody at school stopped wearing their shirts with the Stars of David. And across the street, some of the Christian students rebelled also and stopped wearing their shirts with the red cross.

I asked some of the kids why they followed my suggestion to tear the symbols off of their shirts; most of them said, "I don't know, but it will be fun to do it." I told them to think of the Holocaust and to think for themselves, not to just listen to me. After I said that, all of the kids, both Jews and Catholics, wanted to know more about the Holocaust. After all, they had been safe in Cuba during the worst times.

I asked them, "What would you do if you were told to lie down and get shot in the head or to get on a train to certain death?" The kids who were born in Cuba and who had never suffered or were never hungry were the most curious and helped to rebel against authority. But those kids who were survivors of the concentration camps were just like sheep. I was shocked that the children who had suffered the most during the war were the most likely to follow any order given to them. As a thirteen-year-old boy, I couldn't understand how they could be so passive. It was many years later before I could truly appreciate the horror of their early lives, and how it had affected them.

My education in Palestine had taught me to think for myself and not to be a passive bookworm. Every teacher I'd had insisted that in addition to learning "where, what and when," that I also ask "how and why." Most of the education at the Hebrew Academy in Havana was memorization and never asking the teacher "Why?" The teacher was God and we were disciples, and that was what I was afraid had happened in the Holocaust. Perhaps the Jewish children of Germany, Poland and all the other Eastern European countries captured by the Germans were never taught to think for themselves. So when they were told to line up, or to move to the ghetto, or to lie down and get shot in the head, they did as they were told and never argued, even to their death.

My "revolt" had lasting consequences. After a few days, the parents from both schools had a meeting and they voted that neither school would require the religious symbol to be worn on the students' clothing.

In Palestine I had heard over and over the expression, "Never again!" Even as a boy that phrase had real meaning for me.

# Chapter Thirty, Trying to Be a Man

In Cuba we were not allowed to work until we became citizens, which would take five years. However, we were allowed to invest our own money in the country to start a business and employ Cuban nationals as workers. Once we had a Cuban passport, we thought, it would be easy for us to then go to the United States.

My parents opened a dress factory, just like we had in Palestine before we left, and were able to support themselves and me. I, on the other hand, had a tutor to teach me Spanish and English because the only language that I could read and write when I arrived in Cuba was Hebrew. Once I was able to communicate in Spanish I was enrolled first at the Hebrew Academy and then at a prep school. I was now fourteen and a half.

In Cuba, students at the age of twelve take an achievement test. If you passed the test, then you could start secondary school; if you didn't pass, you could start a vocational school or business school. Since I was already too old to be a freshman in secondary school, I decided to take courses in a prep school to prepare for secondary school. If I passed the entry exam, I would be eligible to take an exam for my five freshman subjects and start the following year as a sophomore.

In the morning, three days a week, I took five freshman subjects. In the afternoon I took ten subjects to prepare for high school. I became friends with some of the students that were the same age and in the same program as me. School was from eight to twelve in the morning and from two to six in the afternoon. I took the bus to school. Sometimes staying at school for lunch was a lot of fun. This was my only contact with my friends.

At school I was able to organize my social activities for the weekend. Because I was a foreigner I didn't have any friends outside the school but I was able to socialize with the kids at school. Just like other normal teenage boys, we talked about sex. The information that I gathered about sex was from my pals in school, not like today where sex education is readily available.

My environment was a macho environment in which I had to prove manhood. I had to prove it by macho behavior. A macho is a person who has a strong sense of masculine pride. I saw what the older boys did and I wanted to be accepted so I followed them. My father didn't guide me about sex. It was a taboo subject.

The boys took me to the gym and showed me how to lift weights. I was embarrassed at my physical appearance. I was bony and unmanly and in disgraceful condition, according to the "Charles Atlas" school of thinking. When we exercised we talked about girls' anatomy. We were safe since this gym was only for men.

One day I was surprised by getting a birthday party invitation from a girl. It made me nervous. I asked some of my friends if they were going. They said, "Free food, free refreshments and, if we are lucky, we will get free necking. Why not?" I didn't know what they meant by "necking." I asked them and they told me that I was a dope.

They grabbed each other's hands and started kissing them, and told me that maybe some girl would kiss me. I felt sick to my stomach. I never had been kissed by a girl.

The day arrived and some of my friends came to pick me up. For parties and other fancy occasions, my friends and I wore dark pants and a *guayabera*, a white shirt worn outside the pants, and a bow tie. Some of the boys who were wealthy wore Panama hats. I didn't.

When my friends and I arrived at the party, several kids had already arrived and there was plenty of soda pop, fruit punch, potato chips, popcorn and candies. The girls were on one side of the room listening to a record player, and the boys were throwing popcorn at each other and trying to catch it in their mouths. The birthday girl came over to us and told us that we should mingle. She then suggested that we play "Spin the Bottle."

I asked my friends what Spin the Bottle was about. They told me to watch what was going to happen. Everybody was sitting in a circle, boy-girl, boy-girl. The hostess spun the bottle and when the bottle faced someone of the opposite sex, she had to kiss that person.

The birthday girl spun the bottle first and the bottle faced one of the most popular boys. Everybody in the room cheered her. She grabbed the boy and took him to the closet and when they were inside the closet, the room became quiet. I thought everyone was listening to hear the kiss through a heavy wood door. The birthday girl and the boy came out of the closet happy and smiling. I wished that the bottle would never face me, but no such luck. A fairly attractive, brunette girl spun the bottle and on the first spin, it stopped and pointed to me. She asked me to join her in the closet. She went in first and I followed and closed the door. We were alone in the dark. I could feel her presence and smell her perfume. I told her, "We don't have to kiss." She told me, "I waited too long not to be kissed. I want to kiss you." I kissed her and it wasn't as bad as I had anticipated. By the end of the party I was happy; free drinks, free food and a few kisses.

The boys who thought that they were big shots were teasing me. They had experienced sex and they asked me if I was a virgin. Being honest was my first mistake; I told them I was. They dared me to have sex and told me that I was at a dangerous stage, that I might become a "homo" if I didn't. I didn't know what they were talking about. I was afraid to ask them since I didn't want to be ridiculed, so I kept quiet.

Every day when we went to school we passed a brothel. Sometimes we talked to the girls there. It was funny that these young prostitutes were my age and that we associated with them, had lunch with them, fooled around with them, and played tag with them. We hugged them and grabbed their purses and played keep-away. We also read them stories and we tried to teach them how to read and to do simple arithmetic. We pretended to arm-wrestle with them. We bought them candy, soft drinks and cigarettes. The young girls told us dirty jokes. We laughed with them and we felt that they were our friends. In Cuba, a decent girl would not go out with you without a chaperone. We felt that we could talk to those girls without watching our tongues.

The young prostitutes were all mulatto, of mixed blood, and they all looked alike. They were slim, had dark hair, dark eyes and dark skin. They had small waists but big hips. They wore girdles at an early age and they tied their waists tightly. They used cheap perfume and makeup and shaved their eyebrows and painted them black, using charcoal, since that was all they could afford. Sometimes they added blue paint around their eyes.

They used heavy makeup to make themselves look older. When we had lunch with them we told them to wash their faces. We told them that they looked better natural, at least to us. And they listened to us and some of them did as we suggested.

We told them what was happening in the world. While we read them the newspaper, the young girls would sit on the bench with their arms around their knees. They looked like little girls. They loved to listen to the radio. They loved to hear novellas (soap operas) and they fantasized about the stories. They were dreaming that one day a prince would rescue them and they would live in a palace. They smoked one cigarette after another, and so did I.

My father wanted me to quit smoking. He put a rubber band loosely around my wrist and he told me that when I had the urge to smoke, instead of lighting a cigarette I should snap the rubber band hard enough to remind me to resist the habit. Soon, he said, the urge to smoke would become uncomfortable and I would lose the desire to smoke. I wore the rubber band but I never snapped it and I continued smoking.

The girls needed the money that they made from prostitution to support their families. Twice a year they went to visit their families on the farms and brought them clothes and money. They told their families that they were nurses, teachers, or secretaries. The girls were the only ones in the family who could read a little. They wore cheap jewelry that they had made themselves when they were not working as prostitutes. They brought their families radios that were treasured by all and they knew the latest songs and dances and they taught them to their families.

The day arrived when I finally decided to show the other boys that I was "normal" by losing my virginity. I couldn't sleep all night. After I finished my homework at nine o'clock I went to bed. I tossed and turned. I started to count sheep but it didn't help. My stomach growled. I heard it say, "Tomorrow is the day." I couldn't believe I was going to do this. I really didn't want to do it, but I wanted to prove to my friends that I was really macho.

It was not a hot day nor a cold day, it was just perfect. The sun was shining, there was hardly any wind and no clouds. I couldn't have picked a nicer day. I could hear the sparrows whispering, "Today is the day that Alex is going to lose his virginity."

It was a school day. I wore my standard uniform; navy blue pants, white shirt, a navy blue tie, navy blue socks and black shoes. I had secretly shined my shoes the night before. I didn't want my parents to know what I was planning to do. If I went to a shoeshine boy, my parents would ask me, "What is the occasion, Alex?"

The morning classes dragged. I didn't want to go to the brothel and at the same time I couldn't wait. My adrenaline was pumping and I really felt alive. My pals were staring at me. Instead of paying attention to the teacher, all of their attention was on me. They seemed to be as excited as I was. They asked the teacher the dumbest questions on a subject that was not even related to what the class was doing. They were driving me crazy.

Finally it was lunchtime. The sun was two hours higher now and it didn't hurt my eyes when I was outside. All the prostitutes at the brothel knew about this, that my friends were treating me. I was very nervous and I wanted to end this before I started it. I was only fifteen years old. I was short and very thin, skin and bones. I wore glasses and I really looked like a nerd. I had hardly started to shave and, since I was blonde, you couldn't see any hair on my face or body. My friends were taller and heavier than me. They played sports like baseball and soccer. Back in Palestine I had been very good at soccer, but now because of my comparatively small size I wasn't too good at sports, and I was the last one to be chosen at any game.

I wasn't hungry even though it was lunchtime. My friends were eating with gusto. I picked up my sandwich, broke off a small piece and started to chew it. Then I picked up another piece and put it in my mouth but couldn't swallow it. I wanted to end the meal. I was able to drink a cup of coffee. It seemed to build up my strength, and I started to smoke a cigarette to make myself feel relaxed.

I kept telling myself, "You don't have to do this." I told myself, "What will happen if I don't go to the whorehouse?" I thought all my friends would laugh at me. Being laughed at was worse than being scared about going. So when they said, "Let's go," I went.

When I entered the brothel, the light was dim. It was lunchtime and the bar was open. The prostitutes were lined up in front of us. I saw some of the young girls I knew from school and I wanted nothing to do with them. They seemed like babies, the same age as I was. Later I learned that there were several old men that chose them in particular.

The minute I went in I was sorry I'd come. I kept repeating to myself, "I don't have to do this. Who am I trying to impress?"

One of my friends asked me, "Who are you going to choose?"

I didn't answer. I was talking to myself. "I can leave the brothel; I don't have to do this. Let them talk about me. But they will tell everybody that I was chicken." I was so nervous that I almost peed in my pants. I almost started to run away but I didn't. I started to smoke. I lit one cigarette, took a few puffs and I stamped it on the ground then I lit another one.

The prostitutes were lined up in front of us almost naked. They wore negligees and were smiling and they whispered "Take me, I am good." Some of them wore colorful bikinis and treated us like we were big spenders. They figured out that once we were hooked we would be their customers for life.

My friends asked me, "Do you like any of them?"

I replied, "I don't care which one."

My friends picked an "older" woman for me. She was maybe twenty-five or thirty years old. They told me that she was hot and was perfect for me. They paid two dollars and they handed me a condom. The prostitute led me to a small room and quickly undressed. I took my clothes off but I was afraid to touch her. She showed me how to feel her breasts and told me not to be nervous. I started to sweat. I couldn't believe how wet I was. The prostitute took a wet towel and dried my sweat. She told me, "Take it easy."

I didn't want to take it easy. I wanted to run away.

She told me, "Don't be afraid."

"I am not afraid." I said.

She asked me, "Is this your first time?"

I told her, "I've done it a million times."

She laughed because she knew better. I wasn't any different than the other school boys that she saw here all the time, but she tried to make me feel at ease. She gently stroked my hair, at the same time kissing my neck. I told her to stop. I didn't want to kiss her. I wanted it to be finished quickly.

She tried to undress me but I resisted.

She told me, "Take me. What are you waiting for?"

I was sweating. She was continuously talking, "Are you afraid? Have I frightened you? Do you want to be in paradise?" She whispered those words into my ears.

The whole thing lasted less than ten minutes; entering the brothel, choosing the prostitute, getting undressed, hanging my clothes on a nail and performing the act. While I was doing it I was afraid the condom would pop and I would catch a terrible disease and die. I felt like a robot. It was mechanical, not an act of love.

When I finished the act and had come out of the room my friends congratulated me. I walked out of the brothel in awe; not so much awe at the act of sex but that I had let them lead me to do it like this.

That afternoon we didn't go back to school. We all went to a movie. Before going home I went to my friend's house. I took a very hot shower for an hour. I couldn't stand the cheap perfume the prostitute used. I felt dirty. I scrubbed myself and I still felt dirty. I washed my hair and I told myself that I was filthy, dirty, scummy, unclean and was crying. I felt ashamed of myself that I had let myself be led just like a puppy. This was supposed to be a happy occasion, but for me it was very sad .I wondered what Ali would have done and how he would have felt. He probably would have bragged about his experience.

The next day when I went to school I tried to avoid walking by the brothel. I took a longer route so the prostitutes didn't see me. I didn't have lunch with them anymore. My friends asked me if I had enjoyed myself. I told them, "Yes, and I am looking forward to my next visit to the brothel." The truth was that I was a phony.

And yet the physical urge made me go again. Several months later my friends asked me if I wanted to visit the prostitutes. I told them yes, but not to the same brothel. When we went to another brothel I didn't gaze amorously at any prostitutes. I knew that I could have any one of them for a price. There wasn't any feeling of love, only the physical urge.

I asked my friends, "How do you feel about visiting brothels?"

They all told me, "Fine, nothing special," or words to that effect.

Then I asked, "Why do you keep going there? Is it just your physical need?"

One of them told me, "In case we ever get married we better know what to do unless we marry a prostitute."

Forty-eight years later I took some of my friends to visit Cuba. We stayed at the old Hilton Hotel in Havana. Now it is called Havana Libre. When we entered or left the hotel we were always approached by prostitutes. They asked us if we spoke Spanish and if we would like to have a good time. I felt nervous. A friend asked me, "If you took one to your room, what's the worst thing that could happen to you, Alex?"

I looked at the girls who were half naked, wearing high heeled shoes, short skirts and short blouses where you were able to see their breasts. I replied to my friends, "I could get a disease, be robbed, attacked or killed." I didn't say any more, but suddenly that afternoon long ago when my school friends had taken me to the brothel came before my eyes. Here it was almost forty-eight years later, in approximately the same place, but now I was with my American friends instead of my school friends.

I went to my room at the hotel and I took a long, long hot shower, just like when I had lost my virginity. A strange question crept into my mind while taking the shower: "How long do you have to go without sex to become a virgin again?"

My thoughts drifted back to the first time I had sex. The room had been a small one. There had been a big bed that took most of the space of the room. There was an armoire, where the prostitute kept her clothes and personal things. On the wall there was a statue of the Virgin Mary. The prostitute had crossed herself both before the act and after the act. She asked me if I wanted to light a candle or pray to the Virgin Mary since I was committing a sin. I told her, "I am Jewish and I go to the synagogue on Friday night."

Every Sunday morning the prostitutes went to church for mass and, after that, to confession. They told me that the one thing had nothing to do with the other. They had a profession and that was the only way that they could make money. When they entered the church they were equal in God's eyes.

I lost my virginity when I was fifteen years old, the same year that I stopped smoking. I thought that having sex would make me a man. After the act, I wondered if there was an invisible mark in front of my head that only grown-up people saw. I wondered if grown-up people whispered behind my back that I had lost my virginity. I was sorry I hadn't waited until I was more mature.

Now, back in Cuba with my friends, I was able to talk to a prostitute as an adult. I noticed that nothing had changed. Like the ones from forty-eight years ago, this girl was the daughter of a farm family. She was young, she couldn't read or write and prostitution was the only way she could support her family. I gave her some American dollars–the equivalent of a month's earnings, and told her to go home. She took the money and laughed at me. She put it in her bra and went to look for her next customer.

# Chapter Thirty-One, Saint's Day

You *can* teach an old dog new tricks. At fifteen I was already an old dog, set in my ways. I was fifteen years old and I knew everything about the world, or so I thought. I thought that I could smoke, drink and womanize because that's what my friends were doing. They expected me to do the same. I didn't want to be the target of teasing, like I was about my Israeli accent. I had a hard time pronouncing double R, so commonly used in Spanish. I pronounced it like the sound of L and it always made my friends laugh.

In Cuba we didn't celebrate our birthday, instead we celebrated our Saint's Day. My saint was Saint Alejandro. My given name was Alexander in memory of my grandfather on my father's side. In Israel they called me Alex, which I didn't mind. When I arrived in Cuba at Havana airport, at the age of thirteen and a half, I was supposed to sign my name for the immigration officer. I didn't know how to write in Latin letters, only in Hebrew. In Hebrew you write from right to left and in Latin from left to right. An officer taught me to write Alejandro, which is the Spanish version of Alexander, and suddenly I had a new name that I loved

In the Jewish calendar my birthday was *Hadar Seva*, which is March 7th in the English calendar and *marzo siete* in Spanish.

Even though I was Jewish I was happy to learn that I was named after a saint. "Alejandro" had been sainted after the following events. Alejandro was very kind to animals. One day when he was walking on the street he heard a pigeon calling for help. A hawk had the pigeon in his claws and was going to kill her and feed her to his children. Alejandro grabbed the hawk in one hand and with the other hand rescued the pigeon. The hawk asked him, "Why did you do this? How am I going to feed my children?" Alejandro, in response, cut a piece of flesh from his arm and gave it to the hawk and told him, "Here is food for your children." I knew then that my birthday was on the right saint's day. He would protect me and I hoped he would help me pass the examination to go on to secondary school. However, he didn't and I failed, and at the age of fifteen I quit school and started to work. Some of my friends passed the examination and started secondary school, others went to vocational school and others went to work like me. We weren't bookworms but we had common sense. My parents were actually happy that I quit school; they needed the income that I could make.

Now I had a chance to see the real world. We weren't losers when I flunked the examination. My parents didn't scold me or spank me. They hugged me and my father told me, "Let's see what we can do." I started working as a salesman selling textile material. My parents needed raw materials for their dress factory. I helped them get the raw materials such as linen, thread, buttons, etc.

As I said, March 7th was my Saint's Day and my parents promised me a party. A good party has something for everyone: good food, good company and exquisite decorations. The room at the restaurant was breathtaking. I had previously seen the room several times when I was invited to different parties, and it hadn't affected me personally. But this time it did since it was my party.

I invited nine boys for dinner at the restaurant. The reason why I invited nine boys was because I was superstitious. Nine boys plus my parents and I made twelve. I could invite one more boy but that would make thirteen. Thirteen was an unlucky number. I could have invited two more boys but I didn't care for one of them.

The restaurant was located in Havana's suburb, across the street from our house. I could walk to it. It wasn't on the main street, it was on a side street, and a park separated my house from the restaurant. Next to the restaurant was a small grocery store, a drug store and a dry cleaner. It was a small park with a tiny bit of green, with flowers, trees, and benches. I remember that the maids brought babies with strollers and walked around the park. Girls gathered in one area of the park looking at the boys who were walking nearby. The boys weren't allowed to talk to the girls. The only way that a boy met a girl was arranged with their parents. If a boy wanted to take a girl out he must take a chaperone with them.

After World War II the neighborhood changed. Most of the residents were European from Poland, Italy and Germany. They were planning to go to the United States. The way they came to Cuba from Europe was by buying a visa. That how was we came from Israel to Cuba. The Cubans called us "Polacos," even though we weren't from Poland.

One of the buildings in the neighborhood had been converted to a restaurant. It had a distinctly Spanish feel. It was the home of a Spanish family. At first Cuban food was served to the residents who lived in the neighborhood. Lard was used to cook the food. Once the Europeans moved in the restaurant changed to Italian and American food and the lard was replaced with olive oil. Besides Europeans we got Americans that went to medical school. They couldn't get into a medical school in the U.S. so they enrolled in Cuba. Once they lived in Cuba, they mixed with the natives, and often married, had children, earned a living and lived in Cuba.

The charming restaurant building had a living room, a dining room, a hallway, three bedrooms, a bathroom and a kitchen. All the rooms faced the courtyard which had a Mediterranean style garden and a fountain. It had lovely rose bushes and other seasonal flowers. The living room had a fireplace and every room had polished wood floors. Prices were very reasonable. This restaurant was a place that young people hung out. There were pinball games and a juke box. I knew the waiters and cook. My parents took me there when they didn't feel like eating at home, even though we had a maid and my mother didn't have to cook.

The place was spotless. You could eat from the floor. The tables were covered with white linen table cloths, beautiful china, napkins and silverware. Every table had seasonal flowers. The flowers were not in a vase but in painted clay pots, reminiscent of Spain or Italy. My favorite flowers were rainbow tulips. They represented the month of March and spring, the season of rebirth and new growth. In February there were red roses for Valentine's Day. Every month, the flowers were changed according to the season.

They had an excellent bakery. The baker was from Germany, a country well known for its excellent baking. My parents ordered a birthday cake for me. It was the best. Once you tasted it, you would never choose another dessert. It was a sponge cake covered with whipping cream, semi-sweet chocolate and sweet dark cherries. On the cake was a written sign, "Happy Birthday to a big boy, love Mom and Dad."

I wanted my father's permission to smoke a cigar. After all, we were in Cuba, the land of the finest cigars, especially the ones called *Cohiba*. My father didn't want me to smoke but I taunted him by telling him I smoked behind his back. In Cuba, kids ten years old already were smoking cigarettes. I wasn't a leader, I was a follower. It seemed hard to be a leader; it was easy to be a follower. That was why I smoked. I wanted to feel that I belonged. Actually, I hated the smell of tobacco.

On my Saint's Day we went to the restaurant for dinner. There was a banner at my table saying, *"Feliz quince a(os,"* Happy Fifteenth Birthday. The table was decorated with balloons and noisemakers. We all ordered by ourselves. We ordered hamburgers, French fries and cokes. We weren't very creative; we wanted to be just like American teenagers, and although we didn't know any American kids, Hollywood was our model and influence. We all dressed alike, ate alike and talked alike. We smoked not because we enjoyed smoking but because there was nothing else to do. We wanted to give an impression that we were older than we were.

We all started eating at the same time and finished at the same time without exchanging a word. Once we started to talk our favorite topic was school. My friends asked me if I was going to our school bonfire. They asked me if I was going to burn my school uniform. Most of them had worn a school uniform–black shoes, navy blue socks, navy blue pants, white shirt and a navy blue tie–for eight or nine years, from kindergarten through six grade and then one or two years in prep school. They were sick and tired and wanted to burn their uniforms. They wanted to show the world that they were mature and ready to face the world. I told them that I was not going to burn my uniform. I felt that since I hadn't passed the secondary school examination

I would donate it to some kid that couldn't afford to buy a uniform.

Now that I was working I also had to wear a uniform of sorts: Black shoes, black socks, black pants, a white shirt called a *guayabera* and a black bow tie. A *guayabera* is a Cuban shirt that has pleated stripes down the front and four pockets, two over the chest, two over the hips, side vents and banded bottom. It is made of the finest linen.

At the restaurant I couldn't wait to open my presents. In spite of not wanting me to smoke, I knew my father bought me a Cuban Cohiba cigar. It was a perfect cigar, not a fake. Living in Cuba you become a connoisseur. My father asked me, "Dessert first or presents?" I was eager to smoke a cigar in front of my friends and parents. I was so engrossed in myself that at that moment the only important thing was to show my parents and friends that I could smoke a cigar. My father convinced me that we must first have coffee and cake.

Cuban coffee is completely different from any other coffee. In the morning when we woke up we had coffee and hard bread. The coffee was brewed and we added sugar and boiled milk to it. We poured it into a large cup and dunked our hard bread.

During the day we had black coffee with sugar in a small cup. We bought it from street vendors. At night we had the same coffee with our dessert.

At the restaurant the waiter served the birthday cake. My friends sang for me and serenaded me. I opened the presents. I got books, clothes, a wallet and money. Finally I got the cigar. I was going to smoke it in front of my friends.

By the age of fifteen what had I accomplished? I had flunked my secondary school examination. I had gone to a brothel, had quit school and started working and now I was going to smoke a Cohiba cigar.

I wondered what Ali, my former best friend in Israel, would say if he saw me smoking now.

My father was a very kind and compassionate man. He didn't want me to smoke but I smoked behind his back. Years earlier he had cured me of being a "candyholic." In Israel, when I was twelve years old, I used all my allowance money on candies. He got me a job during the summer vacation in a candy factory, packing candies. When I started working at the candy factory there was a sign, "Eat as much as you want, but don't take home." The first day I stuffed myself with candy, the second day only a few candies and the third day I didn't eat any candies at all. That was how my father cured me of eating candies. I knew that he would try to keep me from smoking. At first I thought he would try to lecture me and repeat to me the sixth of the Ten Commandments, "Honor thy father and thy mother." But he hadn't done it. Instead, he treated me like an adult.

The moment arrived when my father handed me my most important present. All eyes were on the slim box in blue wrapping paper, a bow and ribbons. I didn't bother to look at the birthday card, I was only interested in the contents of the box. All of sudden the whole restaurant seemed silent. The only noise was what I made when I unwrapped the box. It was a Cohiba cigar.

I had to show my friends that I was a big shot. Since I had started to work, I earned money and I felt I should have the right to smoke…maybe exhale the smoke and make some circles just like a pro.

But there was more to it than that. In Israel during the time my mother had stopped taking care of me and I was filthy, all my classmates had called me *zevel*, garbage, and even though that period came to an end, the feeling that somehow I was still garbage had stuck with me ever since. As silly as it sounds, I felt that by smoking the Cohiba I could finally get rid of the bad smell that had accompanied me ever since.

My father told me it was such a fine cigar that I had better smoke it in its entirety. Everybody at the restaurant watched me. It was a local restaurant and I knew quite a lot of the guests. My father lit my cigar and I started smoking it. So far it was great. I was the center of attraction. I knew how to smoke. I was thinking that I could exhale the smoke and write my name in the air with the smoke. I was wrong. I got dizzy and I started to vomit. I couldn't stop. It was serious enough that my parents took me to the local hospital. I stayed there for an entire week. I could have left the hospital sooner, but my parents wanted to make sure I had learned my lesson. Every time someone nearby smoked I got sick again.

Months later my father confided that he had dipped the cigar into cognac, carefully dried it, rewrapped it and had then given it to me.

For fifty years now I haven't smoked nor do I eat candies. I learned my lessons well.

# Chapter Thirty-Two, Mezuzah

The year was 1949 and my parents and I had lived in Cuba for half a year. Thousands of Jews had immigrated to Cuba from Europe and from the Middle East, planning to stay there just long enough to get into the United States. The magic word was "America."

They were all called transients. Some of them waited patiently for visas to immigrate to the United States, and others, more daring, were able to get tourist visas and then stayed illegally in the States. Some traveled first to Canada or Mexico and then traveled by land to the United States while others traveled by sea. Many of the trips by sea ended in disaster and lives were tragically lost. This is the story of one of those families that I met by accident.

The apartment that we lived in for six months in Havana was on the third floor. I had to climb up and go down seventy steps every day. It didn't have a balcony, but we had a large window with a view of the city. At night, looking at all the lights was something spectacular. For me it was a treat since in Israel we rarely had lights. In the kibbutz electricity was costly and we hardly had any lights. When we moved to the city it was World War II and we had to cover the windows at night so the enemy couldn't see us and so we couldn't see lights. Then before we left in 1948, the Arab-Israel war had started, so again we covered the lights.

Our apartment was divided, partly for our personal use and the rest for our tiny clothing factory. On the roof of the building we had facilities where we could wash the clothes, a room with several sinks that carried hot and cold water, and there were poles with wire strings where we hung the clothes to dry. When you looked at the other nearby buildings you could see that every house had similar poles for hanging clothes.

When we moved out, another immigrant family moved into our apartment. We helped them to get the lease and an electrical connection. We also got them a time slot so they could wash and hang their clothes once a week; the facilities were shared by all the tenants in the apartment house.

The family had arrived in Havana from France. Originally, they were from Poland, and were Holocaust survivors. They had been fortunate enough to avoid the concentration camps and had lived secretly on a farm fifty miles outside of Lyon, France. I don't know how they survived the war because they never talked about it, but I know that they carried internal scars that weren't visible.

The family consisted of a father, a mother, and four daughters, ages fourteen to twenty. Their dreams were to be in the United States. The girls all looked like the mother, tall, pale and blond. Their father was also tall and blond and he enjoyed drinking. I don't know if I could call him an alcoholic but he consumed a lot of liquor.

The youngest daughter was enrolled in the same school as I was. I was very jealous of her when I noticed how quickly she learned Spanish, especially since she already spoke French, Polish and German. I, on the other hand, only spoke Hebrew and a little German. I couldn't read or write Roman letters while she could.

Her name was Emma. I don't know if she spelled it "Ema" or "Emma"; the only thing I know was that she always beat me when she wrote her short name on a piece of paper while I was struggling to write "Alejandro." She was tall and looked like a giant compared to me. At school we had a class in ballroom dancing and, though much taller, she was my partner.

I was surprised that she didn't support me when I rebelled against wearing the Star of David on our school uniforms. I thought that being in Europe during World War II and seeing the Jews wearing the Star of David and being taken to concentration camps, she would support me, but she didn't

One day I saw Emma crying and running out of the class. She told me that the teacher had suggested she was a prostitute. While we were studying geometry the teacher, as part of the lesson, asked her if she would rather be a *curva* or a *linea recta*, a curved line or a straight line. "Curve" in Spanish is *curva* while *curva* in Polish means a prostitute. I told her that the teacher hadn't insulted her at all, and tried to cheer her up. But in spite of that she wasn't friendly and she told me, "I don't want to make any friends because very soon I'm leaving for the United States. Every place I stayed before, I made some friends and as soon as I felt comfortable then I had to leave. That is why I don't want your friendship."

The school year ended and I didn't see her for two years after that. When I saw her again I wasn't sure it was her. She looked much older and she had lost her youthful appearance and had on a lot of makeup.

I knew that the local Jewish organization had supported her family for half a year and then they were on their own. The Jewish organization helped every Jewish newcomer. If they needed monetary help they helped them. They got them houses, furniture, clothes, food, doctors and medicine. They even enrolled their children in school and got teachers to teach them Spanish. But after six months the honeymoon was over and they had to find work and support themselves.

As I have mentioned, immigrants to Cuba were not allowed to hold jobs until they were citizens, and that process took five years. The Cuban government was afraid that foreigners would take jobs from native Cubans. However, it wasn't as hard as it seemed because most of the foreigners, being entrepreneurial by nature, opened their own businesses. My parents opened a women's clothing factory. Emma, her sisters and mother worked in a cantina. I was also working on my own, selling wholesale fabrics. I felt that I was a big shot.

At the cantina they had an all-Negro dance band. They were excellent and in big demand because they played slow dances. The cantina was only a camouflage; it was really a brothel. I don't know why my friends and I went to lunch there, the food wasn't good but the music was great and the girls were beautiful to look at. Besides liquors, they sold coffee. They had big black coffee pots and they roasted their own beans; in Cuba, people drank a lot of coffee.

Emma's father was soliciting prostitution for his own wife and daughters in the cantina. He used to consume a lot of liquor and often asked people in the cantina to buy him drinks. But the same time he watched for the safety of his daughters and wife, and he collected their fees.

Usually a prostitute charged two dollars for her services and paid fifty cents to the cantina owner for using the room. But his wife and daughters were in demand and were able to charge five dollars plus a dollar for the use of the room. The customers also had to pay a nurse for a visual health inspection of both the women and themselves. There was always a full-time nurse on duty.

Emma told me that she didn't like her job. Sometimes if she was lucky she would meet a sexual tourist who would stay with her the entire length of his stay. Sometimes he would buy her expensive jewelry and clothes, and as soon as he left she would exchange the goods for dollars. She was still hoping to immigrate to the United States.

In Cuba everyone had nicknames, like *negrito* (black), *blanca* (white), *gordo* (fat) and *flaco* (thin). The Cubans called me *Polaco* (Polish) even though I was from Israel. Jewish people were called *Polaco* or *Turco* (Turkish). Emma's family were called *blancas* since they were white and blond. Sometimes they were also called *Francesas* (French).

The nicknames were for fun and not taken seriously; you didn't have to be very fat to be called *gordo* or very thin to be called *flaco*.

Sometimes I asked Emma's parents if Emma could go to the movies with me and my friends. They only allowed us to go to matinees, since she had to work later. I felt good that her parents let us go, and for a few hours Emma seemed to like a normal kid even though she had said she was avoiding friendship.

My friends and I knew what Emma was doing, but we were careful to never mention her job. When she was with our group she was careful not to become close to any one person. We never invited her to our homes or to our birthday parties. She only joined us when we went to the movies. She never confided in us and we never knew how she felt about us or anything else, for that matter.

Across from the cantina was the Malecon, a wide boulevard that rounded the bay. The waves crashed against the wall that kept the sea from eating away the pavement. My friends and I played tag with the water, walking until a wave crashed, and then we ran from the spray, sometimes right into the street and the oncoming traffic to avoid getting drenched. Emma watched us with envy in her eyes but didn't join in our play.

Sometimes my friends and I went to Chinatown where you could only find Chinese men who had come to Cuba as laborers for the plantations. The reason they had not brought Chinese women was because the government didn't want Asians to reproduce and multiply in Cuba. Later on, some of the Chinese men moved from the plantations to Havana and married local girls. In Cuba there was a saying, "If you want to live well, marry a Chinese man; he will take good care of you."

They opened Chinese restaurants, tourist stores and movie theaters specializing in pornographic films.

Throughout Havana there were many stalls selling foods and drinks of all kinds; fritters, stuffed potatoes, meat pastries, *guarapo* (sugarcane juice), pork sandwiches, peanuts and coffee. Most of the vendors were foreigners since they weren't allowed to be employed until after the five-year waiting period. Most of the foreigners had little money, but they didn't need too much money to open those enterprises. Many saved their money and invested in real estate. In later years, they owned much of the city.

The Turkish or the Sephardic Jews would buy old furniture from Cuban homes, make them look as good as possible, and sell them on the street. That was how they started their businesses, and many ended up eventually opening large stores.

Sometimes I would ask Emma if she could take a break and walk with me on the Malecon and I would buy her some trinkets. Havana was a beautiful city. We walked on the Malecon and I told her, "When Christopher Columbus arrived at the island of Cuba on October 27, 1492, he wrote, 'I have never seen anything so beautiful.' I, too, have never seen such a beautiful town." Emma didn't reply; she only wanted to go to the United States.

She and I both were required to give our parents whatever money we made; mine from selling fabric and her from selling her body in the cantina.

I was surprised to see Emma's family in temple on the holidays. I supposed that if you are a Jew you should practice your religion, even though everyone in the Jewish community knew that the father was the pimp and the wife and girls were prostitutes.

When my family had moved into our apartment we had placed a *mezuzah* on the doorjamb of our apartment. A *mezuzah* is a small parchment inscribed with verses from the Bible. It is rolled up, inserted in a case, and attached to the doorjamb. It was believed that the *mezuzah* possessed protective powers, that it could ward off evil spirits.

In the Bible when the Jews were enslaved in Egypt, God sent ten plagues to convince the Pharaoh to let the Jews go. The *mezuzah* symbolically takes the place of the lamb's blood mark on the doors of Jewish homes, preventing the angel of death from taking the life of the first-born sons.

When we left that apartment we forgot to take our *mezuzah* with us. When we returned to the apartment and asked Emma's father to give us back our *mezuzah* he became very angry with us and kicked us out of the apartment.

Now that I am older I understand that my parents were wrong for asking a Jewish family to return a *mezuzah*, since the tradition is to pass it from family to family, and even though we brought it from Israel with us, it now belonged to the new residents of the apartment.

When Emma's family applied for tourist visas to the United States, the U.S. Immigration Service asked them to show their bank statements and asked them to show how they supported themselves. It didn't take a brain surgeon to figure out that if they worked in the cantina it was as prostitutes. Their visa applications were stamped, "Undesirable." After living in Cuba for three and half years they returned to France.

At that time, as a young man, I never spoke with my parents about how they earned their living. Even now, I ask myself why the parents had chosen prostitution as a way of life and why the local Jewish population had allowed them to sink so low.

<hr />

Fifty years later when I went back to Cuba with some of my friends, we decided to search for my old apartment house. The night before we began looking I hardly slept because I was worried about being disappointed. But the next day I shouted, "That is it."

I remembered the *mezuzah* and wondered if it was still on the doorjamb.

The building was all rundown. It needed a good cleaning and new paint. In fact all the buildings in Havana seemed to be in need of paint and repairs; hurricanes, rain, sun and salt water, together with a lack of maintenance, had gradually damaged them. My old building looked no better. Several windows were broken and the glass had been replaced by cardboard. At the stairs none of the lights were working because the residents had taken the light bulbs because they needed them in their own apartments.

So far, since I had returned to Havana, it seemed ghost-like. My parents' garment stores and factory had disappeared. The whole shopping center that used to be there didn't exist anymore. It was as though the earth had opened its mouth and swallowed it. The schools that I had gone to weren't there any more. The movie theaters, the restaurants and the cantina that Emma worked in were gone. There was nothing there that I could say was mine.

Now, as I climbed the stairs to the third floor, I remembered the *mezuzah* and wondered if it was still on the doorjamb. I said, "yes" on the first level. On the second level I told myself there wasn't a *mezuzah*. On the third I told myself maybe there was a *mezuzah*. To calm myself I started to pray, even though I wasn't wearing the obligatory hat.

To my surprise the *mezuzah* was still hanging right where we had left it. It was ours; I recognized the Hebrew word *Shaddai* written on the *mezuzah*. It was the original one that we had brought from Israel in 1948. Tears began to flow from my eyes. What a shock! A *mezuzah* where we had left it fifty years ago!

It was made of olive wood and it was well preserved, with not even a crack in spite of its age. It looked proud to be there.

I thought I could explain the situation to the current tenant, offer him a few dollars and perhaps he would allow me to take back our *mezuzah*. Then I could have something to show all my family and friends where I had lived, even though I had only lived in that apartment house for six months. I was so pleased with my discovery that I went to the unscarred door, banged upon it rather rudely, and watched it open slowly.

I saw a mature man behind the door. He was short, slim, dark with a mustache, and he wore a Star of David. He smiled and asked me in Spanish, "Can I help you?" I couldn't open my mouth because I was choking. I was crying, tears were running down my cheeks. Then I took a breath of air and I told him that I and my family were the original tenants of this apartment, and I was surprised to see it still there.

Then he surprised me by asking if my name was Modena and if we'd had a ladies' dress factory. I told him we had. He stepped inside for a moment and brought out a record book and showed me that all the tenants that had lived in this apartment were Jews. He told me that the apartment had become, in turn, a brothel, a beauty parlor, a Hebrew school and was now his. I asked him what he did and he told me that he was a policeman.

Then he surprised me again by asking, "Do you want your *mezuzah*?"

I was overwhelmed by mixed emotions. I thought about how the *mezuzah* had endured all those changes and how it seemed to belong there.

I told him, "No, you keep it." Then I asked, "Is it hard to keep the Jewish faith?"

He replied, "Yes and no. We don't have any prayer books but what we learned we recited by heart. We don't have candles for the Hanukah menorah so we pour cooking oil and we light it. We don't have *matzot* for Passover so we make our own bread."

I leaned forward and kissed him on the cheek, and quickly handed him some money before he could protest. I told him I was happy to have met him, and to keep up his good work. I felt good about myself and thought how good it was to be a Jew and to find a home that signified, by a small object beside the door, that it was a Jewish home, in good hands, keeping the faith...and at least in this small and modest space, all was well.

# Chapter Thirty-Three, Gua-Gua

One must be a Cuban and live in its largest city, Havana, to know and appreciate what *gua-gua* means. The year was 1950 and Havana was noisy and congested with people and vehicles. The smell of gasoline fumes was everywhere.

Why did we need that? Our main form of transportation had been electric streetcars that were very, very slow, and they reflected the slowness of life in Cuba. Before cars and buses many of the older people spent the whole day on the electric street cars. They often had nothing to do and traveling was their amusement. The air was fresh and clean and they even took naps while riding. But that was the past. Now we had *gua-guas*. They were huge buses and they were masters of the roads. Besides the drivers there were conductors who collected the money and helped you to leave or enter the bus.

To Cuban ears *gua-gua* was an awful sound. It wasn't a warm sound, it was not even Spanish. If we look in a Spanish dictionary the word doesn't exist, but it was so much a part of lives that you heard it in our daily conversations. "The *gua-gua* does this" and "The *gua-gua* does that." If I came late to an appointment, I blamed it on the *gua-gua*. I told them, "The *gua-gua* broke down," or "The *gua-gua* never came."

After searching, I found out what *gua-gua* really means and how we got that word. You see, Cuba was a poor country and we inherited the buses from Peru. Peru is populated primarily with Indians and *gua-gua* means a young child or a baby in their dialect. When Cuba received the buses there were signs on them that read "*Gua-gua libre*," which meant a free bus ride for children. The Cuban government was not as generous to the children as the

Peruvians were; anybody who rode the bus, regardless of his age, had to pay a fee. So the Cubans removed the part of the signs that said *libre* and kept the part that said *gua-gua*, and that is how the Cuban buses got their name.

But the word *gua-gua* has many other meanings. When referring to a beautiful girl it can mean, "Wow! What a gorgeous chick!" and when referring to a male it also means a gorgeous-looking guy.

I used to take the bus to school with my friends from Vedado, a suburb of Havana, into Old Havana. The bus trip took forty-five minutes, by taxi twenty and walking took an hour and half. We saw several young girls from other schools who flirted with us. Some of my friends asked me, "Alejandro, what would you do if one of the girls sat next to you?" I was very bashful and I never sat down on the bus for fear of a girl sitting close to me.

My friends teased me and asked me, "Did you ever kiss a girl?"

I replied, "Of course I did."

"Who?" they asked me.

"You don't know her." I evasively replied.

"Did you ever touch her tits?"

I was getting annoyed by their questions and I told them that I had slept with her.

They asked me, "Was she the maid?" but I didn't answer. I didn't want to talk to them about my private life. I was only fourteen years old. I was going to a prep school, studying for my high school entrance examination. I was wearing my navy blue slacks, a white cotton shirt and a navy blue tie and looked very sharp for my age. By my uniform everybody knew what school I went to.

One day I saw a beautiful girl on the bus. She wore a maroon skirt, white blouse and maroon tie. By her uniform I knew which school she went to. She was a brunette with sparkling green eyes. She seemed about my age. She always went to a seat in the back of the bus, near to where I was.

I cursed myself for being so timid, and I blamed the *gua-gua* as well. Here I had the chance to talk to one of the prettiest girls I had even seen and I was speechless. You see, I rationalized that if I was sitting in one of the old electric streetcars I could speak and hear her better. Also, on the electric streetcars, musicians had been given free rides and would entertain the passengers. For a few coins a boy could ask them to serenade a young girl, but before they started to sing they would ask the girl if she would accept a song from one of her admirers. They usually introduced the boy to the girl by singing his name and, as part of the song, asked her if she would like to have a cup of coffee with him or stroll in the park. That is how a romance started

If she accepted the song, I would know what my chances were to go out with this young girl. But in my case we were now on a *gua-gua* and they didn't allow musicians or solicitors because they were afraid that when the bus went fast the musicians could fall and hurt themselves.

So when they eliminated the streetcars it made my life sadder, but I couldn't stop progress. Neither could I keep my childhood; I was growing up.

Months passed and it was the week of St. Valentine's Day. I kept seeing that same girl on the bus but still was afraid to talk to her. On Valentine's Day, she had a rose and I wondered who the lucky guy was who had given it to her.

It was afternoon and we were traveling home on the bus when all of a sudden the bus driver screeched to a halt at an intersection. He had almost hit a pedestrian. She was headed toward to an ice cream store. She was a chunky mulatto, about 5'6" tall and the color of iced coffee with milk. Her green eyes widened when she saw the bus almost hitting her. She was almost naked. She wore a pair of Levi shorts, a skimpy flowered blouse and white sandals that showed her red polished toenails.

The bus driver screamed "Mama mia, what a *gua-gua*!" Then he suddenly turned around and shouted to us passengers, "I've found the woman of my life and I am leaving you." Just like that, he jumped out of the driver's seat and ran over to the ice cream store where he bought two ice cream cones and gave one to her. We could overhear what he was saying, and he told her "I will sweet you and you will sweet me." We noticed that she took the ice cream cone and was licking it. The driver kept talking on and on with no apparent result. But all of a sudden the woman started laughing and shouted to us that he wasn't coming back to the bus. I guess he had traded a four-wheel *gua-gua* for a two-legged one.

The conductor told us that he didn't know how to drive. Several of us leaned out the open windows and begged the driver to come back. But he and the saucy woman kept licking their ice cream cones and walking away.

Then, as if there weren't enough surprises already, that beautiful girl that I had been eyeing for months came up to me and gave me her rose. She must have thought that I was a *gua-gua*, or maybe it was the mood created by the driver's sudden romance. Then she asked me, "Would you like to go to a donut house and have a cup of coffee with me? I'm treating you." I blushed furiously and thought, "What a girl!" She had *approached me* instead of waiting for me to approach her. I guess the *gua-gua* wasn't as bad as I had thought because you could still find romance on board.

Meanwhile, we still didn't have a driver and all a sudden, from the back of the bus a woman passenger stepped forward and drove the bus until she got to her stop. Then another passenger replaced her and drove to his stop.

The girl and I finally reached our destination and we went together for coffee and donuts, where we talked long into the night. I was soooo grateful to the bus driver; if he hadn't left the bus, perhaps she wouldn't have given me the rose and I would have never had the chance to get to know her. Our romance lasted for six months and then we split up. As it turned out, her assertiveness in approaching me was typical of her assertiveness in all aspects of her life, and in the end it proved too much for me.

But such was life in Havana in 1950, with its many surprises and unexpected twists and turns. It was a great experience, and a part of me, to this day, is still a *Cubano*.

# Chapter Thirty-Four, Diabetes

Superstition and ignorance almost caused the loss of my life. My mother had been trained as a doctor and she readily gave advice to strangers and scolded them for not taking good care of their children and themselves. But, astoundingly, in my own case, she succumbed to superstition and shame.

The year was 1951 and I was devastated. For the second time I had failed my exam to go to high school. I couldn't deceive my friends about it because the names of those who passed were published in the local newspaper, but they did not publish the names of those who failed. For several days I was melancholic and wondered what I did wrong; was I just plain stupid or had God punished me, and if so, why?

At that same time I learned, through overhearing hushed conversations between my father and mother, that two male cousins of mine in Chicago had been diagnosed with diabetes.

I asked my mother, "What is diabetes? How do you know when you get it?"

"Sha, sha, don't waste your time talking about this," my mother replied.

In 1951, in Cuba, nobody talked about this killer disease. If you knew somebody who had it you kept away from that person–you didn't want to catch it. On top of that it was considered shameful to have diabetes.

It seemed logical to me that if my cousins had this disease, maybe I should be tested for it. But my parents avoided the subject, and my mother in particular was ashamed that members of her side of the family had it. My mother told me, "If you have it and you don't talk about it, it will go away." This from my medically-trained mother! She told me never to even mention the word. The only reason I could think of for this was maybe because treatment for the disease was very expensive and our clinic wouldn't or couldn't provide care.

Around that time I had been drinking a liter of Coke every day and I still was thirsty. The more I drank the more I was thirsty. I drank and I went to the bathroom. After I drank a liter of Coke I ran to the bathroom to urinate. I noticed that my urine smelled sweet; also, I was experiencing severe headaches, I felt constantly tired and I was losing weight.

I wondered what was wrong. I was only sixteen years old but I was acting like an old man.

Even though I was forbidden to talk about it at home, I became fascinated by the subject. I went to the library and I whispered to the librarian, "Do you have books about diabetes?"

The answer was, "No."

In our neighborhood of Havana we had a clinic where doctors and nurses practiced medicine. I went there and asked them if they had books about diabetes and the answer was, again, "No." The only place where I could find information about the disease was in the local pharmacy because they sold insulin and they had literature about the disease and how the medicine was used to treat it. I discovered that there were two kind of diabetes, childhood and adult. At that time in Cuba in 1951 the only test available was a urine test.

When I talked about it with my friends they called me a hypochondriac. I didn't care. I was looking at the symptoms and I had them all: thirstiness, frequent urination, visual problems, loss of weight, feeling tired, itchy, dry skin and wounds that didn't heal easily.

In spite of my parents, I was determined to prove to myself whether or not I had the disease. I saved my allowance for ten weeks and then bought the test from the pharmacy. There was enough material for several tests. I took some of my friends and we went to the bathroom and I gave the samples to the pharmacist. The result was that all the other kids' urine was normal but mine had very high sugar.

I was diabetic, and I was afraid to tell my parents.

Diabetes, diabetes, diabetes, diabetes, diabetes! How I came to hate the word.

Where we had lived in Israel, both Jews and Arabs alike were superstitious. When we came to Cuba, it was no different. Instead of seeing doctors, the Cubans visited *curanderos*, the equivalent of witch doctors. I went to see one. He told me to eat a lot of ice cream and the ice cream would freeze the sugar and my body would get rid of it. This advice was given after I paid him my allowance for ten whole weeks! After trying the ice cream diet I didn't feel better, I just felt very stupid.

I still thought God had a hand in it. I went to the synagogue every day before school and I prayed to God. I negotiated with him. If he would cure me I would worship him and go to the synagogue every day for the rest of my life. But my symptoms remained. Praying helped me emotionally, but I soon realized that I had to take care of myself.

I knew that I had committed a sin a year ago when I had first gone to a brothel, and that I was still going there. I knew I hadn't gotten diabetes from the prostitutes but I thought that maybe God had punished me because I hadn't saved myself for the woman that I was going to marry.

Besides my undiagnosed diabetes, at that time I had several attacks of appendicitis; that is what probably saved my life. When I went to the hospital to have my appendix removed, the doctors tested me and told my parents that I had diabetes. I was insulin-dependent, with childhood diabetes.

My mother still would not admit I was diabetic. She was afraid to talk about it and didn't allow me to correspond with my cousins in Chicago to find out how they were being treated. It could have been a great help as well as a support for the three of us.

Although not medically trained, my father was more enlightened. He took me to the pharmacy and had the pharmacist teach me how to inject myself with insulin. After two or three months, I was able to take care of myself. Then I found out that the pharmacist was stealing some of my insulin. His daughter admitted to me that he was giving her shots from my insulin supply in order to have her gain weight. After that I went to another pharmacy and stored my insulin at home.

Beside taking insulin and following a strict diet, my father enrolled me in a swimming club. Perhaps it was my astrological sign, Pisces, the Fish, but I quickly achieved mastery in this sport and my bedroom became full of swimming trophies. Practically every week I competed and I won. At sixteen, I was already a well-known swimmer in Cuba.

Diabetes did not cripple me. Instead, it gave me a new outlook on life. I volunteered at school and gave lectures about diabetes. I helped the nurses screen the other students for the disease. I couldn't believe how much obesity was in our school and what a high rate of diabetes existed there. Neither the parents or the students did anything about it.

And still, my mother refused to talk to me about it.

I was lucky that in Cuba there were bakeries that baked with saccharine for heart patients. I was able to buy those loaves for myself. Also, many of the restaurants didn't use sugar in their cooking; they used saccharine for people who were on a diet. Today we know that saccharine increases cancer risk and it is not on the market, but back then it was a godsend.

Once my friends found out about my disease, I became a kind of celebrity. They protected me from fighting because they were afraid that I would bleed to death. I took advantage of it. If I came late, they excused me. If I didn't have any money and I told them that I was going to faint from low blood sugar they would buy me fruit. I took advantage of their generosity and concern and I didn't mind doing it.

After all of this, my mother still refused to talk to me about my diabetes. In later years I made peace with her, but I still don't and probably never will understand how her superstition and prejudice could so blind her to caring for her own son.

# Chapter Thirty-Five, Soccer

Baseball was the number one sport when I lived in Cuba. Every child dreamed of having a baseball glove, bat and a baseball. In some places in Havana, the kids were so poor that they couldn't afford to buy a baseball or a bat or glove, but they still played "baseball." For a bat they used any stick that they could find; usually a broken broom handle or something similar. The ball they used was made of old cigarette cartons. They put the cartons together, one on top of each other and folded them until they made a ball. They played without gloves since they didn't have any, and the carton ball wasn't too hard. They could play for hours. They hoped that they would become good enough to play professionally. If they were that good an American team would help them immigrate to the United States.

However I wasn't any good at playing baseball and I didn't care for it. Soccer was a different thing. Back in Palestine, sometimes my father took me to a park and we played together. We usually kicked the ball back and forth to each other. We didn't have to talk, we knew what each one of us was going to do. It was just like magic. My father was the best. Even though he was still limping from his war injuries, I couldn't take the ball away from him. He showed me how to balance and control the ball without using my hands. I learned to use my feet, head, legs and chest. He told me, "Alex, the ball is just like a bride and you are the groom. Don't ever let somebody take her from you."

When I was playing soccer I shone. This was my game and nobody was going to take it away from me. I joined a league and my team was pretty good. My boss's son, Israel, was on another team in the league. One day our teams faced each other and I played against him. Israel's parents were there, with Israel's sister, my girlfriend, Lupe. I wondered if she was going to cheer for me or for her brother.

Both my parents were there watching me play. The other fathers were shouting and giving advice to their children, but my father was very calm and I knew that whatever I did he would be proud of me. Soccer was our game.

From the first moment that we started playing the game my team had control of the ball. We passed the ball and several times we shot the ball. I couldn't believe that I scored four goals for our team before halftime!

Things were different eleven years ago in Palestine when I started to play soccer. I remember my first game when I faced Ali and his team. Ali was on the green team and I was on the blue team. We were very poor in Palestine and we couldn't afford to buy soccer uniforms or soccer shoes. In Cuba each player on our teams had a uniform and soccer shoes. In Cuba I was on the green team. I wore black soccer shoes, black and green socks, black shorts and a green t-shirt. On each t-shirt our name and number were printed. In Palestine I sometimes had to share my t-shirt and my tennis shoes with other players. We were only five years old then and we played only with nine players on a team and used half the soccer field. In Cuba we were fifteen or sixteen years old, we had eleven players on a team and a full soccer field. Every player owned his own soccer ball. In Palestine we only had two balls, mine and the coach's.

I remember my first game in Palestine. I wasn't aggressive, I was afraid that the ball would hit me. I never stopped the ball and most of the time I was afraid to kick it. Ali, on the other hand, wasn't afraid to hit the ball. At an early age he knew how to stop and kick the ball. When he was playing soccer he was a terror. He would push others and he made sure that he had the ball. He would grind his teeth and make loud noises to frighten his opponents.

The game started and eighteen little kids surrounded the ball, trying to kick it. Finally Ali, after pushing the other kids away, was able to get the ball. He was dribbling the ball forward with his feet and since nobody could stop him he scored the first goal. He repeated it several times. At halftime the score was four to nothing.

Ali's team was in heaven. They were already celebrating their victory. Our team was dejected and at any moment we were going to cry. After our coach's speech we all promised to do better. We started to believe what our coach had told us, that our team was really better.

Ali knew that he could score more goals for his team, but he suddenly pulled off his green t-shirt and put on one of our blue ones. He had decided to switch teams. Both coaches were yelling at Ali but he didn't care, he was going to play for the blue team–he didn't want me to lose. He wanted to tie the game. Both coaches had promised the winning team ice cream.

It was hot and we all were sweating. An ice cream cone would taste great and cool us. With Ali on our team we started to score; one, two, three, four. Ali scored four goals for our blue team. The game ended with the score four to four. Then it was payoff time. Were we all going to get a reward since we had tied the score? Both coaches felt fine with the tied score and bought us all ice cream cones. But ice cream wasn't on Ali's mind when he had switched teams; he cared for our friendship. We both did, and at that moment I knew we were bonded.

Now it was eleven years later and I was in a similar dilemma; but this time I was on the winning team and Israel was on the losing team. Should I exchange t-shirts and try to tie the game? No! Israel and I were never close friends, not like me and Ali. I went for blood. We won, seven to nothing. I played so hard, focused so much on the game that I never did know who Lupe had rooted for.

If Israel and I had been close friends, if we were bonded together like me and Ali, would I have switched sides to help his team win? That was something that little kids might do, but serious teenagers? Not likely.

Was that the difference between then and now? Less concern for friendship and more concern for winning? For years after that, I thought about it every time I played soccer.

# Chapter Thirty-Six, Manuel

"*Mal Ojo, Mal Ojo*," Bad Eye, Bad Eye. That was the curse I heard spoken for years in Cuba. People didn't whisper it, but shouted it. I wondered why people were so cruel to those less fortunate than themselves. They accepted a totally blind man or child and tried to help them, but custom required that anyone with only one good eye was scorned as the Devil's Son.

When I was eighteen years old my parents and I were living in one of the luxurious penthouses in Vedado, a suburb of Havana. After living in Cuba for five years we had been able to become citizens and had also become very financially successful. Our penthouse consisted of two bedrooms, a living room, dining room, family room, a large kitchen, a bathroom and a large balcony. Next to our rooms were the maid's quarters, which consisted of a bedroom and a bathroom.

Our apartment house was in an excellent location. When we were on the balcony we had a perfect view of the city. Our building was a brick building painted light brown. People told us that light colors reflected the sun and heat, and kept the house cooler. It was four floors tall.

We were next to the park and on nice days we often sat on the park benches. The neighborhood was very friendly. In the evening, when it was very hot, some adults sat on the benches drinking beer and others brought folding tables and chairs and played dominoes or chess or checkers. Usually, four people played dominoes. They were the *viejos*, the oldest men in the neighborhood. You could hear the domino chips slapping face down. When a player matched his piece he would shout the domino number or thump domino pieces on the wooden table to intimidate opponents, and erupt in joy after a winning hand. Insults and the occasional fist flew in heated games.

People would bet, and after playing for several hours if you had won a few dollars you were a hero. The older people never let me play with them. They told me that I was too young. The game was traditionally played by men. I did have opportunities to play chess; I had played in Palestine in the kibbutz, but I mastered it in Cuba.

We kids had enough street light to play games outside. The kids played baseball or just hung around and listened to local gossip. We played and stayed out late until it cooled. The parents would yell at the children, "Manuel, Juan, Carlos, Alex, come home!" We shouted back, "We don't want to go home." But finally we all went home and to bed.

Some of the women actually made part of their living spreading gossip. They were called *chismosas* and were proud of their profession. They were sad-looking, old women dressed in dark colored dresses and they were caretakers of many of the apartment houses. They collected rents and made sure that the apartment houses were clean and functioning. For the services that they provided they got a free apartment and a small salary. When they heard some juicy gossip they would try to extort money from the offending individual, threatening to tell the whole town if they weren't paid.

When I lost my virginity, one chismosa tried to blackmail me by threatening to tell my parents, but I wouldn't pay her. She told them, but my parents didn't say a word to me about it.

Across from our building were the local shopping center, a grocery store, a drugstore, a barber shop and a beauty parlor. If we wanted local transportation we could take the bus or get a taxi, since both stations were next to our house.

Our maid, Josefina, didn't sleep on our premises because she was married and had a child. She worked from eight o'clock in the morning to eight o'clock at night, six days a week. She cleaned our house, washed our clothes and made our meals. My mother really liked her because she learned very fast to cook Jewish food. but the most important thing was that we could trust her.

The way my mother met her was that my parents were looking for factory workers. My parents owned ladies' clothing stores and also manufactured ladies' clothes. Josefina couldn't sew and she wanted my mother to teach her to sew. But she was very slow and my mother told her that she wouldn't make enough money since we paid by the piece. Josefina told us that she was willing to iron the dresses but she was very slow at that also. She told us that she was willing to clean the factory and begged us to hire her to do anything we wanted because she had to help her husband support her mother and son.

My mother decided to hire her as a maid. It was a good choice but for me there was a problem, her son, Manuel, who was an irritant to me.

Manuel was seven years old and was small for his age. He had dark skin and Negroid hair. He often wore clothes two sizes too big for him that had been given to Josefina by neighbors, even though my mother gave Josefina extra money to buy him clothes and shoes. Josefina didn't buy Manuel clothes and shoes; she gave the extra money to the church.

Most of the time Manuel stayed with his grandmother, but sometimes his mother would bring him to our house. When he was at our house he was a pest and I really didn't like him. Manuel wasn't a pleasant child to look at. He had several scars on his face and, worst of all, he had lost his right eye. Sometimes he would take his glass eye out and it was frightening. I wished he wore an eye patch. If I was reading or working or writing letters, he would ask me if I could play with him. He didn't have any friends. Kids were scared of him and were superstitious about the meaning of the missing eyeball. The older kids at school bullied him and called him *Mal Ojo*, Bad Eye. When he was a year old an older boy had poked him in the eye with a stick and that was how he lost his eye.

When Josefina brought Manuel to our house I was uncaring and would yell at her, "Why did you bring Manuel here?" Josefina would reassure me that Manuel would behave.

"Manuel, be good, don't bother Alejandro," she said. One day Manuel broke a ceramic vase that I had made. I was ready to kill him. I yelled at him, "You are a bad boy." Manuel cried and went to the corner of the room and was sitting just like a beaten dog. He hit himself and kept mumbling, "Bad boy, Manuel. Bad boy." My mother told me that I treated dogs better than I treated Manuel and that I should be ashamed of myself. I did feel ashamed, especially since I had just spent Yom Kippur, the Day of Atonement, praying and asking for forgiveness, and then I had mistreated Manuel.

I decided to change and to become a new man. At the temple I saw my friend Emma and her family, and I wondered if they also asked for forgiveness for their prostitution.

When Manuel was hungry, Josefina fed him rice and beans. Once I asked him, "Manuel, tell me, what do you have for breakfast?"

Manuel replied, "Rice and beans."

I asked, "What do you have for lunch?"

Manuel replied, "Rice and beans."

I asked, "And for dinner?"

Manuel replied, "Rice and beans."

I asked him again, "Is this is all that you eat?"

Manuel replied, "What more do I want?"

Once I tried to feed Manuel European food but he got sick and vomited, so I stopped offering him things to eat.

Manuel was slow. Neither his mother nor his father could read or write. He was behind in his speech and development. When he asked me to go to the park he would simply say "Park." When he wanted to play ball he would say "Ball." I would take him to the park and play ball with him. When he caught the ball he would start laughing. He was so happy that somebody besides his relatives played with him. I made sure that other kids joined us in the games and played with Manuel. Being with me and going to school, his vocabulary gradually increased and so did his motor skills. After a while he was able to say, "Alejandro, let's go to the park and play ball."

Manuel loved to hear conversation but he didn't listen to words, just to the tone of conversation. When he saw me studying he would ask questions, not to hear the answers but simply to continue the flow of sounds.

"What are you doing, Alejandro?" Manuel asked.

"I am studying." I replied.

"What are you studying?" Manuel asked.

"I am studying for a test."

"What is a test?"

Manuel, who simply wanted to hear talk, had developed a system of making the answer to one question the basis of another. It kept conversation going. When *I asked him* a question, though, he left the room.

At first I had disliked Manuel but slowly I started to like him. I saw that he would fight for things he wanted, and that he wanted to be loved and accepted. But people in our community were superstitious and called him *Mal Ojo*, "Bad Eye." Since having one eye meant he was the Devil's son, they tried to keep away from him. They believed that the Devil had sent him to earth and they also believed that, being the Devil's Son, he had magical powers and that he was a witch.

Sometimes I felt bad for Manuel and I told him that he wasn't the Devil's Son, he had just had a terrible accident and he should learn to accept his misfortune without superstition.

Four or five weeks before Easter, on Saturday and Sunday, the Cubans celebrated Carnival. Carnival is a time for great merriment and fun throughout the island. On Saturday the *comparsas*, the dancers, took part and on Sunday the floats were paraded. Carnival was the beginning of Lent. The name "Carnival" is from the Latin phrase *carne vale*, which means "farewell to meat." During Lent, Christians remember the forty days that Jesus spent in the wilderness.

The *comparsas* were groups of dancers whose tradition dated back several centuries when black slaves held collective marches and dances to commemorate the days of Corpus Christi and the Epiphany. Those long-ago dancers may have been dancing a form of rhumba, mambo or cha-cha.

There were many dance groups in the Cuban capital. In Cuba, where Carnival is taken very seriously, people spend all year designing and making wonderful costumes. Often, the costumes are so elaborate that the people wearing them hardly dare move to avoid spoiling the effect. Each group had its own colorful customs.

In our neighborhood we had one called *Los Hijos de Belen*, The Children from Bethlehem. Their costumes were made of royal blue and white satin. The girls wore long, royal blue satin skirts with white ruffles and white tops. The boys wore royal blue satin slacks and white tops with ruffles. Every group had its own band, with trumpets and drummers playing conga drums.

Our group had rehearsed all year long in the local church. My parents donated the material and laborers to make the costumes. Every group had a female flag bearer accompanied by a male dancer. The flag bearer was traditionally the youngest girl of the group. The parades along the main street in Havana also included *munecones*, which are large dolls, and *faroleros*, dancers who carry a multicolored accessory resembling a streetlight, making it rotate constantly.

Carnival was fun and everyone was excited. The people were on the streets dancing and singing songs. Extravagant, colorful costumes were an important part of Carnival. On the main street you could find vendors that sold food and cold drinks, like beer and rum. The vendors sold cotton candies, ice cream, cakes, pizzas, ham or cheese sandwiches, sweets and bags of confetti. You could also find vendors that sold firecrackers–legal and illegal.

On Sunday the floats appeared. They were carried on *carros alegoricos, special*, large trucks pulled by decorated tractors. All floats carry singing and dancing individuals, all wearing costumes. Most float riders threw candies to the crowd. Most of the floats advertised products like Coca-cola, Pepsi-cola, Pan American Airline, etc.

My father and mother sat on one of the bleachers that had been erected. The kids, which consisted of Lupe, Israel and me, sat by ourselves not too far from the adults. Lupe and Israel were brother and sister and were my best friends, and I thought that I would eventually marry Lupe. We saw Emma with an older man who could have been her grandfather. I guessed she had a steady customer. Lupe didn't like Emma, and when she saw me greet her it made Lupe angry.

Our maid, Josefina, and her family were also celebrating Carnival. They were on the street just like us, taking part in the festival. Manuel loved to play with firecrackers and he looked very happy. He was running with sparklers and waving them in the air. The brighter and noisier things were, the better he liked it.

I was watching Manuel when all of a sudden a firecracker that had been thrown into the air hit his good eye and exploded! I was the first one to rush to him. He was holding his eye and crying. His mother ran up to him and, after a few moments, was able to get him to remove his hand from his eye. Manuel looked around and screamed, "Mami, I cannot see! I am blind!"

A doctor arrived and did a cursory examination. It was enough to determine the firecracker had burned his good eye. I watched, amazed, as his mother kissed him and told him how lucky he was now that he was blind.

Manuel's teeth were chattering but he was able to speak. "Mami, I am blind, I cannot see. Did God take my good eye?"

Josefina replied, "Yes, God took your good eye. You should thank him."

These things were beyond Manuel. He said, "Thanks, God, for taking my good eye."

The following day mother and child went to church to thank God for the miracle. That is, Josefina considered the loss a miracle. Manuel was only a little boy and now he could not see at all. Life was much easier with one eye than with none.

Josefina told Manuel, "Everybody loves a blind man but not a man with one eye. Now when you die you are going to heaven. You are one of God's children."

Meanwhile it was still Carnival. People were decorating the church and it was filled with color. They were twisting and stringing blue, orange, yellow, green and red crêpe paper. There were candles lit, and food appeared. Everybody was celebrating not only Carnival but the "miracle" of Manuel. He was a hero. He was blind. But you could see from the way he acted that he had a lot of pain from the injury.

On the other hand I was very, very sad. People asked me why. They told me this that this was a party, a party for Manuel. The whole neighborhood was celebrating the miracle.

I felt surrounded by ignorant, superstitious people but I couldn't say anything like that. Their belief was very real for them. It was part of Cuban folkloric tradition, taken from the Afro-Cuban religion called *Santeria*.

Manuel was seated on a stage in the middle of the church. The congregation danced around him until several dancers swooned and fell into a trance. The people believed now that Manuel was blind *he had the power to heal them.* Josefina, his mother, was happy and proud because this was partly her day–for she had given birth to Manuel. It was hard to tell how Manuel's father felt; he was drunk and had passed out.

Manuel was tired of all the commotion and attention, and he fell asleep in the middle of the stage, while the dancing continued for a long time.

# Chapter Thirty-Seven, E. H.

I'm not sure of the year…maybe it was 1953 or 1954 and I was eighteen or nineteen years old. One of the things I recall about that time was a long sofa and the strange guest who came to use it. But before I tell that I have to explain where the sofa was and why it was there.

I had just opened my own children's clothing shop called "Little Red Riding Hood." It was in the most expensive shopping center in Havana, called *La Rampa* (the ramp) because it was underground, located underneath the Hotel Nacional. There were thirty or forty shops in the shopping center. The main customers were tourists who stayed at the hotels around the shopping center. The store was open six days a week and was closed on Sunday because Cuba was a Catholic country and no one went anyplace except to church.

My parents had a garment factory close to my store where they manufactured the children's clothing that I sold. I was young and very energetic and enjoyed working at my store. I had the top clientele coming to my store and had two saleswomen who were older than me. My salesladies wore all white clothes in the summer and black skirts and white blouses in the winter. Besides selling and taking care of the store, they crocheted baby sweaters and girls' handbags. I also had a security guard who screened my customers before they could enter the store. If they weren't tip-top in appearance he wouldn't let them in. I guess I was a snob but I could afford to be one since I had more customers than I could handle.

My store was long and narrow, forty-six feet by twenty feet. It was very interestingly decorated. At the entrance of the store the wall was covered with three-dimensional pictures of Little Red Riding Hood. The first picture was Little Red Riding Hood with her mother; the second picture was Little Red Riding Hood walking in the woods with a basket; the third picture was the mean wolf with his fangs dripping saliva; and the fourth picture was the wolf in bed, wearing a nightgown with glasses, with Little Red Riding Hood standing next to him.

The pictures were colorful and made one feel as if they were actually in Disneyland with the characters.

There was a dressing room at the end of the store that was painted like a forest, with trees and pictures of rabbits and chipmunks and other forest animals. The whole wall where the pictures were hanging was a landscape of forest trees and animals, and contained large cuckoo clocks of many different varieties which fascinated the children. They were custom made in Switzerland and each one was one-of-a-kind.

My store also had an exclusive line of Spanish and Italian dolls. I stocked matching dresses for both the children and the dolls that were very popular with wealthy tourists and local people. I had the largest selection of petticoats available anywhere on the island. Any girl who wore one immediately felt like a princess. Once a month I held a fashion show in the mall. Local children modeled our clothes. In addition to being supplied by my parents' factory, I used to import clothes from the United States, Spain and China, and both tourists and locals attended our shows to see the latest fashions. All of this was great for my business, which was thriving.

At the entrance of the store there was a desk where I kept my books, and a cabinet for the cash register. There were four mannequins in the showroom window and behind them was a leather sofa. The sofa was very long, consisting of ten cushions that could be separated individually. The sofa was brown and was a perfect match for the forest decor on the walls. It was there to allow parents and other family members to relax while they watched their children parade in the new outfits

The significance of the sofa to this story? I'm getting to it.

Across from my store were the restrooms. They weren't a hindrance but a benefit for my business because when people came to use the restrooms they noticed my store.

Next to my store was a children's barbershop that also attracted exclusive clientele. The owner was an excellent barber who had a special way with little ones that kept them calm and happy while he was doing their hair. But while his shop had extra chairs for waiting customers, his shop didn't have a sofa.

Besides my children's store there was another children's store nearby owned by the famous Cuban singers, Olga and Tony. This store carried duplicates of the clothes that the artists wore when they were performing, which were authentic Cuban costumes. They didn't have a sofa either. In fact, my store was the only one in my part of the shopping center that *did* have a long sofa.

But with all the security in our complex, I wondered how a bum could be lying on my sofa. He was over six feet tall and must have weighed over three hundred pounds. He was fat and flabby and his large stomach hung over his belt. He wore dirty khaki shorts and a long-sleeve khaki shirt, a safari vest and sandals. He was filthy from head to toe and his breath smelled of liquor. His eyes had bags under them as though he never slept, and his beard was gray and scraggly.

After I noticed him for the first time, I saw that it was five minutes to twelve and we were ready to close the shop for two hours for lunch and siesta. Nobody had stopped the bum from entering; not my security guard, neither of the two salesladies or any of the shopping center guards

Then I learned that one of my salesladies knew him and that "he was all right." Of course I was concerned that his presence would scare away my customers, but I was also fascinated by him. Later, when we struck up a conversation, I became even more fascinated. We went out together for coffee and I learned there were many parallels between his life and my own. We had both been wounded and were survivors...perhaps of different events but with the same emotional aftermath. There was a closeness between us that you can only feel when you both experience similar, traumatic events. He told me that in the First World War he had volunteered for the Red Cross Ambulance Corps in Italy. One day he rode his bicycle to deliver chocolates and cigarettes to the Italian soldiers. Suddenly the Austrians opened up with a mortar attack and hit him. His face and legs were full of machine gun wounds and mortar fragments. He was left with scars on his face, arms and legs.

I, too, had scars on my face, arms and legs. In 1948, just before Israel declared independence, my parents had sent me to the kibbutz for safekeeping from the impending Iraqi attack. I told my best friend, Ali, to come visit me and he came with a hand grenade and left me with scars, both physical and emotional, that I carry to this day..

We both had scars on our faces. I didn't try to hide mine. I thought he tried to hide his by wearing a beard. He had an obvious limp. I had only pain in my knees when the weather was cold; living in Cuba was the ideal climate for me to live with my wounds.

Sometimes we had lunch at a restaurant-bar which was in the shopping center. We enjoyed each other's company. He used to tease me that I would never be able to handle liquor and I would never have a girl friend. He preferred to speak to me in English rather than Spanish. He spoke fluent Spanish but he spoke it with an American accent and you knew he was a gringo. Strange as it sounds, after all this time together I had never asked his name.

When we ate together I always told him stories. I amused him with stories of my adventures with Ali in Palestine. He encouraged me to start writing stories. I started to write and I let him read my stories. I had a notebook where I wrote my first story, "Janine."

He asked me, "Who is Janine?"

I replied, "I thought she was my girlfriend."

He criticized me by telling me that this wasn't a Cuban name. I should call the girl Maria or Helena or Margarita or Linda, but not Janine. I replied, "This is my story, and I can call the girl anything I want."

He said, "Keep reading."

"Janine was a blond with green eyes."

"Stop it!" he said. "Where did you find such a girl? Cuban girls have dark skin like cinnamon, black or brown eyes and black hair."

"In Havana," I said heatedly and I continued reading. "Her hair was long and loose. I knew that when God made her she was perfect. Her nose was in the middle of her face, her eyes were in the right position even though they were always searching and you had to reassure her that they were in the right location. The same were the ears that were listening, and you had to reassure her that they didn't have to change places with the eyes. The mouth was always talking, wondering if it was in the right spot. But when I looked at her, in spite of all that I knew she was contented."

"Cubans have Negro hair which isn't long, but curly," he said, looking at me.

I read, plaintively, "Janine was my life, my love, my whole world."

He looked at me and said, "No women are contented. They always complain to you about something." He had been drinking steadily and I thought he was drunk.

I described Janine wearing a loose dress and I was able to see her breasts.

"Wrong again, Cuban girls wear girdles and they are very tight. Their waists are very small, they have large hips and no way can you see their breasts."

I told him, "Just correct the English and spelling–it's my story!"

Facing me dramatically he said, "Look at you!" He used hand gestures for emphasis. "You are blond with green eyes and you see the whole world with blond hair and green eyes." Then he pointed his finger at me. "You think that is beautiful. Look at the Cuban girls; they are exquisite, but different from you."

I didn't finish my meal. I was frustrated and felt intimidated, and I left him. Before I left, for homework he told me to write one hundred words describing a beautiful girl.

I didn't realize how hard it was to do that. Here are some of my adjectives: bright, lovely, honest, reasonable, gorgeous, grand, ravishing, glorious, stunning, brilliant, divine, holy, supernatural, pretty, beautiful, godlike, heavenly, celestial, transcendent, utopian, paradisaical, nice, good, fair, lovely, charming, handsome, attractive, graceful, elegant, excellent, fine, etc.

Next day we went to lunch again. I wasn't hungry and I ordered a cup of coffee. I also asked for a glass of ice to pour the coffee into. That was how I made iced coffee. My friend ordered his usual: a hamburger and a bottle of rum. I started to read my story.

"I remember the first time I saw the young girl in a bakery store. I didn't know her name. I thought I heard the baker call her

Janine. What an usual name, but I believe the name suited her. She was eating a powdered sugar donut. The powdered sugar was on her dress and I wanted to dust it. Maybe I could feel her breasts."

"Excuse me," he interrupted, "and where did you find donuts? In Cuba we don't have donuts, only *pan dulce* (sweet bread.)"

"Who cares?" I said. "She was spilling the powdered sugar on her dress. She was biting the sweet bread and I wanted to kiss her. She was absolutely beautiful."

I noticed that he hadn't touched the hamburger but he had drunk half a bottle of rum. I asked him if he was going to eat the hamburger. He replied, "We can share it."

I continued reading. "When she finished eating the sweet bread. I noticed that she was looking at me. I bought some loaves of bread and some crackers and I left the bakery. I hated myself that I didn't have the courage to talk to her. I told myself I was seventeen years old and I was the only person who didn't have a girlfriend. I probably would up end being an old, unmarried man."

He laughed at me and was about to make another comment when one of my salesladies came to the restaurant to tell me that they needed me at the store, that we were busy. I thanked my friend for the half hamburger and I told him I would see him tomorrow.

Tomorrow arrived and I didn't see him. Several days passed and I didn't see him. I started to worry about him. I wanted him to finish reading my story and tell me if it was any good. Then once again he came and we went to lunch together. With the hamburgers in front of us, with my iced coffee and his rum, I started reading the story,

"Every week I came to the bakery and when I saw her I never had the courage to talk to her. We were both looking at each other, wanting to start talking but we lost our voices. One day I dropped my bag of breads in front of her. She picked it up and gave it to me. I felt her hand and it was warm and soft. I thanked her and she laughed. She asked me why it had taken so long for me to speak to her. We spent an hour talking, laughing, and promised each other to meet in the next week. I couldn't wait to see her again."

My friend was drinking and was quiet; he didn't correct my English. This time when I started reading the story, tears were in my eyes. I was choking with emotion and I needed to clear my throat. "Finally I had the courage to take Janine to the movies. It was early in the afternoon, because if it was later Janine probably would get in trouble. In the theater there were very few people. We sat on the side of the theater where people wouldn't notice us."

The old man told me, "Very good, but get to it, get on with what happens."

I continued, "When we sat down at the movie theater I held Janine's hand and I was dying to hug her. Finally I had the courage to put my arm around her shoulder. She didn't mind and as a matter of fact she encouraged me. She smelled so good I almost fainted from the combination of nervousness and desire. Being in love was wonderful. Everything about her felt good. I wanted to kiss her. My lips were ready, but I was afraid if I kissed her she would run away and I would never see her again. I told myself that I was doing fine and I shouldn't rush."

The old man interrupted and told me, "Why didn't you rush? You are such a baby. Women love when you are fresh and aggressive."

I ignored him. "While she was watching the movie I was watching her. She looked like a Viking princess. She sat straight like an aristocrat. When the movie finished she asked me what time it was. I told her and she looked nervous. I kissed her cheek. It took enormous courage for me to do that. She looked shocked as we left the theater, and I took her to the bakery store where every week we met. She gave me a kiss on my cheek and told me not to follow her. We said goodbye and we parted."

My friend started talking again "You probably want to know what I am thinking about this story. I tell you, what is the point of this story? I have heard the same story a million times."

I was getting impatient. "Let me finish telling you the story."

"Go ahead, who is stopping you?" When he finished talking to me he poured another glass of rum and drank it. I thought he was drinking it straight but he mixed it with soda.

I started reading again. "I let her go ahead of me and I was dying to find out where she lived. Once again we went to the movie and I asked to kiss her. I felt since I had bought the tickets to the movie and the refreshments I deserved a kiss. She was very cooperative and she seemed willing to please me. I knew that she was falling in love with me. At the same time I was concerned because no decent Cuban girl would go out with a guy without a chaperone. She told me that I was her first boyfriend and she felt great being with me. She told me that she was planning to go to business school and become a bookkeeper. I asked her if I could visit her home. She told me no, since she was only seventeen years old and her parents would never let her go out with a boy. I understood, and I was happy with our relationship. The more I went out with her I wanted to see her more often. Once a week wasn't enough for me. Kissing her felt great; her lips on mine were unbelievably sweet.

One day I got the courage to follow her. I made sure that she didn't see me. I saw her entering a brothel. I was shocked! I couldn't believe that I had fallen in love with a prostitute. I thought there must be some mistake. Finally I entered the brothel and I saw her all dressed up, entertaining older men.

I told myself, "How could I be so stupid?"

The old man looked at me and told me, "Welcome to the real world."

Tears were in my eyes and I scolded him, "What do you mean by telling me, "Welcome to the real world?"

He looked at me and he said, "First love is the most painful. You were looking for something that doesn't exist. Besides, all women are whores."

"Who are you to say such a thing to me?"

"I know. I lived it. You may have read some of the things I've written about it. In all this time you have never asked my name. I am Ernest Hemingway."

And that was how our friendship began.

# Chapter Thirty-Eight, Sugar Cane

The word sugar in Spanish is *azucar*. It was the most loved and hated word that the Cuban citizen could use. The Cuban economy was and still is based on selling sugar abroad. Cuba's biggest customer was the United States. Besides sugar, Cuba exported cigars, fruits and novelties like paintings and artifacts, but those things only brought peanuts to the country. Sugar was its biggest source of income.

Knowing that the Cuban economy was based on sugar, I decided to become a chemical engineer. I knew that I could always get a job in a sugar mill. If everything went according to my plan I would graduate from Havana University at the age of twenty-two and probably marry Lupe, who was the first girl with whom I fell in love. Lupe and I grew up together during my years in Cuba. Her parents were friendly with my parents and our families celebrated holidays together.

After finishing my first year at the university I had to spend the summer at a sugar cane plantation as part of my training. I was dreaming that I would sleep in the master's house in one of the luxurious bedrooms, would get up late, and the servants would prepare my bath and clothes and, after taking a leisurely bubble bath and being shaved by a servant, I would go to the dining room and have breakfast. The breakfast would be coffee and milk, toast, eggs, juice and fruit. I would probably read the newspaper and listen to the radio news. Then a servant would bring my horse and I would check out the plantation. I would probably see the workers cutting sugar cane and delivering it to the mill. By that time, lunchtime would arrive. I would go back to the house and the servants would serve me chicken and rice, and flan and coffee.

Then I would go to my room and take a nap for an hour or two. After all, the temperature by then was probably up to one hundred degrees.

The temperature inside the mill was also over one hundred degrees, but I would be working in a cool laboratory. I would monitor the concentration of sugar in the final product. Sugar changes its coloring; it is born brown and whitens itself. At first it is a brown syrup and in this state pleases the common taste; then it is bleached and refined until it can pass for white. In Palestine, during World War II, I had never seen white sugar, only brown.

Late in the afternoon, I would read my mail, which probably would be from Lupe, telling me how much she loved me and missed me. Later, I would return to the mill and check the production of the sugar. In the evening I would dine with the owner and probably would have a glass or two of brandy or rum.

At ten o'clock, after playing cards or gossiping, I would go to bed, feeling that I had had a full day.

Boy, was I wrong!

I didn't sleep in the plantation house, I slept in a shack with the common laborers. I slept under a mosquito net in a hammock which was very hard to get used to. The shacks were mud houses with palm tree leaves for roofs. Nobody cared how the houses looked since the workers went home just to sleep. They got up early in the morning and went to bed late after working ten to twelve hours a day, six days a week.

As long as I didn't flirt or talk to the women, the peasants left me alone. They were afraid that I was a city slicker and would take young women back to the Big City to work for me as prostitutes, which had happened many times before.

I had to get wood to boil my water if I wanted to take a bath. I had to make my own breakfast, which consisted of coffee with milk and bread. Then I went to the plantation to cut the sugar cane. I learned how to use the machete, and it wasn't easy. I had to hold it at just the right angle to cut the stalks an inch or two above the ground, where the flesh and the juice were sweetest.

To cut properly, you have to bend fully at the waist and swing the machete low with enormous strength. You got paid by the weight of the cane you cut, not by hours you worked. I was sweating and nobody brought me cold water. I had to go and get it myself from the river that was a mile away. I carried five gallons of water each time I went. I knew that if I didn't drink enough, I would dehydrate.

All the cane in the field was cut by hand, using one of two systems: cut the cane just as you found it, with its leaves and grasses; or do a controlled burn to get rid of the leaves and grasses. Cutting burnt cane was easier and that's what I did. But my body became covered with ashes which itched me a lot. I was very proud of myself when I had cut two rows of cane. Everybody told me that I had done very well, but really I was in pain. I could hardly straighten my back, and every muscle in my body ached. The blisters in my right hand had broken open when I washed my hands. I was a mess.

For lunch, if I was lucky, the workers would share with me a plate of rice and beans and supper was the same. While working, I had a chance to watch the workers' children running around naked, barefoot, or maybe wearing some rags. They sucked sugar cane every day, and at an early age they lost their teeth. The girls would hold small sticks and dress them with rags, pretending to be mothers protecting their babies. The boys, on the other hand, would grab bigger sticks and pretend to be soldiers, protecting the property.

None of the children knew how to read or write because they didn't go to school. Schooling was not available. Most of the parents worked and the older children took care of the younger ones. Some of the parents had a kitchen garden and the children helped to grow radishes, onions, tomatoes, cucumbers, etc. The children would carry the crops to the main highway and sell them to passersby. They really were begging, and passersby bought because they felt pity for them. The money that they made was given to their parents, who bought rum. That was the only pleasure that was available to them on the plantation.

The sugar cane workers, known as *campesinos*, looked much older than they really were. Their skin was wrinkled and dark from the sun. Some of them were only in their thirties but looked sixty. Most of them had lost their teeth at an early age from sucking on sugar cane. The water wasn't chlorinated and was infected with many parasites and germs. The *campesinos* looked chronically ill and emaciated. The men all had mustaches, wore straw hats and riding boots, and had sharp machetes slung from their waists. The women's bellies were swollen but their arms and legs were stick thin. They had no makeup and their skin was very dry. When the sun burned them they rubbed lard on their skin. They smelled like cooking grease.

Since they ate beans and rice at every meal, they constantly passed gas. When we smelled it and heard the sound, we laughed. We tried to identify the one who had done it but it was almost impossible. During the two months that I lived on the plantation, I had no eggs, chicken or other meat. The *campesinos* sold their eggs and chickens to the local market.

I noticed that the children didn't play any games like follow-the-leader, jump rope, ball, or hide-and-seek because they didn't have any equipment or knowledge of how to play games. They looked sad and didn't smile much because they had lost their teeth. In a way, they reminded me of Ali and I when we were children in Palestine. We had always been hungry for food; these kids at least had rice and beans, but they were starved for knowledge.

The two months that I stayed with the peasants I never heard them called by name. They were treated by the plantation owner like cattle, not people. They didn't know their own names. They called themselves by primary numbers: *Primero, Segundo*, First, Second, etc.

At the age of 15 the boys were cutting sugar cane full time, and the girls of the same age got married and left the plantation to live on another plantation. The boys and girls met at dances or their parents arranged their marriages. Some of the girls went to cities. They were promised domestic work by shady characters. But once they reached the city, they were put to work in bars washing dishes and other menial chores.

The bars owners showed the girls beautiful clothes and other material things that they craved. They were then told that they could get those things if they became prostitutes and, in addition, they would make enough money to send some to their parents. Many of the girls fell for it. The peasants were desperate for opportunity, and whoever offered them a better life, they wanted it.

Every year the women gave birth to a child. Only the strong infants survived. They didn't have any diapers and sometimes the babies ate their own feces. The peasants hardly washed and rarely wore clean clothes. Soap was expensive and they would rather buy beer than soap.

Those were the people whose miserable lives made Fidel Castro a success.

Sometimes the priest and nuns would come and would teach the children some bible songs. This was the only education that the children got. There were some horses on the plantation and we were allowed to ride them. We had several races and the parents bet on them. We also had cockfights, but they invariably ended in fights between the men.

I remember that every day I got love letters from Lupe and that I drank *guarape*, which was the juice from the sugar cane. Sometimes we mixed it with rum, even though the *guarape*, itself, contained large amounts of alcohol. I was surprised that after consuming two or three glasses of *guarape* my health was not affected, even though I was diabetic. I believe the physical labor kept my blood sugar controlled and, as a matter of fact, in general I had never looked so good in my life. I had a beautiful suntan, I had lost weight and I was full of muscle. But the work was very hard and my whole body was aching, especially my back. The whole day I was bending over cutting cane with my machete, which I had never done before, and my hands were full of blisters. The only way to relieve the blisters was to pop them and cover them with lard. I smelled like a pig but my hands felt better

On the other hand, I kept wondering what I was doing on that filthy sugar cane plantation. I had studied the theory of agriculture for ten months and this was to be the practical application for two months. What a joke!

I told myself that when I went home I would collect clothes and toys and I would send them to the sugar cane cutters' families. But when I went back home and spent a few days there, eating and resting, I forgot the people on the plantation and their horrible way of life. How short was my memory and how self-centered I was.

In my second year, after I had paid my dues by working in the fields for two months once again, I was to be permitted to work in the sugar mill. But it never happened because the University of Havana was closed more often than it was open, and my classes just stopped. We had several student strikes that year that eventually helped lead to a total revolution.

If city people had seen the condition that the peasants were living in and the hardships that they endured, that would justify revolt. Those peasants never were able to earn a living. They never had any money because they had to pay rent and the only place they could shop was in the plantation stores. The plantation owners paid them a small salary, and charged them interest on the money that they borrowed. Since they couldn't read and write, they never knew what they were signing, and since they wanted to work they didn't protest.

Slavery had been abolished in Cuba, but this form of indentured servitude had taken its place. Most of the peasants were Blacks and Mulattos and were descended from African slaves. They believed that when they were slaves their owners had treated them better than now that they were free. When they were slaves, they were the owner's property and were worth money to him. Now they were free, and he didn't care about them.

As more of the students at the University of Havana learned about the peasants' conditions they started to protest. Bautista, the president of Cuba, didn't want any trouble and he shut down the University. Many students gave up and left the country. Nothing was done to help the peasants, but Fidel Castro was very appealing to the masses when he promised land reform and that he would give land to the farmers who worked it. The seeds of the Revolution had been planted.

In Cuba we had large numbers of people who were illiterate. We had a hard time trying to recruit teachers and to open schools on the plantations. The new teachers didn't want to teach in the countryside, they all wanted to teach in the big cities. So Bautista's government decided to furnish televisions and educational programs for the illiterate people. My job was going to be to write educational programs and supervise them. The goal was to fight illiteracy.

In Cuba the best musicians were peasants who cultivated the land. To express their sorrows they made their own guitars and flutes and made up their own lamenting songs. "How sweet the sugar is and how hard our work is to produce it." At first, the owners forbade the singing of those bittersweet melodies, but once the children heard them, they sang them, not knowing what they were, but enjoying the sounds.

Perhaps the strongest lesson I learned from all of this was that there was a large portion of bitterness within the sweetness of sugar once you knew what it took to produce it.

# Chapter Thirty-Nine, Lupe

It was 1959 and I was finishing my second year at the University of Miami in Coral Gables, Florida.

One day I got a letter in a manila envelope from Columbia, South America. I didn't know a soul in Columbia and I thought that it was a mistake. I wasn't eager to open the letter since I thought that it was from some organization soliciting for a donation. Since I had a very limited income I thought to throw the letter away, but I noticed that it didn't have a return address. My roommate, Tom, was a stamp collector and he bugged me for the stamps. I gave him the stamps and I opened the letter. It read:

"Dear Alejandro:

This is one of the hardest things for me to do, to write you this letter. Alex, Alejandro, my dearest friend. Up to now I had deceived you. I had a double life…"

My reaction to the letter was so strong that I ended in the university hospital. My blood sugar was out of control. It took the doctors several days to balance the sugar in my body. I was depressed and I was constantly crying.

It had all begun in 1948 when my parents and I landed in Havana, Cuba. The Sal family adopted us. They showed us where to buy food, furniture, clothes, and got us an apartment. They made sure that I went to the right school and at least I had two friends–their two children.

The Sal family consisted of the father, Jacob, a Russian-Jewish immigrant who had come to Cuba from Europe around 1920. The mother was Carmen, a Cuban native who was a very light-skinned Jewish Negro. Her hair was curly and she was attractive and tall. The son, Israel, looked like the father, no apparent trace of Negro in him. He took boxing and judo and he was very aggressive. The daughter was named Lupe. Lupe had gotten her fine figure and looks from her mother. Her skin was olive brown, her hair was dark and so were her eyes. When you looked at her the first thing you noticed were her eyes. They were huge and black.

At an early age she was already flirting. Her parents had sent her to Alicia Alonzo's ballet school. She looked like a model and when she walked, she swung her hips back and forth in a very seductive manner.

These family members were our best friends. We did business with them and we socialized with them. We went to dinner and we ate at their house and they ate at our house. All the Jewish holidays were celebrated together.

Ironically, Lupe was short for Guadalupe. How come a Jewish girl was named after a Mexican saint, the *Virgen de Guadelupe*? When we asked Carmen why she had named her daughter Lupe, she told us that her first child was a boy, and Jacob had named him Israel. When she gave birth to the second child, she wanted her daughter to be protected from evil spirits and she felt that a Christian saint's name was the best way to do that.

I went to the Hebrew Academy with Israel and Lupe. Israel was two years younger than me and Lupe three years younger. I celebrated Israel's and Lupe's *Bar* and *Bat Mitzvahs* with them. Lupe outdid Israel. She knew her prayers and, having a great voice, she performed well. After her *Bat Mitzvah* performance everybody expected her to become a Rabbi. I was sixteen years old and I fell in love with Lupe. All of a sudden I noticed that she wasn't a little girl anymore but a young woman. When she asked me to dance with her I blushed.

I enjoyed eating Friday night's *Shabbat* dinner at Lupe's house. Carmen, her mother, made all the food we ate from scratch. She made *challah* (twist bread), chicken soup with *matzoh* balls, beef brisket, *kugel*, which is a starchy pudding, while my mother bought everything from a Jewish deli and didn't even serve the food herself–the maid did everything.

When I quit school at the age at the age of sixteen, Jacob Sal hired me. He wasn't allowed to give me a formal job, since I wasn't a Cuban citizen. He made me a deal that I was an independent jobber. Instead of paying me salary I got commission. Jacob had a fabric store and my parents needed fabric for their factory, so lucky for me and for my parents I got the job from Jacob. Whatever I sold I got five percent commission. Most of the clothing manufacturers in Havana bought from me. Besides selling to manufacturers, I sold fabric to department stores. But I wasn't happy. I envied Israel and Lupe because they graduated from elementary school, middle school and they went to high school, but I had dropped out of school because I failed the test. I really had an inferiority complex because of my lack of formal education, even though my natural ability as a salesman was shining.

My parents never pressured me about school. My mother told me, "Alex, in Israel, we didn't need doctors but we needed ditch diggers. There is nothing wrong about your education. You're doing a great job for Jacob."

I said, "Look at Lupe and Israel. They are getting an education and they don't talk much to me because they are intellectuals."

My mother replied, "Alex, do not belittle yourself. In my eyes you are one hundred percent perfect."

Israel went to a private school and when he graduated he continued his education in the United States. Lupe went to an all-girls Catholic school. I wondered why a Jewish girl went to a Catholic school. She told me that she wanted a good education. She also told me that she would improve in her studies if she went to a girls' school instead of a coeducational one. I noticed that she enjoyed spending her free time with the nuns. She told me that the nuns relaxed her and she was at peace with them.

At the age of sixteen I discovered that I was diabetic and then I joined the government swimming team to make sure that I would exercise daily. Lupe also joined the team at the age of thirteen. We both enjoyed swimming and we were considered good swimmers.

Every morning we practiced for two hours, Lupe before school and I before going to work. Swimming was my life and it kept me in good health.

After graduation from high school Lupe said she was planning to go to college. I realized if I wasn't going to college I was going to lose her. I believed that eventually I would lose her because she would get bored with an uneducated person like me.

I wondered if there was some way I could go to a college without a high school education. I found out that I could take an exam and if I passed it I would be able to go to college.

Lupe was very excited for me and she helped me to pass the exam. Until then I hadn't realized how smart she was. I had very little time to study because I was working but she tutored me and made sure that the little time that I did have was used well.

To qualify to take the exam I had to write an essay, "Why do I want to go to college?"

I wrote that I wanted to improve my standard of living; in other words, for selfish reasons. I wanted a good job, good pay and the good life, like owning a house, car, etc. I was surprised that, by being honest, they let me take the exams. I noticed that most of the kids that took the exams were in the same boat as I was. They were Jewish immigrants that wanted to improve their lives. They wrote idealized essays that the examiners must have realized were phony because they weren't allowed to take the exams.

The exams consisted of three groups. If you passed the first group you could go to the second group, and when you passed the second group you would be able to take the third group. The first group consisted of arithmetic, algebra, geometry and trigonometry. The second group, botany, physics and chemistry. The third group, English, Spanish and the history of Cuba.

It would be devastating to fail the exams because the names of those who passed were published in the newspaper, but not the names of those who failed. Everybody who knew me would know if I passed or didn't pass. I was already preparing to bury myself and I tried to avoid my friends. But Lupe and Israel pressured me by continually asking me if my name was in the paper.

Yay, yay, yay! It was! My name was in the paper! I had passed all the exams, and in 1956 I started at the University of Havana studying chemical engineering. Lupe went to a private Catholic college. I didn't know what was she studying but she seemed happy.

The University of Havana was more closed than open in the later years of the Bautista regime, so when I saw an ad in the paper that the Cuban government was offering a four-year scholarship at the University of Miami, I applied and was I surprised when I won the scholarship. Now I knew that I could keep up with Lupe's education.

Lupe was all excited when I won the scholarship and didn't try to stop me. The only person that didn't want me to go was my mother because she worried about me and wondered how I was going to take care of myself in a strange country.

I did very well my first year but I worried that being away from Lupe would break our relationship. I thought some other young men would start to go out with her. Lupe sounded faithful and said that she was waiting for me to return to Cuba after my graduation, and then we would get married.

Now, at the University of Miami, after finishing the letter, I swore. I called Lupe a bitch. I crumbled the letter but then I started reading it again. I probably read it a hundred times. I wanted to make sure that what I read was what Lupe really intended to write to me.

"Bitch! Bitch! Bitch! How could you do that to me? I said it over and over again."

The letter continued:

> "...I had a double life. One was mine and the other one was what people expected for me. You probably expected to marry me once you graduated from college but I lied when I told you the same thing."

I was crying as I continued reading.

"Alex, you are the gentlest, kindest person I have ever met. While my brother was rough with me you were sweet. I fell in love with you when I turned thirteen. I kissed you on my *Bat Mitzvah*. I will never forget the bouquet of flowers you gave me on my first ballet recital. I was fourteen then and all the other girls envied me.

"Friday night dinners were very important to you. You glowed when you recited the wine and bread blessing. You told us that now you knew where you belonged, while in the kibbutz you had never felt good.

"Alex, let me go. Let me go where I know that I belong. Alex, do you remember that at my *Bat Mitzvah* you opened the cage and you let the pigeons go free? Just like we did after every ceremony when reaching a new level and going on to the next. So please open the door and let me go free."

I read over and over this part of the letter and why she was asking me to let her go free. If she had fallen in love with another man and told me, I could try to win her heart back. Why was she in Columbia? I continued reading the letter.

She started again with "Alex," and I started to hate my own name. Why was she writing me such a long letter? She could write me a short letter letting me know who she was going to marry.

"Alex, you never bored me even when you let me win Monopoly, chess and checkers. I knew you wanted me to feel good about myself. You were a gentleman. Alex, the gold bracelet that you gave me for high school graduation I always wore because when I looked at it I thought about you.

"Alex, in the Jewish religion you get your faith from your mother. Neither my mother nor I were Jewish. My mother pretended to be Jewish to please my father. At an early age my mother taught me to practice the Catholic faith. I knew that once I learned about the Jewish faith I would be a better Catholic. I didn't need to convert. I was born Catholic. My happy times in my life were when I went to a Catholic high school and I spent time with the nuns. When I graduated from high school and my mother took me to Vatican city to be near the Pope, I, too, knew where I belonged. When I saw the beautiful painting in the Sistine Chapel I had a dream that God asked me to serve him in devotion for the rest of my life. Anybody can get married and have children, but I have chosen a greater life by becoming a nun. Alex, please forgive me and don't try to convince me to change my mind. I'm twenty-one years old and I know what I want in my mind and in my heart. Both my parents have blessed me and told me that if I ever changed my mind, I could come back to their home.

"Alex, there is a reason why each person was given their name and my name is Guadalupe and I am planning to serve her for the rest of my life. Your name is Alexander and I know that you will conquer the world. You have a great determination and nothing will stop you. You will marry and have children and you will forget me, while I will be praying for peace in the world.

Your friend, Guadalupe"

And suddenly, fierce memories came pouring into my head. "*Zevel, zevel, zevel!*" That's what the kids in Palestine had called me when I was seven and my mother was sick and I had been so dirty and smelly. But even though she had gotten better and I was again washed and clean, the feeling of being garbage had never completely left me.

Now, once again, I felt that I was *zevel*...that I had that horrible smell of garbage that won't go away, and the more you wash, the worse it gets. Maybe I was going crazy. I was obsessed with that smell. I asked myself, "How can I get rid of this smell?" but there was no answer...except: Why had Lupe deceived me? Because I was *zevel*.

❧

Years later my mother told me that she knew that Lupe was secretly Catholic. I asked her, "How?"

She told me, "One day when Lupe was eighteen or nineteen she came to our shop. When she tried several dresses at our store I helped her. I noticed that on her bra she wore a medallion of the Virgin of Guadalupe. I asked her, 'What is that?'

Lupe replied, "For the world I am Jewish and I am wearing the Star of David, but when I need help I pray to the real God, the Virgin of Guadalupe."

I asked my mother, "Did Lupe tell you not to tell me
"No, I didn't want to hurt you, Alex."

Strange as it seems, for several years after she became a nun I received Jewish New Year cards from Lupe. I never replied because I didn't want to open the old wounds.

She was my first love. Maybe it was a puppy love but it was very real and painful to me. And in the secret depths of my heart, a part of it is there still.

# Chapter Forty, Joan

Puppy love or no, I put Lupe in the back of my mind and started to attend every dance available at the University of Miami. I was just like a wild animal released from his cage. Everybody thought that I was automatically a great dancer since I was considered to be a Latino, but really I had two left feet. The girls that I danced with were very kind to me. and I felt happy when they accepted my invitation to dance with them. At that time Americans were dancing rock and roll, but the most popular dances were the mambo, the rhumba, and the cha-cha-cha. These are all dances that originated in Cuba.

Because I was athletic I was able to twirl the girls and lift them over my shoulder and they loved that. The wilder I was, the more they asked me to dance with them.

Dates were very inexpensive. If you were a student you didn't have to pay for the dance admission and the school usually supplied the punch, popcorn and cookies. You were not allowed to bring liquor. If you were found with alcohol, you would be expelled from the university. My roommate and I didn't want to take chances.

One day, during school hours, it was raining cats and dogs. In Florida the rain is not a cold rain but a warm one. It would pour like buckets. I was outside the student union waiting for the rain to stop so I could go back to one of my classes in a different building. All of a sudden I saw a girl running toward the student union. The road was slippery and the girl fell down. I ran to her, helped her up and helped her walk to the student union. The girl was soaking wet and she had scraped her knees and right arm. Her face was red and she was shivering. I put my windbreaker on her and I took her to the infirmary, even though I knew I would be late for my class. When I saw that she was okay I left her and went to my class.

The rain had stopped and I left her without knowing her name. Since she didn't offer to return the windbreaker I didn't take it back before I left her. When the class ended I returned to the student union, looking for her. There wasn't a trace of her. I was angry with myself. Probably, I thought, I would never see the girl or my windbreaker again. That jacket was very meaningful to me.

I didn't have many clothes and the windbreaker was a lifesaver. It was white with blue pockets. I could wear it everywhere. If I wore denim slacks and a cotton shirt and the windbreaker, it gave me a Western look. If I wore dressy slacks and the windbreaker, I looked dressy. The windbreaker was my security blanket. It was the first dressy item that I bought in the United States. If you looked at me wearing the windbreaker I looked like an American. With my windbreaker on I became an American. "America" was the magic word.

A week passed and I still didn't see the girl who had my windbreaker. My roommate, Tom, told me to forget about my windbreaker. I imagined my windbreaker was having a great time, probably covering her naked body, touching her breasts and who knows what else. Maybe she was dancing with it, kissing it and thinking about me. I thought if I ever dated her, instead of giving her flowers I would give her a windbreaker. How romantic!

I usually only ate breakfast and dinner at the student union but now I decided to hang around waiting for her. I told myself that when I saw her I would scold her and yell at her, "What do you think you are?" She reminded me of Lupe. Lupe had also borrowed things and never returned them; but, after all, she was my girlfriend and I knew where Lupe lived. But this girl was a mystery!

The next Monday morning after a long weekend was a time that the sleepy students gathered in the student union for breakfast. There were lunch wagons outside selling coffee, milk, juices, bagels and sweet rolls. Inside the student union you could find hot or cold cereals, eggs, toasts and coffee. It was self-service; you got your tray and served yourself the food. There was a cashier who collected the money and you carried your tray to any available table.

I was sitting with my roommate, Tom, eating eggs and toast and drinking coffee. Suddenly, as if by magic, the student union was transformed from the same old place to a dramatic, exciting world. It was my unknown girl! I was sure of it! I stopped eating and stared at her, my forkful of food poised in mid-air, unmoving. She was wearing a skirt and a blouse, and she looked good, with brown hair and brown eyes. She picked up a tray, selected her food and was looking for a place to sit. I was waiting for her to sit down and then I was going to approach her and ask for my windbreaker. I told myself to be cool and not to be angry with her. She probably hadn't been raised well and didn't know any better.

All of a sudden I heard a crash of a tray and dishes falling on the floor. She had seen me. All eyes were on the "criminal" who dropped her breakfast tray on the floor. She didn't pick up her tray and dishes; she zoomed out the door and I didn't see her anymore.

There was a tradition that whenever someone dropped a tray, the cafeteria workers cheered and clapped. This time the cafeteria workers were not able to cheer and clap in her honor because she was too fast.

Now I faced reality. I knew I had lost my prized windbreaker. A week passed. When I was again in the food line at lunchtime I saw the same girl ahead of me, tiptoeing to a table, carrying a tray with food. I was lost in my thoughts and mumbling to myself about what I was going to tell her. Suddenly my own tray crashed on the floor. Then all the students in the cafeteria were cheering and clapping for me. I didn't care. I took another tray and helped myself to some food. This time the girl had not run away. I went to sit next to her.

In a sulky voice, I asked her, "Remember me?"

"Yes, I do. What is your name?"

"Alex," I replied. "What is your name?"

"My name is Joan. Thank you for lending me your windbreaker."

"Where have you been since last week?"

"For a week I dined alone on nothing more than an assortment of junk food from a machine outside my room," she replied.

I asked her, "Why?"

"I was humiliated, shamed, and I wished that nobody had seen me dropping the tray."

"Why did you come today?" I continued asking questions because I couldn't think of what else to say to her. I don't know if I was angry or happy to see her.

"Because I couldn't take another crunchy-chewy-salty-sweet bite. I needed real food," she said, "Even though I was afraid that I would run into you." We both laughed nervously at that and started eating our lunch.

She asked me, "When are you going to pay the reward?"

I had to think about what she said for a minute, and then remembered that I had put several notes on the student union bulletin board. They said, "Lost: a white and blue windbreaker. If found, reward will be lunch or dinner. Alex. Phone:-----------"

I replied, "As soon as you are going to give me back the windbreaker I will take you out for dinner." She kissed me and told me to meet her at six o'clock at the student union.

Joan wasn't late and neither was I. As a matter of fact, we were both early. I didn't like what she was wearing because she was very sloppy. She was wearing denim pants four sizes too big for her and a sweatshirt, also four sizes too big.

Joan asked me, "Are we eating here?"

I replied, "No, let's take the bus and eat downtown." We took the bus and reached our destination. There were restaurants of every kind: Latin, Jewish, Italian, Chinese, deli, barbecue, salad, etc. Since I was paying and chicken was my favorite food, I took her to a chicken place.

While we were eating we had small talk. I told her about Cuba and at first I was afraid to tell her about my life in Palestine. Sometimes when I had told people that I was from Palestine, now Israel, they told me to go back, that I didn't belong here. Joan told me that she was Jewish. She talked about becoming a teacher and that her major was education

When the meal was over she told me that she was going to the bathroom, but really she went to pay the bill. When I found out, she told me that she wanted to go out with me and the only way she could do that without embarrassment was if she pretended *I* owed *her* a meal as the reward. When we went home we were holding hands. I really wanted to kiss her, but she suddenly asked me, "I know that you kissed many Cuban girls, but have you ever kissed an American girl?"

Before I even had time to answer she started kissing me. It was exciting and wonderful. I didn't want the evening to end but I had to get her back to her dormitory before ten o'clock; otherwise, she would be grounded. She had just turned eighteen years old and she lived in the girls' dormitory where every move she made was chaperoned. When you entered the dormitory there was a guard, and during the week the girls had to be in by ten o'clock and on weekends by twelve o'clock.

The boys' dormitory, in contrast, was open twenty-four hours a day. You could walk in and out anytime you chose. There was also a guard that made sure that you lived in that dormitory but there was no curfew. Now, looking back, I think that the boy's dormitory should have been closed at ten o'clock also!

The romance blossomed. I spent every free moment with Joan. I wasn't rich and Joan understood that. When we went out each one of us paid his share. We were lucky that the university offered folkloric dances that we took part in. For other entertainment we took advantage of the free movies that were shown every Saturday, and they also provided free refreshments. They weren't really free because when we registered we had had to purchase a student union card and this was part of the benefits. Friday nights we went to Hillel, which is an on-campus Jewish synagogue as well as meeting place for Jewish students. I asked Joan if she would mind changing her clothes. Instead of wearing jeans and a baggy sweatshirt, would she wear a dress?

She said, "I can do better than that!"

The next day I saw her wearing a dress with a zipper all the way down and she told me, "I don't want you to overwork yourself."

My roommate Tom made sure that I had condoms with me when I went to see Joan, and he told me, "Just in case you get lucky."

I told him, "Joan isn't that kind of a girl." Tom very sarcastically said, "And just what kind of a girl is she?"

I took the condom from his hand and put it in my pocket. I hoped that I wouldn't ruin it. One day when we were necking on the lake by the student union, Joan's purse fell open and I noticed that she had a box of condoms. I asked her, "Have you ever done it with anybody?" Joan laughed and said, "My roommate gave it to me and told me to use them if I get lucky. I should protect myself. I would never have the courage to go to a drugstore and buy men's contraceptives."

We were necking and nature took its course. We both got lucky. I relieved my tension and so did she.

The frogs by the lake had kept us company. They were noisy and they were everywhere. They clambered up onto the grass, they clutched at each other and some hopped almost right up to us. The frogs frightened Joan and I caught them and threw them into the lake, but they kept coming back. They knew that this was their property and we didn't have the right to share it with them.

After it was all over I wondered why we had done it just like animals on the grass at the lake. I should have taken her to a hotel and had a wonderful meal and a bottle of wine like she deserved. But I didn't use my head. I used my other part, and that was a problem with me.

Once we had done it, we did it all the time. We were always thinking about it. We both were young and I guess our hormones dictated our needs. Sometimes she would smuggle me into her bedroom. The men were allowed to stay in the social room. There were tables and chairs to use for studying. We did study and do our homework, but it was in her bedroom.

Days passed, weeks passed and months passed. We had dated almost a year and I wanted to marry her. If I married Joan I didn't know how we were going to live. I thought love would conquer everything. We didn't have to live in a house, we could live in a tent or on the beach. We didn't need food or clothes, we could live on love.

I knew that over Christmas I was going home to Cuba, and I planned to buy her an engagement ring. She felt the same way about me. I had already met her parents. In fact, her father was my doctor; he was the one that treated my diabetes. I thought he liked me and, being Jewish, he would be honored to have me as a son-in-law. But was I wrong. When he found out we were serious about getting married, he acted to break our relationship immediately. He didn't want his daughter to marry a diabetic. I thought that he was narrow-minded, especially for a doctor. Apparently he wanted the perfect man for his daughter, perfectly healthy. He thought that I wouldn't live long and we would have unhealthy children. If he only could have seen the future, the advances in medicine and the treatment of diabetes!

I never made a fuss about being diabetic. As far as I was concerned, I was quite normal. Every morning I took insulin, I watched my food and I exercised. Once a month I had a blood test and my blood sugar level was normal.

Then suddenly, without any warning, Joan disappeared. I didn't know that she had left school until her father came to my dormitory and asked me if I knew where she was. He thought that we were going to elope and he would never see her again. Although we did not elope he never did see her again, and neither did I.

Some time later I got a letter from Joan that said:

> "Dear Alex, I'm sorry I left you so quickly, but my father was just too strong and I had to get away from him. I was hitchhiking and met a truck driver and we got married yesterday in Las Vegas.
>
> Alex, I don't think that we were ever in love, just lust. I am very happy now and hope that someday you will find somebody to take my place.
>
> Fondly, Joan."

1959 had ended and 1960 had just started. I didn't know what my future held. After fighting a guerrilla war with Bautista's troops for a year, Fidel Castro came to power. I had received a scholarship from Bautista's government but now everything fell apart. I wondered if I would be able to forget Joan. That was not a puppy love, but a more grown-up, more thoughtful love.

Meanwhile, I was left lonely and penniless in a foreign country. Would I be able to continue my education and graduate and be a useful human being?

Sometimes I still felt like *zevel*.

# Chapter Forty-One, The University of Miami

The first year that I went to the University of Miami I got all As, but as the years went on my grades went down. I got Cs and Ds. Now it was 1960 and I was almost twenty-five years old. Beside hitting the books I had to earn enough money to support myself. I remember that my slogan then was, "A dollar a day for food."

I sustained myself by purchasing a loaf of bread that gave me enough carbohydrates for a week. The loaf of bread consisted of twenty-one slices and I ate three slices of bread a day. I also bought several cans of tuna fish that gave me enough protein and a carton of orange juice that gave me vitamin C.

My Cuban scholarship, from the Bautista government, had been paying for my school costs, room and board. Now that Castro was in power, the scholarship funding would expire in two months; after that I was on my own. That put a sudden stop to my search for another woman to replace Joan.

There were a lot of Cubans in the school in the same boat as me and the school helped us a little bit with tuition, but not enough to cover all of my expenses. I had to get a job since my parents were no longer allowed to send me any money.

Spring semester started and the U.S. Immigration Service gave me a permit to work. I didn't know what to do. I needed a job that was able to pay me well because I had a lot of expenses. The essentials were rent, food, tuition, textbooks, laundry and medicine. Since I was diabetic I needed insulin. I also needed regular exercise.

I was able to work at a gym for a few hours each week and I got free use of the gym. My laundry was also free because I worked a few hours at the laundry. I collected the linens from students, delivered them and got paid. Textbooks were easy; I borrowed them from the university library and was able to keep them the whole semester.

The other biggies were food, medicine and pocket money. For a while I tried working as a shoe salesman but I didn't make any money. I went to a local Jewish temple and asked for help. They hired me as a Hebrew and a Sunday School teacher. I made enough to support myself and in the summer, though I lost that job, the temple had a summer camp and I got a job as a counselor. I enjoyed the kids and I discovered that I had talent working with mentally retarded kids.

My first experience with a slow learner and a child with problems had been dealing with Manuel, the one-eyed boy in Cuba. The Jewish children needed patience but lived in a fast-paced world. I had a very, very simple curriculum and I made sure that those children were happy when they spent time working with me. There was no pressure, only praise, and I was amazed at what beautiful work they produced.

When we did finger painting, they mixed the colors and created designs Those designs were so attractive that my boss presented them to a garment factory and that factory produced fabrics from the pictures that my children had created. The children got paid for the designs and the parents were so grateful that they gave me some of the earnings, and the money helped keep me afloat.

When the fall semester started I had made enough money to pay for my tuition and room, but I needed money to live on. I found out that selling soft drinks at the university football games at the Orange Bowl was a good way to make money. With every game I made about two hundred dollars. It was too bad that the University of Miami didn't play at home every week.

The Coca-Cola company really took advantage of us; they never lost any money. In order to work for them we had to rent an apron that cost five dollars. They charged us a ten dollar security fee for the Coke tray, which was a tray with holes that held twenty-five cups of soft drinks. Then they charged fifty cents for each cup, and we sold each drink for one dollar.

I carried the tray of soft drinks up and down the aisles, maybe a hundred stairs–up and down. I climbed the stairs without stopping. The faster I climbed the stairs, the faster I was able to sell the soft drinks. Luckily, I was young and strong and I was able to climb those stairs without difficulty.

I didn't care who the University of Miami was playing. The most important thing that I learned was that when we were winning, the fans were in a better mood and were willing to spend more money. They were very thirsty and bought lots of soft drinks. When our team was losing, the fans often left early without buying soft drinks. That's why I was always praying that our team would be winning.

None of the other vendors helped me; they were cutthroat. Sometimes when the game ended I would take a chance and try to sell a last tray of twenty-five drinks. If I didn't sell them, I lost money. I couldn't drink them myself because they were pure sugar and they would make me sick.

This was my life in the Promised Land. When I sold Coke I would shout "Coke! Coke! Only a dollar." It was hot and the people were thirsty and I sold drinks. Sometimes I would trade a hot dog for a drink. This was the American way.

Some days I was so hungry that I went to a hamburger place and I asked for a cup of hot water. I would pour ketchup and crackers that were on the tables into the hot water cup. After drinking and eating ten cups I was full. The place was air-conditioned while outside it was hot. I was able to cool myself and get free food.

All that time I was afraid that I would run out of insulin. For me, insulin was life. I also needed syringes and needles. A lot of my income went to pay for my supplies so I wouldn't run out and, lucky for me, I never did

All of a sudden I became the most religious man on earth. When you are hungry and you don't have enough money for food you visit churches. I made sure that every Sunday I went to a different church. I had the schedules and I knew which churches served lunches. Sometimes I took a doggie bag back to my dorm. I didn't care if I looked strange; my stomach was going to be full. I wasn't the only one that went for free lunches. In my dorm, several of the students were in the same boat.

Sometimes the local farmers would donate a box of Florida oranges to the dorm. They didn't last long. Like a pig, I grabbed five or six oranges; I was only thinking about myself. At least I was one of the few who wrote the farmer a thank-you note.

Survival then was a constant struggle, and I wondered if a diploma was worth all this trouble. But in 1961 I graduated and got my diploma. I was now an "educated" person, and when I looked at my diploma, which was hung on top of my desk, I knew that by hook or by crook, I had earned that piece of paper.

Maybe, just maybe, I was no longer *zevel*

UNIVERSITY OF MIAMI


Upon the recommendation of the Faculty

has conferred on

Alejandro Modena

the degree of

Bachelor of Arts

August 30, 1961

# Chapter Forty-Two, Havana or Habana

When I came to Cuba in 1948 I was thirteen years old and I couldn't read or write in Latin letters, only Hebrew. I practiced writing my name and address for hours until I learned it:

*Alejandro Modena*
*Calle M #163*
*Vedado, Havana, Cuba*

How do you spell the capital of Cuba in Spanish? You can spell it Havana or Habana, with "v" for *vaca* which is cow in Spanish, or "b" for *burro*, which is donkey in Spanish. I would rather be a cow and live like a cow. All day long I would eat hay or grass and at night I would give milk, which is a life-giving food. I would be happy and healthy. On the other hand, I wouldn't like to be a burro. If I was like most burros, I would be poor and hungry. I would work all day long for a measly meal. This seems to be a fitting analogy for a part of my life.

For ten years, from 1948 to 1958, I knew Havana with a "v." I was wealthy, living in a luxury penthouse in one of the best residential areas of Havana. I wore expensive clothes. I went to expensive restaurants. My parents owned several department stores, made lots of money and life was great.

According to my opinion, cities are divided into two groups: feminine and masculine. Most of the cities in the Middle East are masculine. They are very macho. All those cities consist of big monuments and big palaces. On the other hand, cities in Europe are very feminine. They have small houses with gardens, and although the cities have big buildings they have hanging plants outside the windows and are decorated with landscaping.

Havana, in my eyes, was a feminine city. It had a coquettish personality, with many outside restaurants surrounded with flowers. You could hear radios blaring loudly. Everybody was trying to outdo each other.

Appearance was very important for the Cuban in Havana. At an early age the girls accentuated their waistlines wearing girdles. They wanted big hips and a small waist, so when they walked they had a certain look and a feminine rhythm. The men would flirt and compliment the girls. They would say; "You are so beautiful and you are breaking my heart."

Life was very active in the center of the city. It was alive both day and night. At night you could see lights everywhere. Havana, like Paris, was the City of Light. The department stores were open late and the restaurants only started to serve food at eight or nine o'clock at night. People frequently went to movie theaters, and there were many night clubs, discotheques and gambling casinos that you could visit. Street life was very active and prostitutes waited outside the hotels. You could also find prostitutes along the Malecon, the seawall, after sunset.

In 1959 when the Castro government came to power, everything changed. We started to think of Habana with a "b" because we were suddenly poor and had to live and work like burros. People had been happy and loud. You could hear music on the streets and people dancing to the latest musical hit. Cuba is simply one of the world's most musical places. The musical genres are the fullest expression of the country's mixed African and Spanish heritage. Everybody laughed a lot and life, at least in the city, was great. People drove their convertible cars on the main streets, not to see what was happening on the streets, but to be seen. The weather was nice and people sat in open café houses drinking coffee or beer. They were always discussing politics, local or worldwide.

Havana had been like a prostitute, selling herself to the highest bidder. Havana's wealth reached its highest in the 1950s. Large buildings like the Hilton, the Riviera, and the Capri hotels sprang up then. The U.S. Mafia with the help of the Cuban government controlled the casinos. In 1959 when Fidel Castro took over he closed down all the casinos, lotteries and other games of chance.

Habana with a "b" turned into a poor, ugly, sad city. Nobody trusted anybody. They were afraid if they criticized the government they would end up in jail. The sunny city now felt gray, dingy and sad. The houses became run down and the streets were filled with unrepaired potholes.

In 1948 when we had immigrated to Cuba from Palestine, my parents opened a ladies' apparel factory. Their first customer was Sears Roebuck. Sears' policy was to sell goods that were made in the same neighborhood where their stores were located. At that time, nobody made or sold ladies' ready-made clothes. My mother was the first.

Before our factory opened, women bought the raw material and a seamstress custom made their clothes. Sears had too much inventory in fabrics that they couldn't sell and they asked my parents if they were willing to manufacture garments. My parents made five different styles of dresses and in the first 24 hours that they were available they had sold 200 dresses. It was unbelievable. It was the first time in history that people in Cuba were able to buy ready-made, finished garments made in Cuba.

In a short time my parents were very successful, just like the city of Havana. Their clothes were sold all over the island and abroad. Their "Rivoli" brand became very famous. Money was everywhere and the city was thriving. But drugs were everywhere also, and so was crime. It was hard to tell who was running the country.

By 1958 my parents had saved one hundred thousand dollars and had it in an American bank. They used that money to buy sewing machines and raw materials and brought them to Cuba to build a bigger factory.

Once the sewing machines were installed we had a big party. My parents were on cloud nine. They knew that they had made a name for themselves. Both Cubans and foreigners wanted to wear a "Rivoli" dress. We manufactured two kinds of dresses: cheap ones that everybody was able to buy and expensive ones which were embroidered linen. My parents made sure that everybody was able to afford to buy a Rivoli dress and that was very unique at that time. When you mentioned that you wore a "Rivoli" dress, people knew that you wore the best.

Cuba, under Bautista, had been very corrupt. Doing business in Cuba it was necessary for us to have two sets of books. Like other businesses, we had presented the government with the phony one and paid our taxes based on that but the government was not stupid. They sent inspectors to our factory and we had to bribe them in order to continue our business. If we didn't please the inspectors we would be arrested for tax evasion. My father had been very afraid of those corrupt inspectors. Now he had more than bribes and threats to worry about. In 1960 two soldiers with bayonets on their rifles came to our factory and told my father that this was no longer his property, but if he wanted, for a modest salary, he could continue to run the factory for the state. My father was not allowed to touch the cash register or to collect money for the goods that he had sold.

At that time I was in the United States, studying at the University of Miami. I wasn't thinking about the future and neither were my parents; we were only living in the moment. I thought that the gold tree growing in my family's back yard would continue growing money forever. My parents probably thought the same.

My father had not believed that Castro was a communist. He had thought that, as soon as things settled down, Cuba would be just like the United States. But the reality was very different. The Castro regime stole everything that they could, not only the equipment of our factory, but the doors, windows and even the nails that held them in place.

# Chapter Forty-Three, Jamaica

The year was 1960 and, once again, my family was being separated and uprooted from the country we had called home for twelve years.

It was summer and I came from the United States to spend my summer vacation in Cuba. I had a three-month vacation; it was May and school wouldn't start again until the end of August. I was looking forward to seeing my friends and spending the days at the beach and going from one party to another. I liked to go fishing and several of my friends had boats so we could go fishing or water-skiing. The warm ocean was perfect for either one. After all I was only young once, and if I didn't live it up now, when would I?

But the reality of Cuba was far different. Our kitchen that had been full of food was now empty and you could hardly find any food in the supermarket. Their shelves were more than half empty and whatever you found was very expensive.

The loud music that used to play from radios was now silent. The only thing you heard on the radio were Castro's very long speeches.

You couldn't move around comfortably because you felt that everybody was watching you. We knew that most of the wealthy families were leaving the island. All of a sudden friends didn't talk to you anymore. My parents whispered or spoke to me in Hebrew, because we didn't trust our maid or our workers. We were afraid if we didn't obey the rules we would be put in jail. My ex-boss and our family friend, Jacob Sal, was in jail. Years later, I found out that he died in jail at the age of sixty. The crime he had committed was to exchange pesos for dollars and send the money to the United States.

My father, mother and I had arrived in Cuba twelve years earlier, and we had worked our way out of poverty to become successful. In addition to the clothing factory, we'd had three stores; one for children's clothing and two that carried ladies' clothes, all in the same *La Rampa* shopping center. None of that had come easy–it took lots of hard work. After the Castro government confiscated all of our possessions, what was the purpose of working hard again? We would never be able to regain them.

In 1960, Jamaica was still a possession of the British (it would achieve its independence two years later), and word of our very successful clothing business must have reached the Jamaican government because they contacted my mother and asked if she would be willing to immigrate to Jamaica and open a ladies' apparel factory in the capital city, Kingston. My mother told them that the Castro regime had confiscated all their money but if they would lend her enough to restart a factory she would go.

Once again my mother was packing her suitcase and was leaving our home. She was then 52 years old but she looked much older. Her feet dragged and her hands were shaking. She had lost a lot of weight since the last time I had seen her. Before this she had been a sharp dresser, but now she didn't care how she looked. We didn't know it then but Mother had been afflicted with Parkinson's Disease, which would ultimately take her life.

Some of the first places to be closed in Cuba during Castro's regime were the beauty parlors. He said, "Communist women do not need beauty parlors. They are beautiful on the inside and the government will reward their loyalty, not artificial looks." Mother used to bleach her hair blonde and you couldn't see a trace of gray, but overnight, it seemed to me, her hair was snow white. I promised my mother that I would take her to a beauty parlor in Kingston. Later I discovered that Jamaican beauty parlors didn't dye hair, they only cut it and straightened it by ironing.

Both my father and I were very afraid to let my mother go to Jamaica by herself. We were afraid of what might happen to her there without her family. I didn't know if I was going to continue my education at the University of Miami or work with my mother in Jamaica. My father couldn't go with her. He was very valuable to the Cuban government because he was the only one that was able to run the factory. If they let him leave they would have to shut the factory down and three hundred people would be unemployed.

Finally we decided I should accompany my mother to Jamaica. Before moving, I bought every available book about the country. I talked to every living soul who would talk to me about Jamaica. I sorted the good from the bad and then my mother and I went to Jamaica. I knew that it was safe because it was a British colony. I found out that 77% of Jamaicans are Black, 19% Mulatto, 3% Eurasian and 1% White. I found out that the average Jamaican lower-class couple usually lived together for a long time before they got married, and that, depending on the location, 40-70% of all births occurred out of wedlock. A woman in her 20s who had not had a child was referred to as a "mule" (mules are sterile). Having one or more children insured a steady income of support from the government. The Jamaican men, in general, forbade the women to work, so I knew that most of our workers would be single women.

Mother and I flew on Jamaican Airlines to Kingston. The airport was old and dirty. After a short wait, a government car arrived and took us to a guesthouse. It wasn't expensive, it had a private room with a bathroom and they served three meals a day. There were twenty or thirty guests in residence. Most of the guests were British, some engineers and teachers who were under contract to stay in Jamaica for one year. They seemed to spend their time after work drinking alcohol or smoking cigarettes. The British usually chose gin and tonic, while rum and coke was the Jamaicans' beverage of choice, as well as Red Stripe beer.

The official language in Jamaica was English but the natives spoke their own language, called Rasta, which is a patois of English and various European words, with a rich mixture of African dialects. It is not only the words, themselves, but the very different accent that makes it hard to understand at first–but with time we learned it

Each morning, bottles that had been emptied the night before lay discarded on the ground and the local kids collected them to be redeemed at the local market for money or treats. Most of the Jamaican kids had rotten teeth because they ate so much sweets.

Typical Jamaican food was sweet potatoes, pineapples, coconuts and bananas. My favorite food was ackee and saltfish. The ackee tree was introduced into Jamaica from West Africa in the 18th century. Its leathery leaves, over 20 feet long, are a bright orange-red. The three-inch-long fruit itself is poisonous. Inside the fruit are black seeds that contain a fleshy yellow lump, and this is the only edible part. The "lumps" were very sweet and worth struggling to get to.

For most Jamaicans, religion was a way of life. They ate, drank, slept and dreamt religion. It provided respite from the constant struggles of everyday life. For people living in poverty, anything that gave comfort and hope was welcome. Major religious sects in Jamaica included the Baptist, Methodist, and Anglican churches, as well as Rastafarians, Jewish and African religions.

In Jamaica the Jewish community wasn't as friendly as they had been in Cuba. Kingston had the oldest synagogue in the New World. The Kingston temple is one of a handful in the world that covers its floor in sand, a tradition dating to the time when Marranos needed to muffle the sound of footsteps to avoid detection. Marranos are Jews from Spain who had converted to Catholicism during the Inquisition but practiced Judaism in secret.

The first Jews in Jamaica were Spanish and Portuguese, and arrived covertly after fleeing the religious persecution of the Spanish Inquisition. The British restored their religious rights. Jamaican Jews were primarily white, but the obvious similarities between Rastafarians and Jews are worth noting.

The Rastafarian sect originated in Jamaica. The name of the sect comes from the pre-coronation name of the Ethiopian leader, Haile Selassie, whose original name was "Ras Tafarie." Rastafarians worship Haile Selassie as the Messiah and believe that Ethiopia is the Promised Land. The Rastafarian scriptures are the same as the Jewish Bible. They observe strict dietary rules, often stricter than kosher laws, and they consider themselves to be one of the lost tribes of Israel.

Beyond this, however, they were different, and neither group made much of their similarities. Rastafarians wore long hair and they looked like they never took a bath or a shower. The first time I noticed them I was afraid of them. Usually, I was afraid of the unknown. But once I knew them I felt safe, even though they looked so different from me.

I was surprised that the Jewish community of Jamaica did not want us to mingle with them and they didn't invite us to their homes. They were a very close-knit society and they only accepted their own. Newcomers like us were ignored. I felt the same feeling in the synagogue and neither my mother or I attempted to become a member of the temple.

As I got to know Kingston better, I was surprised at the contrast between it and Havana. Havana was a beautiful city while Kingston wasn't. In Kingston, instead of Latin dance rhythms, you can hear Reggae music from every street corner. In Kingston, it seemed almost everyone was a hustler. There had been no overall plan to build the city. People took any piece of land they could and built a house. Later they put in electricity and sanitation and these haphazard areas became neighborhoods.

Vendors are everywhere, and the sidewalks where they display and sell are known as "Ben Dung Plazas" (you have to bend down to buy).

---

My mother quickly found a place to rent where she opened a ladies' dress store and a factory. She had several orders for embroidered dresses from other Caribbean islands like Curacao, Aruba, and the Bahamas. She wasn't as lucky with the Jamaican workers as she had been in Cuba. They would work for a week or two and then they would disappear. Mother had deadlines but was never able to meet them because of the undependable workers.

Meanwhile, it was nearing time for my classes to begin again. My mother insisted that I return to the University of Miami. She told me that a diploma was my ticket to life, and that I would regret it if I didn't go back. I left her with tears in my eyes. She felt totally alone and I did, too. My father was in Cuba, my mother was in Jamaica, and I was going to the United States to complete my education. I wondered how I would be able to support myself in the United States. I didn't have any skills or enough education to get a decent job. Before, if I'd had a problem, I could fall back on my parents, but now each one of us needed help from the others. My father, who had built an empire, was now penniless in Cuba. My mother had borrowed a large sum of money from the Jamaican government and I wondered how she would be able to repay it, and I didn't have a penny to my name. The only thing that I had was youth and belief in myself.

# Chapter Forty-Four, The Problem

When I was a student at the University of Miami I had a problem. My problem was that I was a man without a country. I had a student visa and I could only stay a short time studying in the U.S. Eventually the United States would kick me out, probably sending me back to Cuba. I could ask them for political asylum, but in my case it wouldn't work–I couldn't prove political or religious persecution. United States immigration might try to send me back to Israel since I was Jewish, but I was born in Palestine and no such country existed now. I could go to Jamaica only as a tourist since I didn't have a profession and my mother couldn't legally hire me.

If I took eighteen credits in the spring semester and six credits in the summer I would graduate. The problem was that some of the classes I needed were offered in the spring semester and others only in the fall semester. I felt that my mother needed my help and couldn't wait that long.

I wasn't the only one who had the same problem; a lot of my friends were in the same situation. I went to the administration and I pleaded with them to help me but the schedule was written in stone according to them.

Every place I turned, in my eyes, there was a big problem.

My father had once told me, "Don't fight the problem–solve it." Well, for starters I knew if I quit I would never go back to school and never earn a diploma. I was constantly worrying. I was worried about my mother alone in Jamaica, my father, under Castro, in Cuba, and myself at school with no scholarship, no money, and no way for my parents to help me.

At night when I saw the moon and stars I wondered if my parents in Cuba and Jamaica saw the same moon and stars and wished the same wish that I did–for us to be together.

Even back then I thought about writing a book about all of this. I would call it "*Yalla*," which in Arabic means, "Let's go." We all had to go. I look at my family's history and I see the Wandering Jew.

There was my father, born in Italy in 1904, and at the age of twenty-nine left in the middle of the night, escaped death in a train wreck, and went to Palestine. He had been a good Italian citizen and when he had come to Palestine he was also. He fought in World War II and was tortured defending his new country. With an Arab-Jewish war beginning, he brought us to Cuba and hoped to call this country his home.

My mother, born in Poland in 1908, hoped to become a doctor helping the needy. But when she finished her studies at the age of twenty-five she was prohibited from practicing medicine. She left for Palestine and adopted that country. After fifteen years of mostly grinding poverty, she almost lost her only son to an Arab suicide bomber. Again she left to go to Cuba. After twelve years of hard work building an empire, she was left penniless and moved on again to Jamaica.

I was born in Palestine in 1935 and was forced to move back and forth between city and kibbutz. Then I was betrayed by my best friend, and after I had recuperated we left for Cuba in 1948. Now it was December, 1960, and I was at the University of Miami.

*Yalla*–let's go! Where would we all be going next?

Meanwhile, Christmas vacation was close at hand. What should I do, work at the shoe store where I had a job and probably make enough money to pay my tuition for the new semester, or return to Cuba to see my father who I worried about? Or should I go to Jamaica to see my mother and help her get settled in her new country?

My friends and my parents all told me to stay in a safe environment, a rich country, where the only thing that worried people was football, basketball and baseball. At school everybody was debating, "Are we going to have a good baseball team this year?" We hadn't done very well the previous year, but we still had hopes of winning the championship this season.

Christmas and New Years were the biggest events of the year. For a woman, shoes are part of her wardrobe and without them she feels naked, so this was my chance to sell a lot of shoes. I didn't get a salary, I only made commissions.

Beside selling shoes, there were private parties that were always looking for students to work as waiters. They paid us the minimum wage, which at the time was $1.75 an hour, plus tips and all the leftover food we could take home.

My friends had a point. I should stay in Miami for the holidays and make enough money for my expenses for the whole next semester, so I could relax and study and make good grades. That sounded good to me for a short time, but I was very concerned about both my parents. Then, the next day I saw in the paper an advertisement for Air Jamaica offering a ridiculously low price, round-trip airfare to Kingston, Jamaica–thirty-nine dollars–which I thought was too good to be true. Some of my American friends who usually spent the holidays in Cuba asked me if I would join them on an adventure in Jamaica, and I jumped at the chance. My friends who went with me had only one thing in mind–SEX! It was on my mind also, but I had to help my mother, so I left them in the city to fend for themselves.

I arrived in Kingston with a backpack and only a few clothes and went immediately to my mother's factory. She was very surprised to see me. She looked even older then the last time I had seen her and seemed very tired. In Cuba she had always been well-groomed, and every week she had gone to the beauty parlor where she'd had a hairdo and a manicure and pedicure. Now I was sure that in the five months that she had lived in Jamaica she had never done this. She was dragging her feet, and her voice sounded very low, instead of loud and bright like I remembered.

The clothing factory seemed more like a prison camp. There was no music, no lively chatter like I remembered in Cuba, only the monotonous sound of the sewing machines. I didn't know why everybody was afraid to talk. It seemed to me they were under tremendous pressure to complete their jobs.

When I had called her she had told me how wonderful she was doing and how happy she was. She told me that she ate properly, slept well, and went to a swimming pool every day; that she had made a lot of friends at the pension where she lived, and that everybody liked her. But things were very different than that rosy picture. And yet, looking back, I realize what a great woman my mother was, in strength and spirit. She was a true survivor. After all that had happened to her, here was a factory that she had single-handedly built in yet another country.

There were two floors in the building. Downstairs was the store with two salesgirls and filled with merchandise. The only thing that was bright was the dresses; they were absolutely astonishing, they were so colorful. Upstairs was a large table that my mother used to cut the material to make the dresses, and ten sewing machines. Both downstairs and upstairs had bathrooms. Upstairs there was a kitchen with a refrigerator and there was a coffeepot and a bottle with mineral water. There were big windows that gave enough light to work, and on every sewing machine there was a lamp.

The girls hardly talked; they seemed hypnotized by the sound of their sewing machines. In contrast, in our Cuban factory we had music and listened to soap operas, and everyone laughed and giggled while they worked. We felt like a family. Here the women looked older, many of them toothless and very worn by their hard lives. I decided to change the atmosphere.

When I first arrived and I ran to my mother, I hugged her and I broke the silence in the room by laughing and hugging and kissing her. The girls stared at me and, for the first time, they laughed also. They asked my mother, "This is your boy?" My mother smiled and said, "Yes, he is my boy. His name is Alex." But none of the girls ever called me Alex; they called me "Sir," and they called my mother "Mrs. Modena."

When the working day ended and we had closed up, we left and my mother drove me to her pension. Lucky for me, they had some empty rooms and I was able to rent one next to my mother. The other tenants were men in their fifties and sixties who worked in the city. Most of them were immigrants that were only staying a year or two in Jamaica on contract.

Some of the men had bottles of whiskey and rum and started to drink as soon as they arrived home. Each room had a balcony where they sat, but they were not friendly with each other. Their main interest was the bottle. Later on I found out that in order to tolerate the heat, you drink; at least that was what they told me. I wished that I could drink alcohol but I couldn't because I was diabetic.

At six o'clock supper was served. It wasn't bad, and then at seven o'clock the tenants went to the sitting room, where we were able to watch television or play games or read books or the newspaper. But most of the men went back to their patios and tried to race each other to see who could finish their bottle first. When I arrived at the pension and saw the trashcan full of whiskey bottles, I wondered how they had gotten there, since the pension was not a bar, but now I discovered the answer to the mystery.

Some of the men offered me a drink and when I said, "No, thank you," they teased me by saying, "Sonny, you can drink with us, we won't tell your mommy." I didn't respond to their teasing. I didn't bother to tell them that I was diabetic and couldn't drink.

I stayed in Jamaica for one month, and during that time I worked in my mother's factory and store. I hired painters and made sure that the whole inside and outside of the building looked nice and clean. I bought two radios, one for the downstairs and one for the upstairs. That made the girls happier. They were actually singing along with the calypso songs. The place became alive, and I told my mother that we should celebrate each girl's birthday by buying a cake from the next door bakery and tell the girl that she was important. All of a sudden, every day a girl announced a birthday, even though there were only ten girls. Production improved and the girls came to work every day, instead of skipping if they felt like it.

The day after payday was a nightmare. We knew that the following day some of the girls would not come to work. They would get drunk, and since they had some money, they thought that they could skip work. We only needed ten full time girls but we had fifty of them on hire because they were so undependable. The girls were living in shacks with no floors, with tin roofs and outside toilet facilities. But this was their life as they knew it and they didn't want to change. I told Mother to tell them to use their money to buy only necessities and a few extra things to make their lives easier, and to open a bank account and deposit the rest. I was able to persuade my mother to provide every girl with basic health care, but the girl had to work for us for three months steady, then she was entitled to coverage. At first they didn't care one way or another, but once we introduced them to the system and they were able to see a dentist, an eye doctor and a family doctor, they understood the value of it.

Then my efforts were greatly helped when the Jamaican government began to provide classes in hygiene for the workers. The instructors came to our factory to do this. They also taught them childcare and nutrition. In a single month, between my efforts and the new government program, the lives of the workers in our factory were turned around. I felt like a *mensch*, a real man, and not once in that month did I think of myself as *zevel*.

Beside working in the factory with my mother, I went fishing and I learned to water ski. I had envied the kids at the University of Miami who were able to water ski while I never had the chance.

When I left Jamaica I felt that my mother was doing much better. I had used all of her extra cash on business improvements, and she was not able to give me any money. So I was still as poor as a mouse and had to find money to support myself. But at least now I could water ski! I was surprised that she had so quickly trusted me to take charge. She told me that she was tired and the business needed new blood, and I was young and full of energy. But once again she reminded me of the importance of a college diploma, and that she could wait a while longer.

And what a wonderful lesson it was for me. It confirmed to me that in order to prosper yourself, you had to treat others nicely and with respect, and if you do that it makes little difference where you are–people are the same all over the world.

# Chapter Forty-Five, The Bond

The year was 1961. I had just graduated from the University of Miami and I was reunited with my mother in Kingston. Having a college degree, I was now qualified to teach Spanish in Jamaica. There was a shortage of teachers and I didn't have a problem getting a job teaching at a technical school in Kingston, which was the equivalent of an American high school.

My mother ran the factory and store where I helped her after school and on my free days. The tourist industry had recently picked up, and several tourist ships docked close to our store. I was successful in getting some of the tourists to visit our shop but in spite of that we hardly made any money because we had a lot of expenses like repaying the government loan, rent, electricity and salaries, just to name a few.

I was young, but instead of thinking about girls and having a good time I thought about my father in Cuba. I knew that by hook or by crook I was going to bring him to Jamaica to be with us. When I had left Cuba that was the last time I saw him. I saw his picture in my eyes, this magnificent person, my father, appearing like a frightened child, crying. He had a gentle face, gray hair and a hairy chest, arms and legs, with glittering eyes. He looked like a Roman warrior, lean and slim. He had a mustache which still covered his birthmark.

Although he knew it was for the best, he didn't want us to leave him in Cuba. I promised him that we would be reunited in Kingston. I couldn't believe that a grown-up person could cry just like a baby. He hugged me and my mother and I felt that maybe this was going to be the last time I was going to see him alive. He told me, "Alex, don't forget me."

"How silly," I thought. He was my father, my own flesh and blood. When he hurt himself, I hurt and when he bled, I bled. I smiled and told him, "I will never forget you."

The stores and factory had been my father's life. He hardly took any time off or vacations and that was one reason why he and my mother were very successful. The factory was open five days a week and the stores were open six days a week. My father had gotten up early in the morning and gone to the factory. He enjoyed calling his customers and getting orders. He loved to draw embroidery designs on dresses. Every morning, six days a week, he went to the post office and collected the mail because he didn't trust anyone else to do this task.

He knew to whom to sell and with whom to do business. He never lost a dime. He employed three hundred people and he made sure that they were always busy. His competitors really loved him because he was fair with them and he always helped them. If they were short of raw material he would lend it to them so they could continue to fill their orders. If he had orders and couldn't deliver them, he gave the business to his competition. He wasn't greedy but was very generous. His motto was "Live and let live."

The business was his life and now Castro and his thugs had taken it away from him. He didn't feel like going early to the business because it wasn't his any more. He lost weight, grew depressed and looked old.

I asked my mother, "Are we doing the right thing by leaving him?" Mother reassured me that we were doing the right thing and that all our lives would become better for it.

I didn't realize that my father had tried to commit suicide when we lost our business. I was at the University of Miami when my mother called me and told me that she didn't know where my father was. A week later they found my father in a hospital in a state of coma. He had registered in a hotel in a resort town called Varadero Beach. He hadn't registered under his own name, so when my mother was looking for him she couldn't find him until she saw that he had used my name in the hospital and that it was written in the medical report that he had tried to kill himself.

It took my mother half a year to nurse my father back to health, but he never was the same. He resented this painful change from being the boss to being a common worker. In past years he had suffered so much from poverty and the inability to provide for his family, and now once again he had to think before he could spend a nickel for a cup of coffee. He told me, "Alex, I don't want to pawn my clothes again for a piece of bread like we did in Palestine."

I was afraid that my father would try to kill himself again. My mother reassured me that he was going to be okay. Once she and I were in Jamaica, we called him once a week. He seemed to be okay and in good spirits. In spite of this we wanted him to be with us, not only for his sake, but for my mother's. Jamaica wasn't a safe country for a white woman to live in alone. During the 1960s Jamaica faced many problems, including inflation, unemployment and poverty. Many Jamaicans were dissatisfied and their discontent sometimes led to riots and violent crime.

By now I had been in Jamaica for six months and my father still wasn't with us. The Cuban government wasn't going to let him leave the country because they still felt that no one else could properly run the factory.

I tried a ploy. We would inform the Cuban government that my mother was sick and ask them if they would let my father come to visit her. The Cuban government didn't fall for it. They told us that we must put up a bond of $10,000 and then they would release my father.

I didn't have the money and I was frustrated. I went to the bank and I asked for a loan. In spite of our factory and store they felt I didn't have any collateral and they wouldn't loan me the money. I was not only depressed at not getting the loan, but they had made me feel like a low person, and my feeling of *zevel* returned. I went to the beach. In the Jewish religion one washed unkosher dishes in salt water and they become kosher. In the salt water I scrubbed myself from head to toe and back again until my skin was pink like raw flesh, trying to get rid of that lingering smell of garbage.

Meanwhile, Christmas was coming and I had a month's vacation from my teaching job. I had been hearing loud noises outside all day long. The Jamaicans believed that the proper way to celebrate Christ's birth was by setting off firecrackers. Chinese grocers everywhere sold fireworks. The Chinese had come to Jamaica as coolies, or common laborers. They didn't remain laborers long. They saved their wages and went into business. Now they controlled the retail grocery trade throughout the island.

In Kingston during the month of December and part of January there were many booths on the main street. Our store was on the main street and so was my firecracker booth. The school where I taught had three hundred students and I knew that some of the students were looking for jobs. I built a booth next to my mother's store and I hired some of the students to work in the booth and some of them to sell outside the booth. The warehouse where I bought the firecrackers on consignment gave me prizes like stuffed animals, toys and other goodies, which I gave to the customers' kids.

Every time I earned a nickel or a dime I knew that money was for my father's freedom. Every day I counted the money I made and I deposited it in the bank and I called it the "Freedom Account." When I made my first dollar I told myself only $9,999 more for my father's freedom. It was good that I was busy working; otherwise, I would have gone out of my mind worrying about him.

I knew my mother was also worrying about him; it wasn't a good life for a married woman to be without her husband. My mother had hardly any friends and the Jewish community still didn't accept us. I guessed that they were afraid that we wanted them to support us and that we would be a burden on them. After living in a kibbutz early in my life I couldn't understand this mentality. I had thought that all Jewish people helped each other.

By the end of the first week I had made $500. I thought to myself, only $9,500 more for my father's freedom. This was after working eighty-four hours in seven days!

I knew that things weren't good in Cuba. Everything was severely rationed. All but the most essential foods had disappeared. When you went to the grocery store the shelves were mostly empty. You could buy food by paying with American dollars, but not Cuban pesos. Every month my mother sent my father a few dollars so he could at least buy the basics to live like a decent person.

I had made a few thousand dollars already, but time was getting shorter. I was desperate because I knew that I had only two weeks left. Everybody told me that I was a dreamer and that I would never make enough money to free my father. That realization was very, very painful for me. I was willing to sell my soul to the devil in order to get my father with us. I knew that in a few days school would start and I needed new clothes and shoes. I didn't want to go to the charity store like I had in Palestine, so whatever I had, I wore, as long as the clothes were clean and the shoes didn't have holes.

By the end of the Christmas season I had made $5,000, which was pretty good but not enough to redeem my father. I was afraid that he wasn't going to last too much longer. I thought and thought how I was going to get the rest of the money. For all the factory and store, Mother barely made a living. I gave her my job salary so we could pay our room and board. I thought maybe I should gamble, or bet on the horses or rob a bank, but those were foolish ideas. The bank had refused me a loan, so in desperation I went to the moneylenders. In America they are called loan sharks, but in the Third World countries they are the normal way of doing business. They charged very high interest, causing chronic and growing debt, much as moneylenders did to sharecroppers in the United States after the Civil War. The loans, known as advances, effectively locked individuals and families into years of virtual slavery as they tried to work off their debt.

There were three groups of moneylenders: the East Indians, the Chinese and the Syrians. The ones that I felt most comfortable with were the Syrians. Since they operated tourist stores, I thought that they would advance us money for the clothing we could sell them, but I was mistaken. They wanted the goods on consignment and that didn't help me; I needed the money right away.

One East Indian family was willing to help me, but as a condition they wanted me to marry one of their daughters and to work the rest of my life for them. The local Chinese were angry with me because I had undersold their price with the firecrackers and they didn't want to deal with me.

The bank had rejected me, but I had a new idea. I asked them, "Aren't you in business to lend money?"

They told me, "Yes, of course."

I said, "Okay, I will give you $5,000 as a guarantee which you can deposit as collateral and deduct each monthly payment from that amount. Plus, in addition to the interest you charge me on the loan, you will be making interest on my $5000!" This time they agreed with me and gave me the money.

I contacted the Cuban government and told them I was ready to put up the $10,000 bond for my father's visit to Jamaica.

Now it was all arranged. I knew the flight number and the time and the day my father was coming to Jamaica. At the airport we were able to see the passengers leaving the plane but I didn't see my father. I couldn't believe that he had missed the flight. We waited for half an hour and we still didn't see him.

When I glanced at my mother I saw a woman in pain. Her eyes were so tightly closed that the skin around them was all wrinkled. She held her handkerchief so tightly that her fingers hurt. She tried to control herself but she couldn't stop crying.

"Alex, what are we are going to do?" She hadn't worn any makeup and she looked terrible. "Alex, are you sure he boarded the plane?"

Again and again my mother was pestering me. It was hot, and the flies and mosquitoes were biting me. I don't know which was worse, my mother or the mosquitoes. For a moment I wished we were Catholics so we could have rosary beads to count that might soothe us, but we were Jewish and our traditions were different–we only prayed in silence.

I left Mother and I went to the information desk and asked them if they could check the passenger list. They told me that it was confidential and they weren't allowed to tell me. We waited a full hour. I thought I was going to die if he wasn't on this plane. I didn't think about the money that I paid for him, just about his health and our family being together. Then, suddenly, my mother was screaming, "Alex, he's here! He's here! Do you see him?"

When we met my father I hardly recognized him. He looked like an old man, just skin and bones. The zipper on his suitcase was broken, so he had tied a rope around it so his clothes would not fall out. He hadn't taken any of his precious paintings or our family albums with him. The Cuban officials had examined his belongings, and he was afraid it would look like he wasn't coming back–suspicious.

Father looked like a pauper. When I had left him a year and half ago he weighed 150 pounds; now he was barely 120. The first thing he did was to kneel, pray and kiss the ground. On the way out he told us how happy he was to see us and to breathe the free fresh air of freedom. He said, "I hope I can call this home."

He was only 58 years old but he looked much older. His skin was drawn and thin, but his eyes were the scariest thing about him. They looked like what I imagined were the eyes of a dead man. I understood. This was the fourth country which he had tried to call home in his lifetime–Italy, Palestine, Cuba and now Jamaica–and now, tired and worn out as he was, he could look forward to the struggle of starting all over once again.

We hugged and kissed him. We could hardly believe that he was really with us. I grabbed his suitcase and I loaded the car and we drove to the pensión. We had told all the tenants that my father was coming and when we arrived everybody was happy to see us. The tenants were in a festive mood. They had prepared chicken and rice for us and had baked us a cake. On the cake it said, "Welcome Home."

In the years ahead they once again gradually built a clothing empire in Jamaica, very similar to what they had done in Cuba. But Jamaica was now close to independence, and with that the resentment of blacks for the ruling white minority was unleashed, and it became more and more difficult for white people to live and work there. Every night we heard gunshots, and sounds of violence were everywhere

After all the work of getting us together, we were destined to part again. I returned to the United States. In 1966, there was so much political instability and violent crime in Kingston that my mother couldn't take any more of it, and she left for the U.S. as well. But my father refused and stayed behind. Once again he had devoted his life to his work and felt that he could not leave it again. He died in 1969 and we buried him in the Jewish cemetery in Kingston.

Before I left for America, I remembered how I had gone to the beach to try to wash away my feeling of *zevel*. But then I thought that maybe that lingering feeling of being garbage had a positive side. Maybe it was that feeling that had driven me, time after time, in difficult circumstances, to overcome problems and to move ahead. Or maybe, I thought, I shouldn't take myself so seriously; it was time to get on with life in America.

# Chapter Forty-Six, Goodbye

The school year in Kingston had ended, and everybody was in the holiday spirit. "No more teachers, no more books, no more teachers' dirty looks," was the general feeling around the campus. Graduation time was in the air and the 1962 class was a big one; over one hundred kids were graduating from our technical high school. We had chefs and cooks and domestic workers that we supplied to the local hotels, because tourism was a major part of Jamaica's economy. My mother's best dressmakers also had been students who had graduated from my school. Very few kids were going to college because their parents could not afford it. The majority of those who did go on to college went to England, since Jamaica was still under the British system. The ones who went to the United States were on athletic scholarships. Jamaica produced some of the best track and field athletes and several of them won gold medals in the Olympic games.

I was also at a turning point in my life. I didn't have a problem renewing my contract with the school, teaching Spanish. As a matter of fact, there was a shortage of Spanish teachers on the island and I was very much in demand. Besides Europeans, our tourists were often from Latin America, and they demanded to be spoken to in Spanish.

Jamaica is very close to Latin America, and Spanish being the official language made my skills very popular.

But there were other problems. The year was 1962, change was coming, Jamaica was about to declare its independence from England, and our family did not feel safe; not very different from 1948 in Palestine. Riots began to occur in Kingston, with white people being robbed in broad daylight and stores being set afire.

The white people began arming themselves for protection, and they slept with pistols underneath their pillows.

I had been very comfortable in Jamaica but now felt it was time to leave. Neither my parents nor I could immigrate to the U.S. We had relatives in the U.S. but they were not helpful people. I believed I could get a teaching permit and if they liked me, a school could be my sponsor to get a "green card." Once I had an income in the U.S. I could bring my parents there as well.

I still owed money to the bank and I had an obligation to pay it back. I went to the school to get my paycheck and clean my desk. Everyone who was around me seemed so indifferent to my going that I felt sad. I heard everybody whispering, "Is he really leaving us?" I answered, "Yes, I'm going to the States." I said goodbye to the teachers who were my friends. They asked me for details, so I gave them the whole story and then I went to the bathroom and cried.

Although it was my decision to go, nevertheless I was angry that, once again, I had to leave my country. I asked myself, "When is this going to end?" I was born in Palestine, where I felt loyal to my country and thought I would never leave it. But after my best friend tried to kill me, I packed and we left for Cuba. I was only thirteen years old then. My parents and I made a new home in Cuba. We were successful and for the first time in my life, I started to really live. Then my wife-to-be suddenly and without warning joined a convent instead of marrying me. Once again, I felt like *zevel*, garbage, that I wasn't worth anything. Then Castro came to power, we lost everything and I packed and left Cuba for Jamaica. After struggling and catching my breath, the whole family was united in Jamaica, a beautiful country.

I wondered when it would all end. Was I forever to be the Wandering Jew without a permanent homeland?

❦

You did not need a lot to survive in Jamaica. You could have lived on the beach, collected some bananas, drunk coconut juice, and lived happily ever after. Our life together had finally been comfortable. Being a school teacher I attended many graduations and other celebrations. There were many parties and Jamaicans were well-known as party lovers. These affairs could last for days. Every excuse not to go to work was taken and enjoyed, and the local slogan was, "We only live once."

We had several bonfires where the kids burned their old school uniforms. Some of these fires were under control but many buildings were burned in others. It was well known that insurance fraud was a way for the owners to make quick money, but then they were forced to pack and leave the country–we were not the only family that was concerned for their future here.

Our school produced local artists that sold their products on the waterfront. They wove straw baskets, hats, mattresses, etc. They also had artists that produced very colorful paintings and wood crafts. The school had an excellent barber shop that I used and a beauty parlor that my mother used. Upon graduation, the students opened their own barbershops and beauty parlors and other small shops.

There was an excellent cafeteria that was open to the public. My family enjoyed eating there because the food was nutritious and very reasonable. It wasn't worth it to bring sandwiches from home. Jamaican food is a blend of African, Chinese, Indian and European cuisines, and very delicious. We ate plenty of fruits and vegetables, especially ackee. If you don't know when to eat it and how to cook ackee, it can be a poison fruit. You can only eat it when the pod is open; unripe and unopened ackee is poisonous. I was warned that if a girl wanted to prepare a meal for you, never ask her to cook ackee for you; if she was jealous she might kill you.

Storytelling has always played an important role in Jamaican culture. There is a short story about Randy and Veronica. They lived together in the same city and went to the same school. Veronica was a good girl while Randy knew that a boy like him could get any girl he wanted. Veronica cooked, washed his clothes and did his homework. Veronica was attractive but she knew she would never win a beauty contest. Randy met a new girl and wanted to make Veronica jealous so he started dating her. Veronica was very jealous and she went to church and asked the priest to get her boyfriend back. The priest told her to participate in a ceremony. Veronica's religion was Animism, a belief based on the idea that animals, plants, and even inanimate objects have souls. If you pray to them they can influence you and you ask them for favors. You must play the drums and the drums used in the ceremony are sprinkled with alcohol. Veronica put herself in a trance and was able to communicate with the spirits. They told her to feed the other girl ackee and make sure that Randy didn't eat it. But Veronica was not careful and Randy and his new girl friend both ate the ackee and dropped dead. Now nobody messed with Veronica.

When I was teaching at school I noticed skin color in Jamaica was the ultimate status symbol in a society that exhibited great admiration for status symbols. The lighter the skin color of the child, the closer the child sat in the front of the class.. Usually the first rows were White, Chinese and Indian kids. The darker skinned kids sat in the back of the class. A black kid never spoke to a white kid or a mixed race mulatto. They waited to be spoken to before they spoke.

My students were well behaved in the classroom. They were so quiet you could hear a pin drop. Education was very important to my students. There were more kids that wanted to go to school than there were schools and teachers available, and the competition for places was fierce. The only bad thing about the school was the teachers' salaries. Most of the teachers who came from England got a larger salary and free room and board and health care, while I got the same lower salary as a native Jamaican and no allowance for room and board or health care.

My parents were worried about me because I was diabetic and taking care of myself–there were few doctors available and no diabetes specialists.

I was twenty-seven years old and I still didn't know how to drive. I took driver's education at school with my own students and they tutored me and helped me to pass the driving test. Now, while they still respected me, they looked at me as more like one of them. Once I got my driver's license my mom and I bought a car. Having a car, it didn't take long for my parents to learn to drive as well and they didn't have to depend on me as much.

Summer was almost over and I told my parents that I would leave the island at the beginning of the month of September. The school didn't have money to hire painters or to buy paint, and I spent most of my summer vacation helping at the store and volunteering to paint the school. Another reason why I volunteered at the school was because I felt guilty about leaving my students. I wanted to be remembered for my teaching experiences and my volunteering.

Some of the department stores donated paint and paintbrushes but not enough to get the job done. We had two choices: we could paint only part of the school or dilute the paint and do the whole school. We decided to do the second one. We didn't paint the classrooms because we didn't have enough paint, but we thought that during the year the school could raise enough money to do them next summer.

We never had any new textbooks; the ones that we had were used ones from England. Our school in Kingston kept the best books. The damaged ones were sent to the country. The kids were so hungry to acquire knowledge that they didn't care about the condition of the books. In contrast, when I started teaching in America, the kids always had new textbooks and never cared about damaging the new ones that they were given. Years later, in junior high and in high school, my grandson was given two sets of books; one to use in school and one to use at home, so he didn't have to carry them back and forth! I was shocked at this extravagance.

In a few days I would be leaving, and I started to pray and I asked God to guide me in my new adventure in a foreign country; I wasn't as confident as I thought I was. Years before, I was in a relatively worry-free never-never-land, but now, I had to face the real world. The University of Miami had an excellent employment bureau that was free of charge to alumni. I started corresponding with them and I had two leads: the first was to go to Oklahoma City, and the second was in Northern California. I kept my file up-to-date. My school grades were excellent and I had several good recommendations from my teachers and also from my employer in Kingston. With a record like this I thought, "Who wouldn't get a job?" But I had a problem; I wasn't a U.S. citizen or even an immigrant, and whoever hired me would have to sponsor me and take a chance that I would fulfill their expectations.

I rejected Oklahoma because I was afraid of the unknown weather; both the climate and the culture. I chose California because in my dream country, where I would be safe forever, everyone moved West.

I packed my belongings in one small suitcase and I flew from Kingston to Miami, and then to San Francisco. There, my new employer greeted me at the airport and took me to San Juan Bautista, where I fell in love with the people, the city and the climate. I knew that this was going to be my home for three years, and I quickly found a place to live.

When I began teaching, the warm welcome from everyone caused tears to flow. I called my parents and told them the good news. I knew that finally I found my home in the United States and I have been living here for more than forty years.

# Chapter Forty-Seven, San Juan Bautista

One of the most charming mission towns in northern California is San Juan Bautista. The mission is the main attraction in town. They had an elementary school that taught kindergarten to eighth grade, a few hotels, a drugstore, a bank, a gas station, a bakery, post office, restaurants, antique stores and a few tourist stores. The population was a little over a thousand people and everybody knew each other.

Most of the people who lived in the town were farmers. There was a large Mexican population. During spring, summer and autumn the population doubled. They were common laborers that came to pick fruits like apples, walnuts, pears, strawberries, tomatoes, etc. Most of the laborers couldn't read or write. They hardly spoke English and I was hired to teach a special class that held fifteen kids who were in the fifth through eighth grades and were ten to fourteen years old. I had to teach different curricula since my students were: five students in the fifth grade, three students in the sixth grade, two in the seventh grade and five in the eighth grade.

I taught from eight in the morning to three o'clock in the afternoon. In between I had an hour lunch. I didn't have a curriculum and I didn't know what I was supposed to do with them. I went to the class cold turkey. The school year had already started two weeks before and my students didn't have a teacher. They were scattered around the school in the regular classes and they hated it. The other kids made fun of them and most of my students hated school in general. Some of my pupils were shy and others, since they weren't successful at school, were discipline problems. They clowned around and were constantly fighting.

The principal of the school told me that out of one hundred and seventy-five teaching days, we could only suspend the kids ten days during the entire year. Corporal punishment was permitted and the principal said that we could only paddle each student three times a year. After hearing this, I was literally sick to my stomach. There was nothing at all positive that the principal told me about my students. In contrast to my warm welcome and feeling at home here, I suddenly asked myself, "What am I doing here?" I told myself that I would never paddle or suspend any of my students. I would try to win them over and make sure that they would look forward to coming to my class.

Next day I went to school where I met the other teachers and my students. It was great that I spoke Spanish and I was able to communicate with my kids. Our schoolroom was a large room with desks, tables and chairs, a stove, refrigerator and a sink. When I entered the classroom all my students were seated, their faces looking down at the floor. I felt that they were shy, sad and ashamed of themselves. They didn't behave like normal kids.

I introduced myself but they were very quiet. They were afraid to open their mouths. I asked them, "What's wrong?" My students complained to me that they were hungry and they hadn't had any breakfast. It reminded me of how I went to school in Palestine–always hungry. But here in America, the richest country in the world, I couldn't believe that children came to school hungry.

My first day at school wasn't a happy day, not when I saw dirty, sad faces reminding me about myself in Palestine. The kids were chewing the pencils and trying to swallow the wood and pencil lead, eating the paper and then spitting it out. It made me sick. I had flashbacks of Ali and me in school, waiting for lunch, which was our only meal of the day. The kids in my class told me that they had only one meal a day, which was supper; usually tortillas with rice and beans, but never enough to fill their stomachs. They had to share the food with their brothers and sisters and parents. The kids who were ten years to fourteen years old looked older because they aged by being hungry.

The worst part of this problem was that free lunches were not available at that time. Being new in town I asked the kids where the nearest grocery store was. Without asking permission, I took the entire class out and we bought bread, peanut butter, jam, chocolate, powdered milk and sugar. I was happy to pay for these items, but soon realized that I would not be able to continue this practice on my modest salary. Nevertheless, I made a pact with them and told them that as long as I was their teacher they weren't going to be hungry, and they wouldn't be sad, either. I wanted them to laugh and be children

Later on, I solved the hunger problem. I asked the school secretary to teach each kid to crochet and knit, so they could make scarves, hats and purses. When we had a sufficient amount we put these things and anything else that they had made, like potholders, piñatas, and corn dolls, on consignment in the mission store where they were sold to the tourists. I couldn't believe how successful we were, and this was how we bought raw materials for our products as well as the food we ate.

Whenever I glanced at my students I wondered what I was going to do with them. They could hardly read and write and could hardly do any math. I soon realized that what I needed to teach them were the essential elements needed to survive in the twentieth century. One thing that they all wanted to learn was how to cook and how to bake cakes, cookies and donuts. By the end of my third year at the school, some of the parents took advantage of their kids' education and opened donut shops, with their children as the bakers. It didn't take very much money to open a donut shop, and the government lent them what they needed.

I was surprised at how hard all the kids worked at school. I realized that my students should be rewarded for doing a good job. On my first field trip I took the kids to Salinas and we went to Sears and to another department store. I told each child to choose a toy and I told them that they could earn the toy if they accomplished all their assignments. The girls selected dolls and stuffed animals. They told me that they had never had any of these things. The boys selected guns and army toys. I remembered that back in Palestine Ali and I had also picked weapons as our first choice of toys. None of the kids selected books, and neither did Ali or I. I guess all kids are really the same, no matter where they live.

I remember one of my older students, Roberto. He was big for his age and heavy. He couldn't sit still for more than a few minutes. He was always looking out the window and was fascinated with trucks, tractors, bulldozers and other heavy construction equipment. Highway 101 was just being built and he couldn't tear his eyes away from the workmen. I wrote to the Sacramento Board of Education and asked them if Roberto could go to school half a day and work the other half as a flag boy on the highway construction. Fortunately, they agreed. Being so big and heavy, it didn't take him long to learn to drive the heavy equipment, and once he accomplished this and was hired, he was very happy. Both of us took driver's education together and we passed the driving test together. I was making only ten dollars an hour as a schoolteacher who had sixteen years of education, and when he turned eighteen he was making twenty-two dollars an hour! "Where is the justice?" I thought.

I taught my kids some patriotism. We started every day with the Pledge of Allegiance, and they didn't parrot me. They knew what every word meant. Holidays were very important to me, especially Thanksgiving. At school we prepared the meal; the turkey, the yams, the salad, the gelatin and cranberry sauce, and we made pumpkin pies. We decorated the room and set the table and invited the teachers and students from the whole school. After that, everybody wanted to be in my class! They didn't call my students dummies anymore. They told my kids, "You're lucky to be in Mr. Modena's class!"

Because I didn't have a car I stayed in San Juan Bautista, but once I could drive and had a car, I moved fourteen miles away to Hollister. I didn't have a private life. My students constantly came to visit me, especially on Sunday, when they arrived at seven in the morning and asked me to go to Mass with them. I told them, "Sorry, kids, but I need my beauty sleep." An hour later they would return and ask again. They were persistent. Finally, I joined them in church. They told me that they wanted to make sure that when I died I would go to heaven.

The three years that I taught in San Juan Bautista were the happiest days of my life. The way that I understood my kids was when I went at harvest time to pick tomatoes and strawberries, and they picked more and got paid more than I did. We also had a kitchen garden where we learned how to cultivate the necessities of life. We raked the soil, prepared it for planting, planted the seeds, watered it and if we were lucky we were able to harvest the fruits of our labors.

Now, when I happen to visit San Juan Bautista, my grown-up students still recognize me, and the whole town looks more prosperous.

# Chapter Forty-Eight, The American Dream

When the nights are longer, the days are shorter, and when the days are longer, the nights are shorter. This happened to me for seventy years. I wonder when I was in Palestine, Cuba, Jamaica and America, did I see the same moon, the same sun and the same stars?

When you write a book like this you feel that a part of you is open to the public, your life isn't any more a secret. I am seventy years old and it is about time to tell my story to the world, and of how people in each country that I was in–Palestine, Cuba and Jamaica–were fighting for freedom. I had to fight for my freedom as well; if I hadn't fought, I wouldn't have survived. My fighting began early, I was born prematurely and weighed a mere two and one-half pounds. In Palestine in 1935 few premature babies survived and under any circumstances my survival was a miracle.

I was a special baby not only because of being premature but because I was born with the protective coating intact all around me, known as a *caul*. In many traditions around the world, this is a good omen. My parents preserved and saved the *caul* and later, when they were destitute and forced to pawn all their possessions, they never parted with it. In fact, from then on my mother wore it as a necklace in a small pouch. Unfortunately, when we were forced to leave Cuba we lost it, and my mother exclaimed, "We're doomed!"

On the other hand I believed this was all nonsense.

Speaking of belief, in the Jewish religion on *Rosh Hashana*, it is written who should live and who should die each year, and on *Yom Kippur* one's destiny is sealed. Even though my mother was starving she was still able to breast-feed me, and though the doctors gave me no chance of surviving I remained alive and grew healthy.

Living in a kibbutz was every child's dream but not mine. I was alone. I didn't have any friends. The only true friend I had was a calf and when they slaughtered him I felt that they killed me. This was the first time I actually learned about birth and death.

In 1940, at the age of five, I was happy to leave the kibbutz. I had had enough sharing to last a lifetime. I thought living in town was better. I was free to wander around and even though we were very poor I had the luxury of going to stores and occasionally buying something that I didn't have to share with all the other kids. And the clothes that I wore, even though secondhand, were mine! I could do whatever I wanted with them, I didn't have to worry that I would have to pass them on to another child. Best of all, I didn't have to share my parents!

I grew up on the street and became street smart, and I learned how to put food on our table. I always took the best of every opportunity that I had. Until the age of thirteen I had a best friend, Ali, my blood brother, who was an Arab. The word "Jew" or "Muslim" never came between us. We were united. We celebrated both our holidays together and for us, as kids, food was more important than the meaning of the holiday. If there had not been a war in 1948, Ali and I would probably have gone to the same high school and lived in the same community, watching the new phenomenon of television and melding the two religions into one. But there was a war, and Ali tried to blow me up with a hand grenade. I believed that my parents wanted me to grow to be a decent person, and so did Ali's parents want the same for him. Until today, I still don't understand what drove him to want to kill me.

In 1948 we immigrated to Cuba. At the age of fifteen I was already in business, selling fabrics to the local factories. Other immigrants chose different paths, such as my neighbor, Emma, who at my same age became a prostitute.

Around that time I discovered that I had diabetes and suddenly my moods were related to the amount of sugar in my blood, just like a roller coaster. Once I discovered my sickness, I fought to survive. I learned to give myself insulin injections, prepare my diet and exercise. But in spite of this condition I was able to compete and represent Cuba in the Big Five (pre-Olympic) Games as a swimmer.

Life in Cuba was easygoing. We never thought about the future, only to have a good time today, and when Castro came, it was a surprise and we were not prepared for the losses that we would experience. It seemed that whatever the trial, my parents and I bounced back, as we had already done many other times in our lives.

In 1958 I won a scholarship to the University of Miami in Florida and that's where I was all alone and I learned how to survive in the United States. In 1960 I lost my scholarship and was penniless in a strange country, but didn't give up and graduated from college in 1961. Upon graduation, I joined my mother in Jamaica, where we were both trying to make a living. By a lot of quick business schemes, fast talking and the American ingenuity I'd learned, I was able to pay off the Cuban government and bring my father from Cuba, which was quite a feat.

I learned quite a bit in Jamaica. Especially I learned how the British school system works and that it is very practical. When a student graduates from a Jamaican high school, he or she is able to begin earning a living. I used this method of teaching to great advantage when I taught special education in San Juan Bautista, California.

Now I am in America, living in Northern California, and have accomplished the "American Dream." It took a lot to get here and to make that dream a reality.